PLAYMAKER

PLAYMAKER

GLENN HODDLE

WITH JACOB STEINBERG

HarperCollins*Publishers*

HarperCollins*Publishers*
1 London Bridge Street
London SE1 9GF

www.harpercollins.co.uk

HarperCollins*Publishers*
1st Floor, Watermarque Building, Ringsend Road
Dublin 4, Ireland

First published by HarperCollins*Publishers* 2021
This paperback edition published 2022

1 3 5 7 9 10 8 6 4 2

A catalogue record of this book is
available from the British Library

ISBN 978-0-00-849537-4

Printed and bound in the UK using 100% renewable
electricity at CPI Group (UK) Ltd

This book would not be possible without the love and support of my wonderful mum, Theresa, and dad, Derek – bless them – who helped me so much throughout my life and not just at the start of my journey. A big thanks must also go to my family, extended family and friends across the years; it wouldn't have been possible to achieve what I have without you all by my side. I have to say it's been a breathtaking journey, with many wonderful highs and a few lows, but without you all it wouldn't have been possible or the same.

I must also thank the two men who have made it possible for me to still be here today and to live in extra time: Simon Daniels and Steve Edmondson. Without your incredible efforts, knowledge and quick thinking, I wouldn't be around to see my wonderful grandchildren get bigger. I am eternally grateful, and words can never repay my gratitude.

CONTENTS

1

FOOTBALL, FOOTBALL, FOOTBALL

I didn't choose football. Football chose me. There was a oneness with the ball, an understanding between two old friends, that lifted me out of my shyness as a child. I was never more creative than when I crossed the white line and stepped on the pitch. As soon as the ball dropped to my feet, I had it under my spell. I knew how to manipulate it. How to control it. How to feel it. The ball was like another part of my anatomy. It was pointless trying to prise us apart. I even had a red ball that went to bed with me when I was really young.

I was eight when my dad Derek took me to a packed White Hart Lane to watch Tottenham play Liverpool. I remember sitting on the barrier at the front, Dad lifting me up and holding me in position. Looking back, it was pretty dangerous. But I was hooked, a complete and utter football obsessive. I watched in awe when I saw the stars on television. Celtic became my Scottish team when I watched them beat Internazionale in the 1967 European Cup final, and I adored George Best, Manchester United's brilliant snake-hipped winger. It was always an event when United or Liverpool came down to London. Football has always occupied a special place in my heart.

Luckily Dad spent countless hours with me in the park behind our house in Harlow, just kicking a ball around, and I have a memory of people stopping to watch and talking to him about this little five-year-old boy who was making it look easy. It just came naturally to me, and although Dad was a good amateur footballer, he would tell me that I was better than him by the time I was eight. 'You could use both feet,' he said, explaining that there was nothing he could teach me about technique. No point wasting time trying to tell me where to put my opposite foot or how to improve my balance.

I appreciated that from Dad, who was at Stoke City when he was 17 and then at Brentford. He had no interest in bothering the coaches in all the years I was at Tottenham. 'They know what they're doing,' he'd say. 'They're professionals.' It was different to the other parents, who would be really busy and say, 'My son plays in this position.' My parents stood back. They wouldn't speak up and I wouldn't ask them for anything. The only thing that mattered was playing football. Poor Dad. He'd come home from a hard day's work and I'd scoff my dinner down before waiting for him, ball under my arm and one eye on the clock.

Sometimes he had to leave me crying in that park. I was always trying to carve out a bit more time. I refused to come in if there was a bit more light in the summer, forcing Dad to hide behind some bushes and pretend that he was going to leave me behind. It was only when I panicked, thinking that he actually had gone, that I went after him.

In all those hours, though, he never coached me. He just offered encouragement, and it was the same with his brother, Uncle Dave, who lived with us. A bit of a flash teenager by his own admission, Dave was an outstanding goalkeeper and spent a year at Tottenham as a schoolboy. He was nine years older than me, more of a brother than an uncle, and he spent hours between these two trees in the park, leaping around and trying to stop my shots.

That was my upbringing: football, football, football. School was a nuisance as far as I was concerned and if I wasn't in the park with Dad and Uncle Dave, I was making up games in the garden. I had my own little stadium long before I pulled on Tottenham's colours and stepped out at White Hart Lane. My imagination was incredible for a young kid. I had a picture in my head. It came to me naturally. I threw a ball against our neighbours' wall, which must have driven them mad, and when it came down I could visualise a defender, whether it was a family member or a player I had seen on television. I didn't know what I was doing or how it was happening, but I could almost see these defenders trying to tackle me and a goalkeeper trying to save my shots.

It was something I took into my professional career. When I lined up a free-kick like the one I scored for Tottenham in our FA Cup semi-final against Wolves in 1981, it was me, the goalkeeper and the goalposts. Everything else faded away: the crowd, my team-mates, the wall. I had this eerie ability to visualise. I loved George Best, even though Jimmy Greaves was my hero as a Spurs fan, and I was always trying to copy Bobby Charlton's moves. Charlton had this lovely body swerve where, using his upper body, he would pretend to go to his right before veering off to his left. I saw it when England won the 1966 World Cup and then I would be outside, trying to perfect it.

My imagination was on fire. My parents told me that I played with my food when I was little, lining up the peas on my plate as players and a referee. Once I was done in the garden, I went inside with a sponge ball and aimed diving headers against the record player. I used the legs of the dining table as a goal. It was how I ended up playing: using my imagination to open teams up and make things happen. I could picture what I wanted to do. By the time I looked down at the ball I had already formulated a plan.

I always wanted to create something different, both as a player and a manager, and later in my life many people wrongly mistook that desire for self-indulgence. I wasn't understood in England, often being dismissed as a luxury player because the mentality at the time was centred around flying into 50–50 tackles, hitting long balls and playing in rigid lines.

My mentality was 80 per cent attacking when I stepped on the pitch. 'What can I create today?' I'd think. 'Can I score? Can I create things for the team and play with confidence?' If I could, then I trusted my team-mates to benefit from my imagination. Everything I did was to help my team win. I wasn't a show-off. I played with purpose and positive intent.

I wasn't going to change for anyone, even though standing out from the crowd isn't easy. I was strong-willed and had faith in my talent. I wanted to play beautiful football. I wanted to paint pictures, to entertain. I wanted to perform. I wanted to be myself.

I have often wondered where that imagination came from. Instinctively, I assumed that I inherited my ability from Dad. Now, though, I think about Mum. Her name was Terri – short for Leticia Theresa, which we used to tease her rotten about – and she was fierce. She didn't hesitate if I needed disciplining and she hated injustice, which I get from her. Yet she was also extremely creative and loved performing. She was a great amateur actress. 'With this name,' she'd say, 'if it wasn't for meeting your dad and having you early, I'd be out on the stage.'

A beautiful soul who would do anything for anyone, Mum was a good athlete in her day and was excellent at the long jump. It's her acting that intrigues me, though. When you act you pretend you're someone else. You visualise. Your imagination comes alive and that's exactly what I was doing in the garden. I had a whole arrangement, an imaginary crowd cheering me on, and I even provided my own commentary, much to the amusement of our neighbours. They told my parents that they used to peer over to check where the noises and voices were coming from, only to find that it was me playing.

I might as well have been in the theatre: 'Here's Hoddle ... he's gone past Bobby Moore, brilliant skill ... and it's another goal for Glenn Hoddle ... what a player!' It was a bit bizarre, but I liked to put on a performance. One day I bunked off school with three mates, went home, rolled out the carpet and made goals at both ends of the lounge before starting a two-on-two game. I wasn't expecting Mum to come home early from work. She was livid when she opened the door and found the lounge in a state of utter chaos. Our pleas for mercy fell on deaf ears. Mum kicked us out, even though it was tipping down with rain and we couldn't exactly go back to school. We had to keep a low profile for the rest of the day.

Football influenced our family from the start. I was born in Hayes in 1957, out in west London, and Dad played for Hayes Football Club. If we had stayed there throughout my childhood, everything might have turned out differently. But when I was four we moved east, across London and out to Essex, ending up in Harlow New Town. Dad was a toolmaker, and the chairman at Hayes, Jack Kavanagh, had just become the housing developer for Harlow council. Somehow this guy managed to swing it so that eight players from teams around west London moved with him. There were council houses and jobs waiting for them when they arrived – and, most importantly of all, places in Harlow Town's squad.

My primary school was St Alban's, which was a quarter of a mile away from our house and next to my comprehensive, Burnt Mill. It was a quick walk to both in the morning, so I started to test myself when I was 11. It was me, the road, a small ball and a piece of chalk. The challenge was simple: juggle the ball all the way down the road, never letting it touch down the ground. There was a slightly busy road to cross, which was the trickiest spot, and every time I dropped it I used the chalk to mark the spot on the pavement, giving myself a target to beat the next day, then the day after that. Then I did it on the way home.

It wasn't easy but after about a year of persevering I reached the holy grail without making a single mistake. You should have seen my face when I reached school. It was an achievement, even though I was late for class. That's what I was like. I wanted a challenge, even though people thought I was mad.

I was always looking for something to keep off the ground. If I found a tangerine, I took it into the garden and practised keepy-uppies. If I could keep a grape up 10 times, great. I loved playing with smaller balls and it was something I introduced when I started to coach in England, where they never used it. We had 20-minute sessions with a small ball, working on skill and technique. That feel for the ball was rooted in me. I had a gift.

I was eight when I played my first ever match, turning out for St Alban's with boys who were 10. Although I didn't quite realise it, I could sense that I was different. I could use both feet, I could keep the ball in the air, and people were stopping on their bikes to watch me in the park. The only skill I wanted to master that was beyond me was catching the ball on my neck. It kept rolling off, which really annoyed me. Otherwise I had everything under control and I liked it when people stopped to watch. I knew they were talking about me and it gave me confidence, although it was all internal. I knew I was good, but I needed to compare myself against other players. I needed competition.

I had to start somewhere. I joined Potter Street Rangers when I was 10 and must have impressed the manager, who nick-named me Georgie Best because I could go past opponents easily, although I thought that I was more like Charlton. I was an attacking midfielder, usually starting on the right, but it wasn't too structured in those days. We had a goalie, a back four, a midfield and two strikers. It was nothing special tactically and all I cared about was having as much of the ball as possible. That was it: give me the ball. It always annoyed me if my team-mates didn't pass to me and I carried that mindset into my career, often getting frustrated when I found myself on the fringes while playing for England.

I had a lovely, balanced childhood. I adored my little brother Carl, who was born when I was nine, and Mum and Dad always came to watch me play, even in the wind and snow. More importantly, there were other people keeping an eye out for young talent. There were these twins who refereed in the Harlow Recreational League, Jim and John Higgins, who had a job on the side scouting for Tottenham. They spotted me when I was 11 and one day there was a knock on our door from Jim and John, who wanted to see if I fancied coming to train at Tottenham.

I swear that I was doing somersaults. I was over the moon at the thought of playing for my team, and my parents were so excited. But six months passed and we didn't hear a thing. I was absolutely distraught. I was lost in the system and my parents were too reserved to try and find out more. That was it. My career as a Tottenham player was already over.

When I was 12, though, I moved to Spinney Dynamos because Potter Street Rangers were starting to fall apart. It was pure at Spinney. We were a really good team and everything changed when we reached a cup final in Harlow, six months after that first conversation with Jim and John.

There was a buzz before the game because two Tottenham players, Martin Chivers and Ray Evans, were coming to watch as somebody at Spinney knew Ray. Suddenly I had a second chance and I made sure that I took it, scoring twice as we won the final 3–1.

My performance was enough to wow Martin, who had broken the British transfer record when Tottenham signed him from Southampton for £125,000. He went back to the chief scouts at the club and told them that they had to check out this kid in Harlow. They asked for my name and because it was unusual it rang a bell. They went back to check the files, found me buried away in all that paperwork and got back in touch with the twins, who made sure that I didn't slip through the net this time.

'Right,' they said. 'You come every Tuesday and Thursday night, 5.30pm at White Hart Lane.' My life was about to change.

At 12 I was too young to sign on schoolboy forms, but Tottenham had me and another kid, Andy King, training with boys who were 15. My technique was already better than theirs and it was clear that school was going to take even more of a back seat. It had never been high on my list of priorities and now it was even more of an inconvenience. I didn't boast about training at Tottenham or even tell many people about it, but people knew that something was up when I started to rush for the exit when class finished at 3.55pm on Tuesdays and Thursdays. I had somewhere else to be and a train to catch at 10 past four.

The problem was whether I would make it in time. Thursdays were fine because Mr Thomas, my history teacher, was a football fan and let me leave five minutes early. Tuesday afternoons, though, were pure torture. Ironically it was geography, one of the few subjects I enjoyed, that stood in my way. My stomach would be churning throughout the lesson because I was worried that Mr Levitt was going to hold us back. If someone was talking in class, I was in trouble.

I was so nervous. If I missed the train, I missed training. I only had 15 minutes to rush to the station and I was ready when geography finished, ready to sprint across the pitches and across the park, busting a gut to get my seat.

Mr Levitt was fairly bewildered by my behaviour. But when he asked me one day why I was always in a rush, I finally had a chance to curry some favour with him.

'I have to get across to the station,' I said, thinking that he might treat me differently if he knew I had a 5.30 appointment at White Hart Lane.

But Mr Levitt wasn't much of a sportsman. 'Ah, football,' he said. 'You want to be a footballer?'

'Yeah.'

'Hoddle,' he replied, 'you've got no chance of being a footballer. Get your head on your lessons and knuckle down.'

It was a bit of an own-goal on my part. It was different with Mr Thomas, who used to give me a wink to signal that I could leave, which always wound up my classmates. But Mr Levitt would not budge and I was distraught whenever I missed the train. At that age I couldn't see things in perspective and realise that it didn't matter if I was absent for one session. I thought they were going to forget about me if I wasn't there, which is ridiculous given that I was already training with 15-year-olds. It was because I wanted it so much. My dream was becoming a professional and I was scared stiff that Tottenham were going to discard me. My parents had a difficult task trying to lift my spirits on the afternoons when I came home distraught after missing the train.

I couldn't relax on Tuesdays. The journey, which involved getting to Edmonton before catching a connecting train to White Hart Lane, wasn't simple. If everything went to plan, I would arrive with 15 minutes to spare, make my way down Tottenham High Road, reach the ground and change into my kit. Then I was in my element.

Even the journey gave me a bit of fear, though. I was doing it on my own when I was 12 and it wasn't pleasant. There were skinheads and prostitutes on the train, and I saw plenty of fights. If I had been more of a cheeky chappy, the type to answer back, I would have got a pasting. It was a bit of an eye-opener, and I couldn't wait to get to the safety of the stadium.

Once I was there, I was at ease. I might as well have been back in the garden, kicking a ball against the wall. We trained in the gym at White Hart Lane and the coaches gave us various tasks to complete. There were circles, squares and lines on the wall and the floor in the gym. One exercise was chipping a ball above the line when it came to you. We spent ages aiming half-volleys or volleys into the circles and squares, doing the drills in pairs.

It all came naturally to me, and the only time when I really doubted myself at that age was when we watched the first team on a matchday. Tottenham used to put the schoolboy talents on the benches in the front row at White Hart Lane, which was either because they didn't want to waste the good seats on us, or because they wanted to give us a proper taste of the real thing – a coach saying, 'Put them down there, let them see what a real game's like.'

Either way, it was a brilliant education. When United came to White Hart Lane, I was sitting by the touchline, right behind Best when he took a throw. The physicality of the game was incredible. I can still remember the smell of the liniment on the players' legs. You heard the clashes between the players, the collisions, the thud of studs going into shinpads.

There was a night game against Chelsea, a proper London derby, and their striker, Peter Osgood, going up against our centre-back, Mike England. I was a young kid watching Osgood challenge for a ball and elbow Mike right in the face, who retaliated by raking his studs down the Chelsea forward's calves. The players got away with so much in that era and the verbals were incredible. Joe Kinnear, our right-back, was an expletive machine. He did it to put the opposing winger off.

It's impossible to explain this to a 12-year-old. Tottenham needed us to feel it for ourselves, even though it was the worst view in the ground. It was real football: no open spaces like there are on television. It was a shock to the system. 'I don't know if I'm going to be able to make it,' I told Dad after one particularly rough game. 'I'm really worried. I can't believe how physical it is.'

It made me realise that the game wasn't just about technique. I would have to be strong as well. If I was thrown in at a young age, nobody was going to leave me alone just because

I was a teenager. There were points to fight over and livelihoods on the line.

At least Dad, who had played amateur football, was under no illusions. Typically, he didn't panic. He was always a steady hand. 'Look, it's good that you've seen it,' he said. 'You're going to have to deal with it.'

It takes immense dedication to make it as a professional. Those years from 12 to 15 were harder than when I became an apprentice. Anything can stop you in your tracks, as I discovered when a freak injury on a cricket pitch almost ended my football career when I was 13.

All I remember is a red blur coming my way before I hit the ground. A decent all-round sportsman, I was captain of our school cricket team and was looking to seize the initiative during an away game against Mark Hall. We had one fast bowler, Dave Tait, and I decided that I needed to put myself at silly mid on, in position to catch anything off their batsman.

Dave was such a good bowler, but this time he delivered a full toss. There was a bang and this red blur hit me just under the eye. I was out stone cold. There was no blood but I don't know what would have happened if it wasn't for Mr Godsman, the assistant headmaster. He drove to my house once I got home to check on me and he took charge as soon as Mum opened the door.

'Get him to a hospital now,' he said. 'You've got to get him to a hospital.'

I'm not sure if my parents would have taken me without Mr Godsman's insistence. They might have tried to let it settle down overnight, which would have been a disaster. The enormity of the situation was clear when I arrived at Harlow hospital and they said that I had to be taken to the specialist eye unit in the hospital in Bishop's Stortford, because they suspected a haemorrhage behind the eye.

It was horrendous. There was no open wound, but everything was happening beneath the surface. I felt out of it. I remember the ambulance moving so slowly, a 20-minute journey that took an hour, and the doctors at Bishop's Stortford confirming the original diagnosis when we got there.

I was in that hospital for two weeks, under strict instruction to lie in bed, keep my head still and do nothing other than stare at the ceiling. 'If he moves his eyes he loses his eye,' the doctor said to my parents.

Although I knew that I was in trouble, I wasn't yet aware of the haemorrhage. When my parents came back the next day, I wasn't doing my job. There was an old guy in another bed and we were talking about cricket. I was lying down, but my head wasn't still and Mum broke down.

'You've got a haemorrhage behind your eye,' she said. 'There's a 50–50 chance you're going to lose your eye.'

That got my attention. Nobody said it out loud, but my first thought was that my football career was over. The fear of God went through me and I immediately changed my attitude. I had an eye-patch over the injured eye, and all I did for two weeks was lie on the bed, staring at the ceiling and drifting in and out of sleep. I thought about Tottenham and I wanted to cry, but it would have hurt my eye. People visited, but I was on my own a lot, staring, scared to move, in total fear of losing the thing I loved most in the world.

I couldn't lift my head or feed myself. It was so boring. The old guy had cricket on the radio, which I liked, but I couldn't study or do a crossword. It was just me against the ceiling.

Sometimes I thought about my old matches or training sessions at Tottenham, and that just got me going. There were so many times when I nearly broke down. But I had to stay positive, and it taught me discipline. 'I have to do this,' I thought. 'I've got to do it.' It became like breathing; keep your head still and, as Dad kept saying, the injury would calm down.

With encouragement from my parents and the doctors, it healed after a fortnight and I was allowed to go home to recuperate. Initially my vision was impaired because of the swelling. There was a strain on the eye and it was months before everything got back to normal again. The first time I went in the garden was a bit nerve-wracking.

But the haemorrhage had cleared up and because it was the summer holiday there was no training at Tottenham anyway. They had no idea. There wasn't as much contact as there is these days. It was up to me to feel my way back and decide when I was ready to return, a huge challenge for a 13-year-old.

Setbacks teach you valuable lessons about life. If you're prepared to learn from bad experiences, you can turn negatives into positives. I recovered from my eye injury and continued my development at Tottenham, confident that they were going to give me an apprenticeship. My parents weren't particularly worried about my education. The general consensus was that I was going to become a professional footballer.

But every aspiring footballer faces times when it seems that the world is against them. The most innocuous incident has the potential to ruin everything and I found myself back at square one when I was 14, in absolute agony after injuring my knee during a training session on a summer's evening at Spinney Dynamos. I went in for a tackle, only for my foot to get caught in the ground, giving me no time to react as the other player came in hard, bending my right knee backwards.

The pain was excruciating and for days I could barely walk. The end of the season was approaching and I was back on the treatment table. So much for the people who reckon I was a luxury player.

I went to see my GP, who reassured me, saying it was nothing more than badly strained ligaments, but his diagnosis was way off. After four weeks there was no sign of any improvement and I could almost see my leg disappearing. The muscle was shrinking because I was hardly using it, which should have been the cue for my parents to contact Tottenham and ask them to check me out. In the end it took Jim and John, the scout twins, to get in touch with my parents, who told them that I'd been out of action with a knee injury.

There was no hesitation from Tottenham, who wanted to examine me straight away. I went down there and met the physio, Cecil Poyton, and the doctor in the first-team treatment room. I was in agony while they were checking me out. It was obviously worse than strained ligaments – I needed an operation to remove the damaged cartilage.

At least Tottenham's concern showed that they wanted me to stay. Not all players would have been treated that way, but they looked after me. They did all the tests and booked me an appointment with a specialist in London. Dickie Walker, the chief scout, joined Mum and me on the day. We took the underground into London, an alien place to me at the time, and had some time to kill when we arrived.

'I'm taking you to the shops,' Dickie said, directing us down Regent Street and stopping at a place with the Queen's coat of arms above the front door. 'Look, the Queen shops here. You can choose anything you like. I'm buying.'

I picked out a polo neck, a burgundy number, and it was honestly the only gift that Tottenham ever gave me.

Dickie, a great character and a proper cockney lad, must have wanted me to relax before the appointment with the surgeon, who looked at the X-ray before saying that I had a bucket-handle tear of the cartilage. The whole thing had to come out and I couldn't go home straight after the operation. I was stuck in hospital for almost two weeks, during which time I wasted a lot of muscle. I could hardly lift my leg and I had an unforgiving physio, who didn't care that I was desperate to go home.

'You ain't leaving this hospital until you can lift your leg up and do these exercises,' she said, refusing to take no for an answer.

The pain was excruciating and I was terrified that the stitches were going to give way, but I knuckled down and did the exercises. My character was being tested; I might as well have been staring at that hospital ceiling again. Tottenham told me that I had to build my muscle up before I could kick a ball. They had me working with weights and gave me a sandbag to put over my foot before swinging it up.

I wasn't sure why they were asking me to do it, but now I know that it was vitally important. Your muscles have to be so strong and my legs were already thin after I'd had a growth spurt. I had to work tirelessly, putting myself through the pain and the monotony, and I didn't feel great when I played again after six months out.

It was touch and go for a while. I was very fragile, so it probably wasn't ideal that I took a big risk when I was 15, leaving Spinney Dynamos and moving into men's football to play for Longmans, Dad's team.

Tottenham would never have allowed it if I'd told them. But after seeing that battle between Mike England and Peter Osgood at White Hart Lane, I had outgrown youth football and needed to test myself at a higher level. It was too easy for me at Spinney as I could score six goals in a game if I was in the mood.

Men's football was tougher. After watching Dad when I was a little kid, it was fantastic turning out with him as he was a cracking player. I was in midfield and he was at the back. It was emotional for both of us – Dad was so proud, although he had to have a word after the first game.

'Don't call me "Dad" on the pitch,' he said. 'Call me "Del".'

I thought that was great – 'Del, give us the ball!' – although Dad wasn't happy when I tried it on when Mum was serving us Sunday lunch after we got home.

'Del, pass us the salt!'

'I ain't on the football pitch now. Call me "Dad".'

'Oh, come on, Del.'

Mum wasn't impressed either, but I cherish those times playing alongside Dad. He was so placid, so unassuming, but when it came to me he was cautious. Paternal concern took over when he asked if I was sure that I wanted to join him at Longmans, although I was certain it was a good idea. Uncle Dave was on my side, arguing that I was in danger of picking up bad habits if I stayed at Spinney.

Despite Dave being more fiery than Dad, he was right. Footballers have to get out of their comfort zones and push the limits. I wasn't going to be able to beat five or six players at will anymore. That's why players like Diego Maradona and Lionel Messi are incredible – they can do it as and when they please.

The rest of us mortals have to pick and choose our moments to shine. For me, it was another chance to learn a valuable lesson about the game's harder realities, and I had to figure out when to take risks. There was one game, down at the Bank of England pitch in Loughton, when I discovered that some players weren't going to take kindly to a skinny teenager making fools out of them.

It was a fantastic pitch, smooth like Wembley, perfect for my style of play. It was a hard game, full of verbals, but we were 2–1 up and I fancied myself. I picked the ball up on the halfway line, dropped a shoulder to beat their midfield destroyer, went past four players, skipped round the centre-back and left the goalkeeper on his backside before tapping into the empty net.

I was feeling pretty pleased with myself. Our fans were on the touchline, clapping and laughing at the audacity of the goal, and even their big centre-back tapped me on the back-side to congratulate me. I was on top of the world – until I came face to face with the midfielder I'd left on the floor at the start of the move.

'You fucking do that again, son, and I'll break your leg,' he said.

I thought he was messing around and tried to laugh it off.

'No, I fucking mean it,' he said. 'You do that again, I'll break your fucking leg.'

I felt like telling Dad, but I had to learn to handle it myself. Instead, I asked our coach how long was left. Twenty minutes. Twenty very long, dangerous minutes. The guy was on a mission. He was trying his best to injure me, and that was when I learnt how to play one and two touch.

'You know what?' I said to Dad when we were driving home. 'That fella's done me a right favour.'

'I wasn't happy,' he said. 'If he'd done something I think I would have lost it.'

'Dad, it made me play one and two touch. I just played one and two.'

Dad saw my point. The higher you go up the ladder, the more the good play is between one and three touches from the best players. Messi's Barcelona were like that at their peak – ones and twos, bang, bang, bang, no messing around. For me, a skinny teenager, it was a fabulous way to learn that football was a tough game.

It was slightly different when I started playing youth team football and for the reserves at Tottenham because I was playing against better players, who held back and made me think more. But that one angry guy taught me so much, and it stayed with me. If it was a really physical game, I started playing one and two touch. It was about adapting to the circumstances. Sometimes I would be looking to pass and an opponent would dive in, allowing me to skip round him. Then the next move would be a pass.

Footballers have to see pictures quickly. My vision was going to be an asset. I had it as a young kid, ever since those days on my own in the garden, and it was going to help me achieve my dream at Tottenham.

2

TO DARE IS TO DO

I was never going to relax after recovering from my knee injury. Although Tottenham were making encouraging noises about offering me an apprenticeship by the time I was 15, my dream had almost died on two occasions. Having seen the harsher side of life, I knew that it was going to take more than natural ability to succeed at the highest level. It was also going to be about character and mental fortitude, hidden qualities that are difficult to quantify but just as important as the ability to hit a 50-yard pass or whip a free-kick into the top corner.

I could take nothing for granted as it only takes one bad tackle to ruin everything. My world almost caved in on me twice and although I believed in myself, I was not immune from self-doubt. My fingers were crossed as the moment of truth drew closer, and it was an overwhelming feeling when, six months after turning 16, I signed as an apprentice for my boyhood club. That day, 17 April 1974, is etched in my memory. I could not have been prouder.

It was reward for all of those Tuesday and Thursday night sessions, not to mention the frantic dashes to make the train to White Hart Lane after geography with Mr Levitt. At home, though, the reaction was typically steady. Dad wasn't one for popping open a bottle of champagne. The focus was less on celebrating my achievement, more on the importance of keeping my feet on the ground. It was a quiet chat in the garden, with Dad matter-of-fact in his advice, telling me that I had to work towards earning a place in the first team.

He was right. The apprenticeship was hardly a walk in the park. It was another challenge, only this time in a harsher environment, and there was more to it than training with the ball. They gave us unappetising jobs, tasking us with cleaning everything from the toilets at White Hart Lane to the muddy boots scattered around the first-team dressing room. No job was beneath us. One summer we painted all the crash barriers on the terraces at the stadium. Mum took one look at me when I got home one day, covered in silver paint, and said, 'I thought you were training to be a footballer, not a painter and decorator.'

It was hard to explain to an outsider. The jobs were menial but the Lane became like a second home. We were earning the right to play and building our connection with the club. I didn't even mind it when Johnny Wallace, the first team's boot man, told me and another player to climb up to the top of the East Stand at White Hart Lane and clean the cockerel on the roof during the summer.

It wasn't exactly health and safety friendly. We had to climb up a ladder at the back of the stand on a hot, sunny day, and when we were up there we could look all over London. Being Tottenham apprentices, it crossed our mind to see if Highbury really was within spitting distance. We had a laugh and didn't mind that the cockerel clearly hadn't been cleaned in years.

The experience stayed with me. That beautiful cockerel looking over the pitch was a reminder of my roots once I broke into the first team. I looked up at it when we ran out of the tunnel to warm up before games, and I told myself not to forget my upbringing.

They were character-building times and it could be tough inside that dressing room. I wasn't the type to come barrelling through the doors, cracking jokes and having pops at people. I was more likely to be on the receiving end. We were all climbing up the same mountain and it was inevitable that some of us weren't going to make it to the top.

The ferocity of competition made us suspicious of each other at times. Team-mates were forced to view each other as rivals, as obstacles blocking their path to the first team, and this juxtaposition caused mixed emotions. It was dog eat dog during training, even though we had to play as a team in the FA Youth Cup or South East Counties games. Everybody was fighting to keep their place and it was a natural human reaction to worry when a newcomer arrived.

Some players were too keen to catch the eye. I noticed that when I was a young apprentice and some of the older players refused to give me the ball, presumably because I represented a threat. They tried to do too much and eventually came unstuck. Unless you're going to beat three or four players, there's no point trying to play as an individual. Football is a team game, and although I had to be better than the other midfielders, I reminded myself that I also had to play alongside them.

After all there were enough teams capable of making me doubt whether I was going to reach the right level. I had a jolt when I was a raw 16-year-old and came up against an older, stronger Arsenal side, who were more than happy to hand us a footballing lesson.

We were an inexperienced team, while they included players who were going to be signing as professionals. It was the cream of Arsenal's crop – Liam Brady and David O'Leary played and they destroyed us, barely allowing us a kick. We were left chasing shadows and Arsenal were merciless, beating us 7–0. I went home utterly deflated and opened up to Dad, saying that I feared that I wasn't going to be good enough.

I was, of course, overreacting. Two years later the boot was on the other foot when a younger Arsenal team played us at our training ground in Cheshunt. This time we handed out the punishment, winning 6–1, and I knew how those Arsenal kids were feeling. If they had played for anyone other than Arsenal, I would have told them not to worry. In fact I brought up that story a lot after becoming a coach, reassuring nervous youngsters by telling them that I'd had doubts too when I was their age.

Every footballer has those negative thoughts after a bad game, and it takes a lot of mental strength to overcome them. It happened to me, even though I was naturally talented, and it's why I really admire players who compensate for their lack of skill by making themselves invaluable to the team through sheer grit and application.

John Pratt had that ability to dig in for Tottenham. John was a youngster trying to break into the first team when I joined as a 12-year-old, and he used to come down on Tuesday and Thursday nights because he was studying for his coaching badges. He taught me so much. He was a decent player but he wasn't the most skilled, and the crowd always got on his back when he gave the ball away. Some players crack under that scrutiny. Not John, though. He had such a sharp character and the criticism every week was like water off a duck's back to him. He kept seeking the ball, never hiding, and he won the UEFA Cup in 1972 and the League Cup in 1973.

Paul Miller, who was two years younger than me, was similar to John. When he came in as an apprentice I admit that I thought he was limited. Who would have imagined he would go on to score in a UEFA Cup final? Paul was shrewd and knew how to handle himself. I always told him that he must have already been nine years old when he was born. Paul was switched on, full of common sense, and his determination meant that he won two FA Cups and a UEFA Cup.

Ability is not enough on its own. Young players have to show will and desire. And nobody was going to hand me anything for free.

Games in the South East Counties division weren't for the faint-hearted. There was a lot of long ball, which wasn't conducive to my style of play, and some players wanted to shut down my creativity through sheer brute force. It was an era where physicality dominated English football, and I had to work hard to get the ball down and play. At least it was giving me an early taster of what I could expect as a professional; I definitely wasn't going to be unprepared.

It was just as well that I was coming through at Tottenham, whose vision of how the game should be played suited me down to the ground. I think it was destiny to start out at a club that placed such a high value on aesthetic qualities, and I could sense the connection between us from a young age. The club's motto, 'To Dare Is to Do', summed it up. Their traditions demanded that players were willing to be brave, willing to create and take risks with the ball, and I found fitting in as easy as slipping my hands into a comfortable pair of gloves.

Our visions aligned. I saw Holland playing Total Football at the 1974 World Cup and although they ended up losing in the final to West Germany, I knew that Johan Cruyff and his team-mates were playing the game in the right way.

Tottenham also wanted to play beautiful football, and I was fortunate to have coaches who believed in me. I learnt a lot from Pat Welton, a former goalkeeper who went on to become a first-team coach, and loved playing for Peter Shreeves when he ran the youth team. I had a special relationship with Peter because he coached me at every level at Tottenham, watching me grow from boy to a man. He loved skill, knew his football and was such a creative coach. He had a lovely left foot and made us laugh when he joined in the five-a-sides because he always wanted the ball. 'Give me the ball, I've got a plan,' might as well have been his motto in life.

Meanwhile I was able to continue doing my thing. I impressed the coaches with my ability to see a picture on the pitch, which is a major asset for a footballer, and knew that I was on the right track when I was called up to the reserves. Once again it was dog eat dog. Reserve-team football was like a tumble dryer, with everything thrown in together. There were young players like me and then there were older players coming back from injury.

Some players didn't want to play because they felt it was beneath them and others treated games like they were in the World Cup because they were coming back from injury. I played against Alan Ball, a World Cup winner in 1966, and with Martin Chivers when he was feeling his way back after a knock. It was very competitive and an interesting way for me to find out if I was ready for the real thing.

It was also a case of staying with the current that was flowing into the first team. I was making a name for myself within the club and was hoping for an opportunity to impress the great Bill Nicholson, who was managing the first team at the time. The set-up was different in those days. Whereas modern managers can easily check out youth-team players by watching their games back on analysis tapes, I was relying on Bill turning up to watch me in the flesh.

Although he sometimes wandered over to watch us train, I wanted him to see me in a proper game. My best hope was in the FA Youth Cup, and my chance arrived when we played Middlesbrough. I knew that I had to up my game for his benefit. A legendary figure at White Hart Lane, Bill led Tottenham to the Double in 1961 and was one of the greatest managers in the history of British football. Although I was only 16, I couldn't go into my shell with him watching.

I told myself that I had to perform. Fortunately, his presence had a positive effect on me. After drawing the first game at their place, we ran Middlesbrough ragged in the replay back at White Hart Lane, smashing them 5–2 on a cold, wet night in north London.

I was in my element, scoring three lovely goals, even rounding the goalkeeper when I completed my hat-trick. I was walking on air and was still buzzing when I spotted Bill walking down the corridor at the ground the next day.

Normally that would have been the cue to dive into the nearest cupboard and get out of the headmaster's way. But after my exploits against Middlesbrough, I thought it was time to introduce myself properly. I gathered up all my courage, puffed out my chest and nodded at him.

'Mr Nicholson.'

Surely a pat on the back was on the way. Maybe even a 'Well done, Glenn,' or 'You'll be in my midfield soon, lad.' A hat-trick in an FA Youth Cup tie – that had to count for something.

I might as well have been asking Mr Levitt if I could leave school early to get to training.

'Ah,' the manager said in his Yorkshire accent. 'Young Hoddle.'

I waited expectantly, prepared for the inevitable compliment.

'Your third goal,' he said.

'Yes,' I said, feeling the excitement rising.

'You should have passed it. You shouldn't have gone round the goalkeeper. You had the last defender. You should have passed it to your team-mate. He was in a better position.'

That was it. End of conversation. He didn't wait for me to reply. He just strolled off, leaving me totally deflated. I walked away in a daze, wondering what I was going to have to do to impress this living legend. If a hat-trick wasn't enough, what hope did I have of playing for him?

But I think he was looking to teach me a valuable lesson. Those were the standards he set at Tottenham and it was up to me to reach them. From my conversations with Steve Perryman, it seems that Bill never went over the top with anyone. Even players as good as Pat Jennings, Martin Peters and Martin Chivers took notice if they got a 'well done' after a game.

The one consolation was that Bill had noticed me. But it was clear that I couldn't rest on my laurels if I was going to play for his team.

Along with waiting in vain for that elusive bit of praise from Bill, I was waiting to sign my first professional contract. I had to hang on until I was 17, and it was so exciting when they finally put that piece of paper in front of me. As an apprentice I was on £8 a week, while Mum received £6 a week for expenses at home, but this was nothing compared with what they were going to pay me as a professional. The jump was extraordinary to a kid from Harlow. I was going to be on £60 a week, a crazy sum given that I probably would have been happy to pay them to let me put on that famous white shirt.

It was such a buzz when I put pen to paper. Although I'd seen the club release so many kids along the way, I'd worked really hard and the thought of doing something else with my life had never once crossed my mind. I'd had one summer job, helping a neighbour install TV aerials for a bit of cash on the side during the close season, but my parents never put any pressure on me to complete my exams. It was football all the way after I left school at 15, and I felt immense pride at lasting long enough for Tottenham to give me a contract, although Dad still wanted to make sure that my ego wasn't going to get too inflated. 'You're only starting over,' he said. 'You've got to make sure you make an effect now.'

Dad had a way of cutting straight to the point. But everything was moving quickly. I hadn't taken long to become a professional and they didn't make me wait too long before calling me into the first-team squad for the first time.

Unfortunately I hadn't timed my run well enough to make the leap when Bill was still in charge. It was a difficult time for Tottenham. We made a poor start to the 1974–75 season, losing our first four games in Division One, and Bill was under growing pressure. When we lost our fourth game, at home to Manchester City on 28 August, it was the end for Bill, who handed in his resignation the following day.

Bill's departure shows how harsh football can be at times. In shock, the club turned to the former Arsenal defender Terry Neill as Bill's replacement. I just had to keep my head down. I was probably low down the agenda for a new manager looking to establish himself at one of the biggest clubs in the country.

While Neill focused on steadying the ship, finishing 19th in his first season, I was still doing unenviable jobs around the club. Friday afternoons could be a grind for the young players. We would train in the gym at White Hart Lane, doing a bit of running round the track, but we were kidding ourselves if we thought we were going to be allowed to leave early. We were the ones lumbered with the dressing rooms and it was particularly harsh if you landed the home one, going in to clean up after the first team had finished training and gone home.

It was the school of hard knocks. I arrived early one day, hoping to finish the job quickly, and was unprepared for the frosty reception when I entered the dressing room. A few players were already inside and they weren't happy to see me, telling me that I wasn't welcome until I was good enough to put on that white shirt.

But one Friday afternoon at the start of the following season was different. There I was, waiting to sweep the floors and scrub the toilets, when I had a quick look on the team sheets pinned to the wall outside. I looked at the reserves, and realised with a start that my name wasn't there.

'You're with the first team,' a mate said.

He wasn't joking. I was in the squad for the first time and I made sure not to disappoint. A couple of Fridays later I went through the same routine, putting my gear on before going to wait outside the dressing room. Tottenham were at home to Norwich City on the following afternoon and for some reason I sensed my moment had arrived. I scanned the names, looking down from 1 to 11 until I reached the bench.

My stomach was in knots. I was in a daze, gazing at the team sheet on the wall, staring at the No12 next to my name.

I walked outside, jumped in my car and somehow made it home. I honestly cannot remember the journey, I was completely spaced out. I was already playing the game in my head, imagining myself coming off the bench and introducing myself to the Tottenham fans, repeatedly telling myself that I was going to get on the pitch.

It was a mixture of nerves and excitement. I had played a few reserve games at White Hart Lane but I hadn't ever seen anything like this before. I had never experienced playing in a full stadium and on that afternoon, 30 August 1975, it felt like the pitch was half the size, with 40,000 spectators surrounding us. It felt claustrophobic, enclosed, and I remember my heart almost jumping out of my body while I warmed up on the touchline before replacing Cyril Knowles, who injured his knee so badly that he never played again.

Cyril went down early and John Pratt, who started in midfield, was filling in at left-back. I was so full of nervous tension when I ran on that the Tottenham fans must have thought they had some wild animal on their hands. I got on the pitch and saw the ball spinning in the air on the edge of the Norwich area. High on adrenalin and determined to make an instant impact, I came steaming in to challenge for the ball and had a 10-yard run on their hard-as-nails centre-back Duncan Forbes, who had a standing start. I won the header, bulleting it into the Park Lane end behind the goal, and was so pumped up I accidentally caught Duncan in the nose with a stray elbow.

It wasn't the first time that his nose had been in the wars, but it was probably the first time Duncan had been flattened by a skinny 17-year-old debutant. There was blood everywhere and his nose had gone again. Duncan was lying on the floor and I heard a sharp intake of breath from the Tottenham fans, who were wondering where this tough guy had been hiding.

Of course, it couldn't have been further from the truth, especially at that age. I was a beanpole of a kid and I was trying to say sorry to Duncan. Call it crisis management. In my head I was telling myself off for apologising to him on my debut. Meanwhile Martin Chivers, the Tottenham hero who had spotted me all those years ago, was concerned for my safety. 'I wouldn't come back up here again if I were you,' he said.

It was wise advice. I stayed back and ended up playing quite well, passing nicely as we drew 2–2. Gradually the crowd started to realise what I was about. It was wonderful when they applauded a piece of skill or a clever pass, which never happened in the reserves. It gave me a buzz, making me feel like I could do anything. I fed off it, growing in confidence, and almost scored a wonderful goal, catching the ball with my right foot before flicking it over a defender's head and volleying it towards the top corner with my left.

The whole stadium went nuts. If only the ball had gone in. As it was, their goalkeeper, Kevin Keelan, tipped it over the bar. 'Bloody hell,' I thought after the game. 'You're going to have to do something special to beat these keepers.'

But it was still an incredible experience. The hairs on my arms were standing up and my spine was tingling for the rest of the game. After feeling so claustrophobic at the start, I realised that I loved playing in front of a crowd. I wasn't egotistical, but I relished the reception from the fans. It was like a drug. I wanted more.

* * *

Desperate to experience that high again, I grew frustrated with Terry Neill for not giving me another chance straight away. All the same it was brilliant training with the first team every day. I looked across at the reserves and, although a lot of my old mates were there, I told myself that I couldn't go back there. I needed a ruthless mindset. I was training with great players every day and had to make the most of it.

Of course, there was a lot of banter in the dressing room. Big Willy Young was a character and Terry Naylor was hilarious. But I remember watching Steve Perryman. He was the ultimate professional during training. I wanted to follow his example as I waited for the manager to remember to give a few minutes to that skinny kid who'd almost scored a wonder goal against Norwich.

Months passed. I kept my head down and eventually Terry turned to me again, naming me in the starting 11 for a trip to Stoke City towards the end of February. It was a special day. My parents and Uncle Dave made the journey up to the Victoria Ground, and I also had a lot of aunts and uncles who lived in the Midlands. Somehow I managed to secure tickets for everyone and spotted them when we came out to warm up, adding to the sense of occasion.

That mixture of nervousness and excitement returned. Sitting in the rough and ready away dressing room, I watched how my experienced team-mates were preparing. Steve was quiet, unassuming. Others were taking the piss. I tried to take it all in. I felt like I was watching a film. It was like I was somebody else, a young kid watching the grown-ups, documenting it all and not really present.

I had to snap myself out of my reverie – 'Get yourself ready, you're playing,' I thought. But I was still in a daze when we went down the tunnel. Alan Hudson, one of my favourite players when I was growing up, was playing for Stoke. As we lined up I was thinking, 'I'm with the first team,' when it would have been more professional to be focused on winning. It didn't feel real. At best I was an extra on set.

It felt more relaxed when we strode on to the pitch. Playing in central midfield, I settled when I got a touch of the ball. Jimmy Neighbour and John Pratt were there. I knew the shape of the team. I felt confident. Then we went 1–0 down after five minutes, conceding a sloppy goal to Jimmy Greenhoff.

But it was our day. John Duncan, our striker, equalised from close range and half-time was approaching when my moment arrived. I was waiting, 25 yards from goal, when the ball ran free after a scramble in their area. John Pratt, my old coach from the youth team, was lying on the floor nearby and I heard him shouting 'Hit it, Hod!' as the ball approached me. I didn't need to take a touch. The pace was already on the ball. Relying on my technique, I met it first time and it flew off my left foot like a spring, whistling towards goal and flying past Peter Shilton, the England goalkeeper, before whizzing into the left-hand corner of the goal.

It was such a pure strike and some way to announce myself. 'Did that just happen?' I thought as my team-mates mobbed me, with Martin Chivers giving me a cuddle. I jogged back to the halfway line, trying to pick out my family in the stands, feelings of pure elation running through me. Even Hudson was impressed. 'Great goal, son,' he said as he jogged past shortly after the game restarted.

At that stage, though, I had to focus again. It was about being professional as we held on to our 2–1 lead. After all it was only one goal and I still had so much more to prove. Plenty of young players have faded away after a brilliant start, failing to live up to the hype. I couldn't afford to get carried away. I had a few more games and played OK as we finished ninth, but the fear was still there. I was heading into unknown territory. Was I going to stay with the pace? Was I going to be good enough?

Chivers was a big help. 'Glenn, you're going to be a good player,' he said one day at training. 'A top player. Setting a standard is one thing. Keeping it is another.' It was a great piece of advice from a great player – a reminder that I had to stay grounded, especially as difficult times were on the way at Tottenham.

Change was in the air at White Hart Lane, arriving when Terry Neill resigned out of the blue during the summer, soon joining the old enemy, Arsenal. Before he left we went on a tour at the end of the season, visiting Australia, New Zealand, Canada and Fiji. I didn't play in all the games and was still helping carry the kit off the bus, which wasn't a problem. During training, though, Terry was on my back all the time. Perhaps he was testing me, but I didn't feel comfortable with the relationship and there was a good chance of me leaving if he had stayed. There wasn't a lot of communication between us. I wasn't sure where I stood – in fact I thought that he didn't like me – so I didn't shed many tears when he left, making way for Keith Burkinshaw.

I was happy with Keith, who had been first-team coach under Terry. He was never a skilful player and didn't play at the highest level, spending most of his career at Workington and Scunthorpe, but he wanted to create a team that was everything he couldn't be. Given time, his vision came true. First, though, he had to suffer.

We were in transition going into Keith's first season. Big players like Mike England, Alan Gilzean, Martin Peters and Martin Chivers had gone, and we were a mixed bag, short of finishers and often playing without any real method. The season started badly, with consecutive defeats to Ipswich and Newcastle, and after that we never found our feet. Home games were a struggle. The crowd were on top of the team and it wasn't ideal when a bad pass met with jeers, even though the criticism made me stronger in the long run.

I was fighting through it, trying to cut out the noise, following John Pratt's example, but it was a constant struggle. In October we travelled to Derby County after picking up only six points from eight games. We imploded, losing 8–2.

The defeats kept coming, leaving us in danger of relegation, and the atmosphere in the dressing room became frayed. Although we tried our best to stay together, it's difficult when you're losing matches. There were confrontations and the blame flew around. The defenders and attackers were pointing at each other, and we became fragmented when what we really needed was to pull together on the pitch.

I was still a teenager at the time and it was hard to speak up. I was a shy and undemonstrative kid. But when push came to shove in meetings, I had my say if I felt that fingers were being pointed in the wrong direction or if a defender wasn't looking to pass to the midfield.

It didn't come naturally and sometimes I felt strange as we walked out to train, wondering if I had caused offence. It was a learning curve and I think that was Mum's character coming out in me. I've mentioned that she despised injustice, and I couldn't sit by if I thought criticism was unfair. As I got older I became more confident making my point and standing my ground. Learning how to deal with adversity before tasting success was important for my development.

Every so often a positive result came along, raising everyone's hopes. In March we thought that we were going to escape relegation after beating Liverpool, the champions, at White Hart Lane. Then we won two of our next eleven games.

We were running out of chances by the time we hosted Aston Villa in our penultimate home game. There was hope in the crowd that day and the atmosphere was reminiscent of a European night. We turned it on, winning 3–1 thanks to goals from me, Chris Jones and Peter Taylor, and briefly felt euphoric as we dreamt of survival.

But it wasn't to be and we died a slow death. We had too much to do and the teams around us – Bristol City, Coventry, Norwich, QPR and West Ham – were doing more. A week after beating Villa we travelled to Maine Road to face Manchester City, who were challenging for the title. City, who ended up finishing second to Liverpool, were far too strong and smashed us 5–0, confirming our descent into Division Two.

I was in tears in the dressing room. I was overcome by guilt after failing to save my boyhood club from relegation and letting the fans down. It was a dreadful feeling, scarring me inside. As a Spurs fan, I felt embarrassed and devastated to have finished bottom of the league, and the journey on the coach home was horrendous – you could have heard a pin drop. I felt so sorry for Keith, worrying that he was going to lose his job. There were no guarantees that he was going to be allowed to oversee a rebuild.

But these are the times when players have to dig in and fight. It's easy if everything's running smoothly. Although I was distraught, I had to scrape myself off the canvas and start swinging. That failure made me even more hungry to lead Tottenham to glory. Life was testing me. I had worked so hard to become a professional and I couldn't allow one setback to knock me off course. I had to respond. Tottenham needed me to respond.

Keith was under immense pressure. Tottenham were one of the biggest clubs in the country, famed for playing attractive football, and hadn't been in Division Two since 1950. We had become the first English club to win the Double and the first British club to win a European trophy, winning the European Cup Winners' Cup in 1963. We were the club of Danny Blanchflower, Jimmy Greaves and Bill Nicholson, and we weren't supposed to be in Division Two. Relegation wasn't just a huge story, it was a shock to the system, and I wouldn't have been surprised if the board had decided to fire Keith after our ignominious display at Maine Road.

Instead they kept faith in him, giving him time to pick up the pieces and lift us back into the top flight. Yet we were kidding ourselves if we thought that winning promotion was going to be a walk in the park. We were by far the biggest draw in the league. Everybody wanted to watch us and everyone wanted to beat us. It was going to be a slog. The memory of Maine Road haunted us, and there was so much talk about what would happen if we didn't win promotion straight away.

Early on, though, we played without fear, which allowed our class to shine. Turning out in front of packed crowds gave us a buzz. We fed off it at the start of the season and played some glorious football at times, even thrashing Bristol Rovers 9–0 in October. I was in my element that day, finding space, creating chances and getting on the scoresheet.

Playing like that, we could have been forgiven for thinking that we were certainties to finish in one of the three automatic promotion places. Indeed we were in the top two for much of the season. But the league was tough and uncompromising, and we started to draw too many games. The anxiety about not going up, about getting stuck in the second tier for years, started to affect the team, choking our football.

A decent run in March, three wins on the spin, should have calmed us down. Instead we hit a wobble and failed to win our next three games. We couldn't relax even after beating Bolton, one of our closest rivals, 1–0 at home. We had another huge game a week later and we faltered, losing 3–1 at Brighton.

The momentum was with Brighton after their fourth win in five games. By contrast, we were crawling over the line. The walls were closing in on us, and a day before our next game, at home to Sunderland, Keith started speaking like a man who was ready to throw in the towel when he came into the dressing room.

'Well,' he said, 'you've blown it.'

I never found out if this was an inspired piece of reverse psychology from Keith. Either it was genius man-management or he was genuinely panicking. Whatever the truth, his words riled us, making us determined to prove him wrong. We left the meeting rejuvenated and defiant, even though a 3–2 defeat to Sunderland left us fretting in third place. There was a feeling that we could still do it as the season entered its final week.

Yet our rivals weren't giving up either. On Tuesday night Southampton all but secured promotion by drawing with Leyton Orient, while Brighton's chase continued with a 1–0 win over Charlton. The following evening, on the same night Bolton clinched promotion by beating Blackburn, White Hart Lane was an anxious place for a crunch game with Hull City, who were already down. Playing for nothing but pride, the visitors managed to stifle us, and we were mightily relieved when Steve Perryman popped up with a controversial late winner that could easily have been disallowed.

It was a huge goal from Steve, one that would shape the club's destiny, not that we knew it at the time. Yet the final day promised more tension. We still needed a draw at Southampton, who were all but up thanks to their goal difference, to be sure of finishing third. While Southampton were relaxed, we were terrified. 'This is the biggest game of my life,' I thought as we travelled down the M3, watching the Tottenham fans stream past our coach. 'The biggest.'

The pressure was building on the journey, even though we tried our best to keep it casual. The Dell, a tight little ground, was a tough place to visit and Southampton had a good side. Alan Ball was playing for them, and although my first thought when I received possession was usually to be creative, I knew this wasn't an occasion to try anything complicated. I didn't take risky positions or get ahead of the ball. With Brighton beating Blackpool at home, we needed to protect the point and be professional.

I didn't care about playing well. Normally I was proud about the aesthetic side of the game and determined to express myself. This was different. This was about grit. At one stage I felt like a spectator, as though I were a fan watching everything unfold. If the ball went down the opposite flank I was almost just gazing across. It was all about surviving.

The last 15 minutes were hellish. While it was the most stressful game I ever played, Southampton were carefree. Alan Ball was laughing at us. 'You lucky bastards,' I thought. 'You're playing with no pressure at all.' Southampton could afford to mess around and they turned up the heat near the end, creating a few chances. We were under the cosh at times and had a lucky escape when Ted MacDougall got caught on his heels with the ball bouncing around our six-yard box. My heart was pounding. I thought we were done for until

MacDougall delayed his shot, allowing Barry Daines to come out and smother the ball.

It was pure relief when the final whistle blew. Two wins from our last eight games? We were like a golfer crumbling on the back nine on the last day of a major and crawling over the line. But who cares? All that mattered was clinging on to third place and pipping Brighton on goal difference. Southampton were celebrating with their crowd and our fans wouldn't go home until we came out to salute them. We went up to the directors' box to avoid the melee down on the pitch and felt the pressure melt away. After the pain of Maine Road, we could look forward to better times.

3

EYE ON THE BALL

I was delighted that Keith had justified Tottenham's decision not to sack him. With promotion in the bag, he could turn his attention to building a genuinely competitive team. Keith knew that we needed to strengthen if we were going to make an impact in Division One. I just wasn't prepared for how big a statement he was going to make that summer.

My focus was on the 1978 World Cup in Argentina, who had a brilliant little whirlwind of a player in midfield. It was the first time I had seen Ossie Ardiles play. I watched him charging around the pitch during the early games and thought he was different to anything I had seen before. Ossie was unique. A greyhound in blue and white stripes, moving so quickly with and without the ball. At times he looked like he was skipping along the surface.

With Ossie impressing in midfield, Argentina reached the second round. Ricky Villa hadn't played yet, but he had a new fan when he came on at half-time against Poland. 'Who's the big fella with the beard?' I said to Dad. 'He's got some great skill.'

It turns out that I wasn't the only person paying attention to Ossie and Ricky, which I discovered when Keith asked me to come to the club for a chat during the middle of the tournament.

'Are you watching the World Cup?' Keith said. 'What do you think of the little one in Argentina's midfield?'

'Ardiles?' I said. 'He's amazing. He's so quick.'

'Yeah, look how much ground he covers,' Keith said. 'So much energy.'

After a while the conversation moved on to Mario Kempes's performances up front for Argentina and whether Holland were going to make up for their defeat to West Germany in the 1974 final. The meeting ended and I left Keith's office thinking that it was slightly unusual. I didn't normally chat with him like that. But I filed it away. There were no hints of what was about to happen next.

But Keith was on the move. Obviously he had been to Argentina without telling us. The deal was already in motion and the news broke a few days after our chat. I couldn't believe it. Two World Cup stars were on their way to Tottenham. 'That's why Keith got me in,' I thought, realising that the manager wanted to make a point to me about my game. Keith was always on at me about tracking back, and there he was getting me to agree with him about how hard a world-class player like Ossie worked without the ball.

Not that I cared. Foreign players coming to play in England were almost unheard of in those days and we were beside ourselves with excitement at the prospect of playing with Ricky and Ossie. It didn't feel real. It was only when they came to meet us at White Hart Lane that I truly believed these two brilliant players were going to be my team-mates.

Unfortunately they needed an extra holiday after winning the World Cup and couldn't join in straight away. The rest of us had to go to Holland for a pre-season training camp and I was like a little kid on Christmas Eve while I waited for them to arrive. My room-mates, John Gorman and Jimmy Holmes, were just as giddy.

It was wonderful when Ricky and Ossie finally turned up. Although they couldn't speak English, we did our best to help them settle. Once again Keith was talking about Ossie's work rate and telling everyone to follow his example before announcing that he was going to test us with a long warm-up, revealing that we were going to do laps of the five pitches outside. 'But we'll start the first lap slow,' he added, acknowledging that we were going to be really working hard to develop our sharpness before the new season.

That concession meant it was really four pitches. But after the first lap I turned around and looked for Ossie, who was lagging behind. By the time we got to the second pitch the lads were starting to take the piss. Ossie was nearly a lap behind us and it got worse from there. He disappeared further into the distance and I couldn't help but bring up everything that Keith had said to me about Ossie's fitness.

'Keith, you know that fella we were talking about,' I said. 'You didn't sign his brother, did you?'

The boys were cracking up at Ossie. He couldn't run at all. He'd given so much to the World Cup and had nothing left in the tank. Yet the mood changed when the balls came out later in the session. That was when Ossie came alive. Ricky was quickly into the swing of things as well, much to my delight. His quality was obvious from the start and it felt like I finally had someone who could connect with me on the pitch. We played Antwerp in a friendly, and although Ossie wasn't yet fit enough to play, Ricky was playing one-twos with me and returning my passes with easy accuracy.

I was delighted to have someone on my wavelength along-side me and the signs were promising when we earned a 1–1 draw at Nottingham Forest, the defending champions, thanks to a debut goal from Ricky. Yet my initial optimism proved misplaced. Four days later the club attempted to replicate the atmosphere at the World Cup by treating Ossie and Ricky to a ticker-tape welcome for their first game at White Hart Lane. It was a nice thought, but I was annoyed to have all that paper under my feet during the game and the mood fell flat when Aston Villa ruined the party, beating us 4–1.

It was a struggle for Keith to find the right balance with Ricky and Ossie in midfield. Although we played some lovely football at times, we took some right drubbings, losing 7–0 at Liverpool and 5–0 at home to Arsenal. Finishing 11th in our first season back in the top flight summed up our inconsistency.

Our second season was nothing special either. It must have been hard for our supporters to imagine that the glory days were on the way when we lost our second game 4–0 to Norwich. Keith still hadn't hit upon the right formula and we endured more difficult days in the league, losing 5–2 to Southampton and 4–0 to Nottingham Forest on our way to finishing 14th.

Yet we had enough individual talent to cause any team problems on our day. Our unpredictability made us a danger-ous cup team, and although we were up and down in the league, we had a good run in the FA Cup in 1980.

It started with a third-round tie against Manchester United, who snatched a draw after answering Ossie's excellent opener with a Sammy McIlroy penalty. Forced to go to Old Trafford for a replay four days later, we were up against it. United were going to come at us in front of their fans and they must have thought it was going to be their night when our goalkeeper, Milija Aleksic, had his jaw broken in a collision with Joe Jordan, who was one of the most physical centre-forwards around.

We didn't have a goalkeeper on the bench so an outfield player had to put on the gloves and the responsibility was obviously going to fall to me. It was my fault – I had already shone as an emergency goalkeeper earlier that season, landing myself in it when Barry Daines went off injured during a game against Leeds at Elland Road in October.

I hadn't planned to don the green jersey against Leeds. But I only had myself to blame, sealing my fate by wandering over to listen in as Steve Perryman and Don McAllister were discussing who should go between the sticks as the medical staff tried to get Barry onto a stretcher.

There was no big plan. Keith hadn't shouted any instructions from the touchline and our only substitute, John Pratt, was sprinting towards us with every intention of taking one for the team. It was typical John, totally unselfish, but there was no way that someone who was smaller than a grasshopper was going in goal.

'Fuck off, John, you're shorter than me,' Steve said, turning around and looking for a more suitable victim.

It was then that he noticed the young busybody standing nearby. Steve looked at me and I realised there was no escape. 'Well, I used to like going in goal in the park,' I said. Idiot. Steve didn't need another invitation to hand me the gloves.

My stomach dropped out. I felt sick but I'm six foot one. I couldn't say no when I was actually holding the gloves. Before I knew it I was putting on the green jersey. 'What have you got yourself into?' I thought. 'Why didn't you stay away from that little conflict?'

I had no idea what I was doing. Although I loved going in goal, I had no idea about where to stand in an actual game. I was like a cat on a hot tin roof. It was total panic.

Fortunately the lads defended brilliantly and we managed to make it to half-time unscathed. All I wanted to do in the dressing room was seek out our assistant manager, Pat Welton, who used to be a goalkeeper, and ask him for advice.

'Corners,' I said. 'Where do I stand with corners?'

'Well, don't go in the centre,' Pat said. 'Go a little bit towards the back post. Not completely at the back post, but a little further than centre. Free-kicks, you've just got to organise your wall.'

I was totally confused. Pat gave me a crash course in the art of goalkeeping in the space of 10 minutes and we still needed to see out the second half. When we went back out, I was thinking that I couldn't remember anything Pat had said. I simply had to play off the cuff and I even made a diving save as we somehow clung on to win 2–1.

I have no idea how we managed to beat Leeds. But I had clearly convinced the lads that I was potentially as good as Gordon Banks and there was no doubt that I would have to go in goal when Milija went off against United.

'Crikey, we've got it on here,' I thought as I took up my position in front of the Stretford End. With Joe Jordan leading their attack, I was worried. My nerves were on edge when they won a corner. 'Hod, you know where this is going,' Ray Wilkins said as he ran across to take it.

I pretended not to hear him. I focused on organising my defence and making it seem as if I knew what I was doing. United were trying to crowd me. Joe was in the six-yard box and Gordon McQueen, their big centre-back, was nearby.

'Joe!' Gordon barked. 'Do you want me to do him or are you OK? You've done the other one.'

I tried to drown it out. Ray whipped the corner in and I shut my eyes as I went for the cross, thinking that I was going to wake up in hospital. I went to punch the ball and didn't get close. But while I got knocked, I didn't get an elbow. Somehow we scrambled the ball away and dug in, dealing with everything United were throwing at us.

Yet the threats weren't just confined to the pitch. At one stage the ball was up the other end and I was standing on the edge of my six-yard box when someone in the Stretford End sent a snooker ball zooming past my ear. 'They're trying to kill me,' I thought. I spent most of the game 10 yards past the D, well clear of the United fans.

My team-mates were baffled by my positioning, but I could claim that I started the trend of the sweeper-keeper. The mood in the dressing room was jubilant thanks to a late winner from Ossie, whose goal took us into the fourth round. I was becoming a lucky charm when I went in goal, finishing my career as an emergency keeper who never lost a game after I went in for a third time when Milija suffered a horrible injury during a 2–2 draw with Norwich at the end of 1980. Although I let in a penalty against Norwich, I could hold my head high.

I was prepared to sacrifice myself to help the team. It took a mammoth effort to beat United and we fancied ourselves after knocking them out. But although we reached the quarter-finals after beating Birmingham and then Swindon, our run ended when we lost 1–0 to Liverpool at home. Terry McDermott scored an amazing goal, flicking the ball up on the edge of the area before volleying it into the top corner.

Liverpool had too much for us that year. It was frustrating, especially as we beat them 2–0 in the league a few weeks later.

In the dressing room we said it would have been nice to have reversed the results. Losing to Liverpool stung. We were desperate to make up for it as soon as possible.

Although that defeat by Liverpool motivated us, we had to improve before thinking about winning anything. For all the excitement about Ricky and Ossie coming to England, we were yet to click properly and we needed better balance in midfield. It was a struggle to find the right position for Ricky.

But Keith was about to unveil his masterpiece, with a slight tweak to our system into something resembling a midfield diamond working wonders. When Tony Galvin went down the left, giving us balance, energy and work rate, it was more fluid. Ricky slotted in behind the front two, Ossie was in the middle and I often floated from the centre to the right. I wasn't a winger but I had licence to drift back and forth, with Steve Perryman providing security after moving from midfield to right-back.

We were growing stronger and Keith was making smart signings like Graham 'Robbo' Roberts, a tough-tackling defender. Other players were emerging. Chris Hughton had pace to burn at left-back and Paul Miller was dependable in the centre of defence. And it helped that Keith had finally found two sharp strikers, bringing in Garth Crooks from Stoke and Steve Archibald from Aberdeen.

Sometimes I wondered how we were going to function defensively, but it worked. We often played off the cuff, and our main strength was having such fantastic invention behind Archie and Croosky. It was a breakthrough moment for me because I finally had two strikers whose pace and movement allowed me to drop dangerous balls behind unsuspecting defenders. That was my real art: always looking to play forward and be creative in possession. Previous team-mates weren't quite on my wavelength, or they didn't have the pace or movement to make my through-balls come off. But these two had pace and they knew where to run. They made pictures for me.

It must have been great for them because the ball would come nine times out of ten. Crooksy was electrifying and Archie had an eerie ability to sniff out a goal. We could score from nowhere and that made us a threat. The goals were finally flying in and much of the credit had to go to Keith, who was putting that difficult first season behind him and showing that he could build a proper team. It's the beauty of management in many ways. Although Keith wasn't a skilful player, he admired talent and allowed it to flourish as a coach. It takes a lack of ego to think that way.

That was Keith. His honesty made us want to play for him and he had a good relationship with Steve Perryman, who was the best captain I ever had. Everything was coming together: we had a real camaraderie, which was enhanced by Keith bringing in a couple of sports psychologists, John Syer and Chris Connelly, to work with us. This was unusual in the 1980s and we found it difficult during the first few months. We weren't sure about them or if we needed their help. But Keith had taken a chance on them and he left them to do their work. They held individual sessions, and after I had my first one I came away thinking that I needed to give it some time.

The rest of the team had a similar view. The more work the psychologists did with us, the more we felt the benefits. My mind went back to our relegation season and the fractious mood in the dressing room. Arguments are natural in a team environment, but the difference between success and failure is working out how to channel conflict in a positive way – and that was beyond us during that season. As a consequence we ended up suffering on the pitch. We weren't a unit. We may have been a family, yet we didn't know how to express ourselves.

With the psychologists on board, however, we discovered how to communicate. All of a sudden we were in pairs and little units, speaking in ways we never had before. I learnt so much about myself. John spoke to me about the mental side of the game and he took me back to when I was still a child, visualising skills and moves. He brought that carefree, imaginative side out of me, allowing me to think like that kid in the garden again. His visualisation techniques were incredible. He taught me how to compartmentalise. If I had a problem, like an injury or an off-field issue, he told me to write it down on a piece of paper and picture it, open a drawer and lock it away. It wasn't about pushing the problem away, it was about putting it to one side. I felt safe. Working with him helped me on a subconscious level, and I soon realised that I didn't fret over problems that could affect my football when I stuck them in that drawer.

I began to feel free. When I was younger my shyness often stopped me speaking up. Although I have always been strong willed – and I had to show character to break into the first team – there were times when I wished that I expressed myself more. When the psychologists arrived, though, I began to find my voice. If something had to be said in a team meeting, I was more prepared to say it and less worried about the consequences.

It wasn't just me. We became more honest with each other as a team. Criticism was delivered with a purpose. The trick was realising that we all had the same goal on the pitch. Better communication was only going to make us more likely to be successful. We were spending hour after hour travelling to games, but we weren't speaking about football. We weren't talking to each other about our job. There were no conversations between players about whether someone held on to the ball too long. The manager and his assistant might tell us what we were getting wrong but we would never sit down as a team and discuss it.

This was Tottenham thinking outside the box. Even bringing in two Argentinian players was unusual, bearing in mind how few foreign players came to play in England. I connected with Ossie. When we had team meetings he also asked why the ball was in the air so much, and people had to listen given that Ossie was a World Cup winner. He had clout and his English came on quickly, so he didn't have a problem expressing himself.

Ricky and Ossie soon settled in and became part of the group. Even now Ossie tells me he's more English than me. He still lives here, and his children and grandchildren were born in England. They were both humble characters, very down to earth and very funny. More importantly, they could play. Ossie was such a smart footballer. If a game was tactical and tight, you could see his mind take over. He could create, he was quick, he could score and he could tackle, often coming out of nowhere to win the ball.

I loved playing with Ossie and enjoyed watching Ricky develop in the free role. He had lovely technique. But I look back and wonder how we managed to pull it off. Ossie was supposed to be in the holding role, but in reality he was charging around everywhere, while I wasn't going to stick to the right wing. Tony Galvin was the only one who was really giving us positional balance. Garry Brooke, something of a super-sub, was another attacking player and Micky Hazard was naturally talented and so creative.

Most of us couldn't tackle our own grandmother, but Keith wanted us to play. Although we worked hard together, we often left the defending to the defenders, who knew what we could do with the ball. Somehow it clicked. We became a unit and a lot of it was down to the psychologists. We had a connection. I don't think it was a coincidence that we became more successful after Keith brought them in.

It helped foster a strong team spirit. It's not that we were all best friends. Personality clashes are inevitable in that sort of environment. For instance Archie was quite an insular striker on the pitch and that was his personality in a social setting. If we went out for a meal or a beer as a team, Steve wasn't up for getting involved – and that created problems at times. But working with the psychologists enabled us to find out more about Steve's character. Everybody is different. It was like we were a collection of different seeds, waiting to bloom. We just needed someone to sprinkle water over us before we could flourish.

We were playing beautiful football and we had an inkling that it might be our year at the start of the 1980–81 season. Beating United with me in goal gave us confidence in the FA Cup and losing in the last eight to Liverpool fired us up. Instead of deflating us, it only made us hungrier to maintain Tottenham's long tradition of doing well in the cups.

There was a positive vibe in the dressing room, a belief that grew as we advanced through the early rounds. The run began with a replay win against Queens Park Rangers of Division Two, clinching victory when Archie played me in to make it 3–1.

Hull put up a great fight in the fourth round, giving us a scare before Garry Brooke scored late to make it 2–0.

We beat Coventry 3–1 in the fifth round, playing well, but our quarter-final against Exeter was a slog. Our Third Division opponents were desperate to impress at White Hart Lane. Defending with their lives, Exeter held on, only to crack in the second half when I lifted a cross to the far post for Graham Roberts to head in the equaliser. The relief was immense when the ball hit the back of the net. The anxiety poured out of the stadium and we knew that we were through when Len Bond spilled my free-kick, allowing Paul Miller to bundle in the second goal.

It had taken two defenders to see off Exeter but we didn't care. We weren't at our free-flowing best but we were through to a semi-final against Wolves at Hillsborough. It was a huge step for us. If you've played in countless semi-finals, it's just another game. But we were totally inexperienced. We were hardened professionals, we believed in our game and we knew that we were a good side, but this was a new feeling and it's easy to lose your way when the desperation to win takes over.

The atmosphere was unreal. We saw so many Tottenham fans driving up the motorway to Sheffield, and a lot of them didn't have tickets. There actually could have been a catastrophe inside the ground. This was eight years before 96 Liverpool supporters lost their lives during the Hillsborough Disaster; it's hard not to wonder if vital lessons could have been learnt after our experience in the same stadium. Both ends were packed and some of our fans ended up spilling on to the pitch. It was bewildering. We were defending a free-kick at our end, and as I was lining up in the wall I saw all these people wearing Spurs hats wandering behind our goal. There were so many of them. They ended up sitting by the side of the pitch and I remember thinking that something must have gone wrong in the stands. It was such a strange scene. The fans were close enough for us to hear them shouting at us. At the time, though, I had to put it out of my mind. I had to concentrate on winning the game.

It was a cracking cup tie, an end-to-end game with both teams going for it on a tricky pitch. We started well, taking an early lead through Archie, but Wolves then woke up and quickly equalised when Kenny Hibbitt smashed in a cracking shot from the edge of the area.

The tension increased. It was tight but there was good play from both teams and we had a chance to regain our lead when Ossie went down on the edge of the Wolves area just before half-time. It was made for me. Our fans were singing my name because they knew what I could do with free-kicks. The pressure was on and I was thinking: 'Come on, where are you going with this? Where are you going?'

It helped that I understood the importance of taking my time. I never panicked over a dead ball. It was just me, the goalkeeper and the goalposts whenever I lined up a free-kick. Everything else just faded away while I stood over the ball and thought about what to do next. I knew how to drown out the noise. Sometimes my team-mates would be in my ear, offering advice, but they couldn't help. They might say, 'Try this' or 'So and so's waiting at the far post'. Or they'd ask if you were going to shoot. But I wasn't really listening to them. I was in my own little bubble, totally oblivious to the outside world. You've got a decision to make and not much time to make it.

I had to be totally focused because a set-piece is the only time when a ball is still during a match. You become like a golfer. Your mind takes over, and if you allow yourself to become distracted you end up blowing it. Different things start running through your head and you get caught in two minds. You have to take a step back and believe in yourself. I liked to take the wall out of the equation. I saw a goal and I saw a goalkeeper. All I thought was: 'It's just me versus you and a goal.'

My ability to visualise came to the fore. I almost floated away from the stadium to have a conversation with myself and although this all happened in the space of a split second, it was almost like time slowed down. I couldn't rush it. I was in a good position, maybe a little too near, and in those days the wall would never be 10 yards away. The opposing team would always edge forward, making it even harder. It was so close, centrally placed and right on the 18-yard line, with the Wolves players almost on top of me.

Various scenarios ran through my head while the referee was trying to get the wall back and my team-mates were trying to talk to me. Did I need to blast it? Or were they waiting for that? Could I catch out Paul Bradshaw, the Wolves goalkeeper?

I had to think quickly and make sure that I wasn't going to miss the best route to goal. I looked at their wall to see if it was arranged badly, making it easier for me to curl it around their defenders. As I studied them more closely, though, I realised it was going to be tough to whip it to the left. I needed an alternative plan.

In the end, sometimes you just have a hunch. 'I'll shape up as if I'm going around the wall,' I thought. 'But what I'll do is I'll go back the other way. I'll take a risk. If he stands still, he's just going to catch it.'

I wanted to deceive Bradshaw. I had a feeling that the position of the ball would make him think I was going to use my right foot to curl the ball towards the top-right corner. Shaping my body that way hid my true intentions and I could see that the keeper had inched to his left as soon as I lifted the free-kick over the wall. 'I've scored,' I thought as the ball left my foot and sailed towards the right corner. Bradshaw was helpless, wrong-footed and in the wrong position, and unable to adjust in time.

It was all about decision-making in the heat of the moment. I took a chance because Bradshaw would have had an easy save if he hadn't moved to his left. But it was all down to me. My team-mates couldn't help. I had to focus and make a call. I decided to take a chance and it was a fantastic feeling when it came off.

We were 45 minutes from Wembley. The second half was about protecting our lead and doing enough. We missed a couple of chances to make the game safe but we were still 2–1 up as the final whistle approached. Yet Wolves weren't going to stop chasing an equaliser before time was up. They attacked with a minute to go and the ball approached our area, reaching Hibbitt, who went down in a heap when I intervened with a perfectly timed tackle.

As I toed the ball away from Hibbitt, I thought that we were home and dry. I couldn't believe it when Clive Thomas, a referee who liked a bit of controversy, pointed to the spot. It was pure devastation. 'This cannot be,' I thought. No way was it a penalty. I was aghast and pleaded with Thomas to change his mind. In my heart, though, I knew that he wasn't going to bail me out and we went to extra time when Willie Carr stuck the penalty away.

Fatigue took over. Injustice too. My head had gone and all I wanted to do was have a go at the referee. Yet that would have been pointless and after five minutes of fulminating I pulled myself together. We needed to show character to make sure that Wolves didn't score again. 'Get on with it,' I thought. 'We've still got a job to do to get to the final.'

It finished 2–2, and the replay was four days later. This time we had to go to Highbury, which was strange. Either we reached Wembley by winning on Arsenal's turf or we crashed out by losing at the home of our greatest rivals. Yet while that was in our minds at the start, it was great to see the ground packed with Tottenham fans. We were inspired on the night and Wolves couldn't live with us. Crooksy was on fire. I set up his first goal, lobbing a ball over the top, and Crooksy headed it in when Wolves hesitated.

Wolves were terrified of his pace. Crooksy was always on the move when I had the ball. He knew that I could pick out his runs and I knew he was quick enough to reach my passes into space. He sped away from defenders with ease and I set him up again for his second goal, using the outside of my left foot to bend a pass away from their defenders and through for Crooksy to finish. I rate it as one of my best assists.

The ability to play the right pass was one of my biggest strengths. I wasn't being flashy by choosing to hit the ball with the outside of my left foot – in my head that just represented the easiest way to beat their defence. It was about making the right choice under pressure. When the ball was in front of me in a central position, it was hard to manipulate it with the inside of my right foot. The space was narrow, so I needed to use my ankle and cut across the pass.

It took me back to when I was a youngster training at Tottenham. One night I had to speak up to Ron Henry, who was a fearsome coach. We were doing a simple drill, standing 15 yards apart and passing to each other with the inside of both feet, and after a while I decided to mix it up.

Outside of my left foot, outside of my right foot. I was still hitting the target. But when Ron saw what I was doing, he wasn't happy.

'The drill is inside the left, inside the right,' he said. 'That's what I want.'

I could have stayed quiet. But I believed in my ability. Although I was shy, I summoned the courage to answer back.

'Yeah, but if I take it to the other side of my foot, I'm taking it earlier,' I said.

'Inside the foot,' Ron said, clipping me round the ear.

But I think he knew that I had a point. Outside of the foot? It made sense. It gave me so many more angles during a game and it took time away from defenders.

It wasn't arrogance. As I grew older I realised that I became an actor when I stepped over the white line. I became ultra-confident in my ability and was willing to try things. I trusted in the technique and how much power you put on the pass comes naturally. It was about feeling the ball and using my visualisation in those split seconds. When the ball was set properly, I just needed a moment to think. I didn't really see the ball. While I looked at it, I was really seeing a picture in my mind and working out which team-mate was in the best position for a pass.

In my mind's eye I saw Tony Galvin running by their full-back. I could have switched it to the left. But I could also see Crooksy running through the middle. I looked up and it was happening. As I went to hit the ball, curling it and cutting across it, I could visualise where I needed to play it for Crooksy. If I got the ball round the defender, I knew that he would be off.

I always had that ability to see a pass. Kevin de Bruyne is similar. I'd love to know how he comes up with some of his assists. It's about knowing where the ball needs to end up and being able to execute it. Obviously it doesn't always come off. But if I could visualise where a defender was going to be and where our forward was going to be running, I was in business. It was similar with shots. I saw the goal and worked out whether to hit it right or left.

In this case I saw Crooksy scorching past a defender in my mind's eye. It summed us up on the night. With everything working in perfect harmony, we were 2–0 up at half-time and the place was going nuts. We were playing Wolves off the park, and there was no coming back after Ricky cut inside before hammering in our third goal. Game over. Wolves were beaten and at that stage my mind drifted back to the first game. In a way I was grateful that Clive Thomas awarded that penalty. Tottenham wouldn't have taken over Highbury without that decision. We were on our way to Wembley.

I dreamt of playing in FA Cup finals when I watched them as a boy. Making it to Wembley was a massive achievement for every member of the squad. Ricky and Ossie, who had played in a World Cup final, were blown away by the enormity of the occasion. It was new territory for everyone and although we tried to keep saying that it was just another game, it was hard not to become distracted by everything around us.

There was so much going on. Ricky and Ossie did television interviews with their families back in Argentina on the night before the game. There were events with sponsors and constant questions about how many tickets we needed for family and friends. We even appeared on *Top of the Pops*, singing 'Ossie's Dream' with Chas & Dave, and I think that we struggled to keep our focus on the most important thing, which was beating Manchester City at Wembley.

Although it was all enjoyable, it didn't help our preparations. We were an inexperienced side at the highest level and we needed someone to snap us out of it, a wise head to come into the dressing room and deliver a few home truths. We were training and we were analysing City. We knew how we were going to play. But we weren't mentally prepared for going down Wembley Way with television cameras on our bus. We weren't ready to walk out of the tunnel in our suits. We weren't ready for the pitchside interviews.

It was completely different to a normal game. As we emerged from the tunnel before kick-off, we were waving to our families and there were handshakes with a member of the royal family, but were we truly focused? All the distractions affected us subconsciously, preventing us from reaching our top level.

We didn't play badly. We had a few chances and City needed Joe Corrigan to make some good saves. But City were physical and they succeeded in disrupting our rhythm for long spells. They targeted Ossie and were in the lead going in at half-time thanks to a powerful diving header from Tommy Hutchison.

When the goal went in I thought that we had to raise our game. We had to produce more. It had to spark us into life. But it just wasn't happening for us. To an outsider, it must have looked like City had a greater hunger than us. Although we were the more skilful team, they got stuck in and made it awkward.

Joe kept making saves, and with 15 minutes left I was getting frustrated. As a Tottenham man, I knew that we had never lost a final before. But the fear of losing didn't make me play better. We were drifting towards defeat.

It looked like City's day until we won a free-kick with 10 minutes left. This one was over to the right and further out than in the semi-final. I had to come up with something else. I thought hard and remembered one that we had scored in training. 'Let's shift it,' I said.

Steve Perryman and Ossie looked at me. 'Stevie, Ossie, we're going to shift it,' I said.

I stepped back and at the last moment, just as Ossie was about to play it, I saw that Steve was too far away.

'Steve! Closer!'

Ossie touched it and it wasn't the greatest set from Steve. Now it was up to me, and it was then that I thought that Joe Corrigan must have seen me whip the ball over the wall. This made up my mind to go round the outside and inexplicably Hutchison decided to move away from the wall. He appeared out of nowhere, popping up just as I hit it towards the left corner. It was such a strange position. Joe had already dived to his left and although he guessed correctly, he couldn't do anything when the ball veered towards the opposite corner after taking a massive deflection off Hutchison.

It was pure luck. I was like a little kid, jumping up and down, ecstatic when the ball went in. But we still had to make it through extra time. Technique went out of the window and it simply became about character, a pure mental battle. For once I was playing with my socks down. So was Chris Hughton. The Wembley pitch was so big and even Steve, who was such a fit player, was battling with cramp. Both teams were absolutely shattered and in the end it became about holding on for a replay.

The overriding feeling when the final whistle went was relief. Although Mum credited our goal to me, it went down as a Hutchison own-goal and we were lucky to have another shot at glory. We had to regroup before the replay. It was time for the psychologists to get to work. We admitted that we had taken our eye off the ball. We got carried away. We went out as individuals and forgot the qualities that had taken us this far. We agreed that our attitude had to be different during the replay. We weren't going to wave to our families or have cameras on our bus. We needed to get our heads down and focus.

There was a real buzz at training. I knew that we weren't going to lose. I also had faith in Ricky to turn up after having had a shocker in the first game. Keith had to take him off and there was a lot of debate over whether Gary Brooke should come in for Ricky before the replay. Stevie P was talking to Keith and Peter Shreeves was giving his input. But Ossie summed it up well. 'He's up there or he's down here,' Ossie said. 'If he isn't wonderful, just forget about it.'

I agreed with Ossie. I knew that Ricky was going to play well. The way I saw it, his stinker was out of the way. I saw it from him in training all the time. He was either brilliant or hopeless. There was no middle ground. It was how he lived his life.

In the end Keith went with Ricky. I felt for Brookesy, who was a cracking young player. He was distraught not to start, but that's management. Keith had to make difficult calls all the time and he must have been relieved when Ricky put us 1–0 up after eight minutes.

We had gone out with a much steelier attitude. We were determined to get our tackles in and didn't want City to bully us. Ricky's goal was our reward. Ossie started the attack with a lovely piece of skill, Archie had a chance and Ricky was in a world of his own after tucking the rebound away. He went off on this solo run and we all jumped on him when he stopped. It settled everyone down.

But City responded really well. It was one of the great cup ties, an all-time classic, and they levelled when Steve MacKenzie scored a stunning volley. I tried to get across to stop him but he struck it so sweetly Milija didn't have a chance.

We had to stay cool. They tried to kick us but we evaded their challenges. While it felt like we'd been playing uphill in the first game, this one had a flow. I hit the post with a free-kick and we put together some lovely moves. We were in control. We just needed to hold our nerve.

Yet it doesn't matter how much you control a game if you can't take your chances. You have to be clinical in a final and we found ourselves chasing the game when City won a penalty after Keith Hackett penalised Chris Hughton for a shove on David Bennett in the 50th minute.

Panic took over when Kevin Reeves scored. We lost our heads for the next 10 minutes. We were doing stupid things. I was rattled. Someone raked their studs down my thigh and I responded. Ossie came in kicking someone. Ricky got involved when Ossie got fouled. We were all over the place. It was pure indignation at being 2–1 down.

But we were playing into City's hands. I realised that we were definitely going to lose unless we put our anger aside and started playing again. I said it to Ossie. Ossie and Stevie P were saying it to the others. We knew we had to calm down. Our minds weren't on the ball and it was turning into a repeat of the first game, which suited City down to the ground.

It helped that we had spoken about the importance of focus before the game. We knew that we had to revert to our original plan. There was no point trying to fight City. The only way we were going to win was by playing beautiful football and creating chances.

The mood changed. I had a shot saved and we built momentum. We won a corner and the ball came to me on the edge of the area. I had to be sharp. I wanted time, but the blue shirts were closing me down. I set the ball nicely before chipping a pass over the top for Archie. Joe Corrigan came out and although the chance ran away from Archie, Crooksy was in the right place to equalise.

The goal shifted us up another gear. I doubted us at 2–1 down, but I knew we were going to win at 2–2. It was time for Ricky to take the stage. The rest of us watched transfixed when he set off on his run. I was far away and shouted 'Hit it' twice. On the edge of the box Garth pulled back his leg, almost as if he was willing Ricky to shoot. But he kept going, weaving inside and out, leaving their defenders for dead. It was an incredible run. We were witnessing history in the making and could hardly believe it when Ricky snuck his shot underneath Joe.

What a way to win the cup. Ricky was on one again. I tried to grab him but he was like a bar of soap. He went past Archie as well and just sprinted towards the halfway line, like a rugby player. We were all chasing him and it was wonderful that Ricky had his moment after playing so badly in the first game.

Everything had balanced out. We held on, surviving a late effort from Dennis Tueart, and going up the steps to collect the trophy in the Royal Box was a dream come true. Eventually we returned to the dressing room and jumped in the big Wembley bath. We were drinking champagne and celebrating. It was already mayhem before Ossie, who couldn't really hold his drink, came in holding the cup.

We were singing 'Ossie's Dream'. Ossie saw the bath. He didn't wait. He took a huge run-up, not realising how deep the bath was, and threw this famous old trophy into the air as he landed in the water.

Oh, Ossie. The cup hit the ceiling, fell in the water and had a dent on the rim. Ossie was splashing around in the water, completely oblivious, and we were pretending we were going to kill him. 'What have you done to our FA Cup?' I said. 'What have you done?'

We had no idea what to do. Deciding it was best to do nothing, we just put it in the middle of the dressing room and hoped nobody would notice. But Johnny Wallace, our kitman, was paying attention.

'Have you seen this cup?' he said.

'No, John. What cup? What's the matter?'

'Look, there's a dent in this cup,' he said.

We had to play dumb. We had to get to the after-match party at the Chanticleer, the luxury restaurant that was more or less part of White Hart Lane, and we'd sort out the trophy situation with the coach there. We couldn't let the dent appear in any pictures. We covered it up when we were having our photos done, although we told the FA in the end. They had to change it thanks to Ossie.

But it was a great night. My mind went back to winning promotion against Southampton. Ricky and Ossie certainly wouldn't have come to Tottenham if we'd stayed in Division Two, and Ossie told me that he wouldn't have joined if he'd known that we were a promoted side. So it was destiny.

That goalless draw with Southampton changed so much. When the final whistle at Wembley went I became a Tottenham fan again. I looked at Crooksy, who was jumping up and down like a little kid. I was too knackered for that. I was contemplative, remembering that I'd experienced the most painful day of my career against City two years earlier. I looked to the heavens and it hit me. I felt so proud. I had come so far since joining the club as a schoolboy.

4

BLUE AND WHITE BLOOD

There was a buoyancy around the club after Ricky's heroics at Wembley. We were on the move and Keith wanted to strengthen. I was excited when I realised that his search for a new goalkeeper had led him to Ray Clemence, who was interested in a new challenge after winning the European Cup with Liverpool. I'd played with Ray for England and knew that something was up when he started talking about moving down to London while we were off on international duty at the end of the 1980–81 season.

I was desperate for Ray to sign for Spurs. Although Milija Aleksic and Barry Daines had done great jobs for us, Ray was the best goalkeeper I'd played alongside. It gave us a huge lift when the deal went through, elevating us even more. Ray was still at his peak and he had such a big presence. He made incredible saves look easy and his winning mentality was another injection of positivity.

Our confidence grew, as we were more solid with Ray between the sticks. He organised the defence and took responsibility, holding his hands up if he made an error. He didn't have a big ego, nor did he put pressure on us by talking about winning all that silverware with Liverpool, who ruled

European football at the time. His view was that his time at Anfield was over. 'What I've done at Liverpool's one thing,' he said. 'This is a new challenge.' He was a great guy and a lovely character. I loved him to bits.

We were fighting on so many fronts in the 1981–82 season, challenging for the title, reaching both domestic cup finals and testing ourselves in Europe. It was an exhausting campaign, starting with us sharing the Charity Shield after a 2–2 draw with the reigning champions, Aston Villa. At one stage we were in with a shout of winning an unprecedented quadruple but the workload caught up with us. Every game felt big and it took a mental and physical toll. We couldn't sustain our title challenge, finishing fourth, 13 points behind the winners Liverpool, who we also faced in the League Cup final.

We were unbeaten in 20 games when we returned to Wembley to face Bob Paisley's outstanding side. We had just won the first leg of our European Cup Winners' Cup quarter-final against Eintracht Frankfurt and had come from a goal down to win our FA Cup quarter-final against Chelsea a week earlier, beating our London rivals 3–2 at Stamford Bridge.

We trusted in our ability. There's a difference between being a good side and being confident enough to win a trophy. We were losing our inconsistency and began to believe that we could win, even when we didn't play well, the mark of all great teams. We played lovely football, but we also had grit. If we went a goal down, we didn't lose faith.

Beating Chelsea summed up our spirit. The pitch was horrible and the place was going nuts when they went in 1–0 up at half-time. This wasn't Roman Abramovich's Chelsea. They were a Division Two team going through a rough period and they got carried away. Their fans were behaving like they'd already won, but we knew that we were going to turn it around. Archie equalised and we went 2–1 up when I banged one in from 25 yards. We were inspired. The atmosphere changed, and we pulled clear when I laid the ball back for Micky Hazard to score from the edge of the area.

This was us at our best, turning on the style, with individuals stepping up their game under pressure. We were tougher. Ray made us more solid, Robbo and Paul Miller gave us grit, and Tony Galvin added balance in midfield. We knew how to turn games round.

But taking on Liverpool at Wembley was a different proposition to outclassing Chelsea at Stamford Bridge. They didn't lie down when Archie put us 1–0 up after 11 minutes, and we couldn't put them away. Archie had a shot blocked on the line, then Liverpool equalised with three minutes to go, Ronnie Moran capitalising on an error from Ricky Villa.

It took the wind out of our sails. We'd invested so much energy into protecting our lead and that big pitch drained our legs. Liverpool completely dictated extra time and we ended up losing 3–1.

It was a bitter disappointment to let the trophy slip from our grasp. But our season wasn't over yet. Four days later we travelled to West Germany for the second leg of our Cup Winners' Cup tie against Frankfurt. Europe offered us a chance of swift redemption.

European nights were special. My mind went back to when I was a kid, watching European ties on the little pitchside benches at White Hart Lane. I saw us beat Wolves in the UEFA Cup final in 1972 and I was desperate to test myself against the best players on the continent. The thought of Ajax, Barcelona and Bayern Munich coming to town sent a shiver down my spine. I couldn't wait to play those games in front of our fans. It was going to be a huge test of our skill, intelligence and technique.

The quality of play far exceeded anything we had experienced in England. The style itself wasn't a shock to us. It wasn't that different from international football, and I'd already played for England, making my debut in a 2–0 win over Bulgaria in November 1979. As a team, though, we knew nothing about Europe. We had to step up our level and make the most of the raucous atmosphere at White Hart Lane.

Every European team played on the floor. They looked to play out from the back and focus on technical football, even if they weren't good enough. Michel at Real Madrid, the team that knocked us out of the quarter-finals of the UEFA Cup in 1985 thanks to a Stevie P own-goal, played with such freedom. Karl-Heinz Rummenigge was a threat when we played Bayern. Everyone was comfortable with the ball, even the defenders. We've caught up in this country in the last five years, but European teams have been playing that way for ever. We had to be so switched on. The foreign teams could pick you off if you lost concentration for a split second. We had to wise up quickly.

It was different to the English style, which was more rough and ready. Even Tottenham were a little direct at times, mixing our creativity with a more physical approach. It was the English way of thinking. Crowds wanted to see the ball move forward at pace and we used the atmosphere at times, placing visiting sides under pressure and seeing if they could handle the heat. The fans were close to the pitch, making it more intimidating, and I think this was partly why English sides had a lot of success in Europe during that era.

All the same I admired watching the European teams. It sparked something in me: a desire to test myself on the continent one day. 'Crikey, this is how I love the game played,' I thought. 'This is how I play, really. I want that challenge one day.'

It eventually happened when I joined Monaco in 1987. But I had opportunities before moving to France. Cologne, who were one of the best teams in Europe at the time, were close to buying me when I was 21. I even brought my wedding forward by a year because I thought that I wanted to go abroad, but it was too early in my career. One morning I woke up, looked at myself in the mirror and decided that it wasn't the right time to move.

I pushed it to one side and focused on Tottenham. We were heading into the unknown when we drew Ajax in the first round of the Cup Winners' Cup in September 1981. It was a glamour tie against a European giant. Although Ajax weren't quite as strong as when they won three consecutive European Cups in the 1970s, they were no mugs. They had Søren Lerby, an excellent Danish forward, and one of the challenges was that we didn't know much about them. There was no in-depth analysis available, so it was essentially a case of finding out if we were better than them on the night.

It worked both ways, though. They probably weren't sure about us either, and we gave them a shock, winning the first leg 3–1 in Amsterdam. Ricky Villa scored and Mark Falco, who was competing with Crooksy and Archie up front, was a right nuisance. Mark was such an important striker for us. He scored twice that night and we went through after winning the second leg 3–0 at home.

Yet we came crashing down to earth when we played Dundalk in the second round. The first leg in Ireland was a massive struggle. It was at the height of the IRA Troubles and security was intense. It was hard not to be distracted by everything going on around us. It was a test of character at Oriel Park, a cramped little stadium with an awful pitch and dodgy floodlights. The place was packed an hour before kick-off and the tension off the pitch made us jittery while we were warming up. I was worried when a voice came over the PA saying, 'We have an important announcement.' I froze and saw that Crooksy was panicking as well. We looked at each other and I could tell that we were having the same thought: bomb threat. We were both looking for somewhere to run and were about to leg it when we heard the second part of the announcement.

'In the West Stand, Bovril will be served at half-time.'

Everyone in the West Stand went mad. Meanwhile Croosky and I couldn't stop laughing. One minute we were looking for the nearest exit, the next we were thinking about half-time Bovril. It lightened the mood and, if anything, relaxed us too much. Dundalk gave everything. They didn't make it easy for us and earned a 1–1 draw when Mick Fairclough cancelled out Crooksy's opener in the second half.

We were relieved not to have lost. But we were wrong to assume that their moment in the sun was over. They were incredibly defiant during the second leg at White Hart Lane and we needed another late goal from Crooksy to calm our nerves.

It was another reminder not to take anything for granted. Dundalk gave us a fright, but we were in the zone when we met Eintracht Frankfurt in the quarter-finals in March, winning the first leg 2–0 and squeezing through when I scored a left-footed curler in the second leg to ensure we went through 3–2 on aggregate.

Yet the semi-final against Barcelona was such a letdown. A lot of their creative players were out and they adjusted by putting in their hatchet men for the first leg at White Hart Lane. Although we thought that we'd caught them at the right time, their injuries worked in their favour. They just wanted to take us back to the Nou Camp and they got away with their thuggish tactics thanks to a weak performance from the Dutch referee, Egbert Mulder. He let them get away with an incredible amount. Every time you beat someone, they responded by hacking you down. The tackles were knee-high at times and we had a blatant penalty waved away. It reminded me of when I was a kid playing in the men's league and the referee wasn't strong enough to restore order. We pleaded in vain for Mulder to take action.

We lost our rag in the end. Although Mulder sent off Juan Estella in the 57th minute, we lost focus and they grabbed the vital away goal when Ray somehow let a hopeful long-range shot from Antonio Olmo slip through his grasp. A late equaliser from Graham Roberts did little to lift our spirits before the return leg. 'Animals!' was the headline on the back pages the following morning. But it could be like that in Europe at times, and there was no happy ending against Barcelona. Although Robbo's equaliser in the first leg gave us hope of reaching the final, the Catalans edged the second leg at the Nou Camp, winning 2–1 on aggregate thanks to a goal from Allan Simonsen.

Losing was disappointing. After coming close to European glory, we were in danger of ending the season empty-handed. Liverpool had broken our hearts at Wembley, Barcelona had beaten us cynically and our title race was running out of steam. Everything was riding on our defence of the FA Cup.

*   *   *

Our comeback in our quarter-final against Chelsea convinced us that we were going to retain the FA Cup. We won our semi-final against Leicester 2–0 and went into the final against QPR thinking that we simply had to win it for the sake of our season. We deserved to win something after fighting so hard, but we knew that nothing would be handed to us for free.

The positive was that we were used to Wembley after our finals against Liverpool and Manchester City. This time we weren't affected by the fuss around the game. We were focused and we ignored the politics around Ricky and Ossie, neither of whom played because of the Falklands War, which was still being waged at the time.

Ossie, booed by Leicester fans during the semi-final, had already joined Argentina's training camp for the World Cup and Ricky was under pressure not to play from people back home. The FA Cup final was an English affair, and Argentinians didn't want to see Ricky shaking hands with members of the Royal Family or standing during the national anthem. After much deliberation with Keith, Ricky decided it was better to sit it out.

It was a difficult situation and we were gutted not to have our two Argentinian midfielders with us, especially as Ricky had been so influential against City the previous year. But it was out of our hands. It was nothing to do with us and we trusted in ourselves to win without them. Micky Hazard – a wonderfully skilful player – replaced Ricky, Robbo gave us steel in a midfield lacking Ossie, while Gary Brooke always offered something from the bench.

We had to be single-minded. We spoke about it as a group and reminded each other that Ricky and Ossie obviously wanted us to win. We used their absence as a motivational tool and made sure that all the hullabaloo didn't distract us.

Although I was interviewed on the bus taking us to Wembley, our attitude was first class. Recording another cup final song wasn't going to knock us off our stride.

But QPR, who were managed by Terry Venables, had a decent side, including Tony Currie, Gary Waddock and my mate Glenn Roeder, and we were under pressure as favourites. Although QPR didn't find playing in their first final easy, they caused us problems. Terry had clearly identified me as a threat and he had Waddock following me everywhere. It was irritating. Gary had a few digs and I was lucky not to be sent off after deciding to meet fire with fire. Keen to show that I could dish it out, I went into a two-footed tackle and left Gary in a heap.

It was a red card by modern standards. But play went on, the ball bounced to Robbo and I got up, leaving my man-marker behind. I was free at last. Robbo advanced towards the area and I was screaming at him to find me on the edge of the area. He cut it back, I took a touch and my shot took a nick off Currie's hamstring, enough to take the ball spinning into the right corner.

I sank to my knees, utterly ecstatic, and Chris Hughton jumped on me. My legs were bent with cramp and I jumped up to shake it off. I was exhausted but I thought it was the winner. QPR had other ideas. They equalised straight away, Terry Fenwick scoring, and took us to another replay.

QPR were unlucky. They played so well in the second game, and we had to show character after I gave us an early lead from the spot.

Robbo won the penalty, driving into the area before being fouled by Currie.

There were only six minutes on the clock and I wasn't really in the game, so I wanted to take the penalty quickly. Peter

Hucker, their goalkeeper, should have delayed me. He should have walked out or kicked his post a bit – anything to put me off. But as soon as I put the ball down I knew where I was going to go: bottom-right corner.

It felt right. I fought myself to stay positive and – bang. I took it so quickly that the television almost missed me giving us the lead. It was the perfect start and we were canny enough to hold QPR at arm's length. We knew how to play a final and European football taught us to be smart. It wasn't about playing the Tottenham way and trying to chase a beautiful second goal. Ray was in goal, screaming at everyone to concentrate, and we dragged ourselves over the line by defending properly.

It was a great battle. Gary man-marked me again and he was gutted at the end. We respected each other and I didn't think twice when he asked to swap shirts on the pitch. I didn't hesitate, which was a mistake. I should have waited until we were in the tunnel. QPR were in their away kit, which meant that I was wearing a red shirt when we went to the Royal Box to collect the trophy. 'You idiot,' I thought. 'What have you done? You look like an Arsenal player.'

But it was a minor disappointment. I had blue and white blood running through my veins. Life could hardly have been better for everyone associated with Tottenham.

Once again Europe was the next mountain to conquer. We disappointed in the 1982–83 season, suffering an early exit from the Cup Winners' Cup after losing 5–2 on aggregate to Bayern, but our league form was good. We had aspirations of winning the title and finished fourth in the end, which was enough to qualify for the UEFA Cup.

Yet that was a tough time in my career. A persistent Achilles injury was holding me back. I played with it for two years.

The sheath was strangling the Achilles, making it tight and inflamed, and there were mornings where I couldn't put my foot on the floor until I jumped in the bath and put it in hot water, just to get some respite from the stiffness.

Injections didn't help. By April 1984 there was only one option left: surgery. They snipped the sheath and removed the scar tissue.

It was awful timing given that we were on a roll in the UEFA Cup. I was heavily involved during the early rounds, particularly when we faced Feyenoord in the second round. They were no pushovers. They had just signed Johan Cruyff from Ajax, and although the Dutch wizard was approaching the end of his career, we knew better than to underestimate him.

I was excited to pit my wits against a player of Cruyff's calibre. I remembered watching him win a penalty for Holland in the first minute of the 1974 World Cup final. West Germany's Berti Vogts, who was man-marking him, didn't know where to turn. Cruyff stopped, started and stopped again, bewitching Vogts, who brought him down. Although Holland didn't win, it was a fabulous plan from Cruyff. He played with such style and imagination. As a kid I watched in awe when I saw him invent the Cruyff turn against Sweden. I watched it with Dad, and we were both trying to work out what had happened. It was beautiful. Cruyff sent the poor defender off for an ice cream and the dummy was amazing.

I was smitten and went straight into the garden to try it out, even though it was pitch black outside.

'What are you doing out there?' Mum shouted.

'Don't worry, Mum, I'm just practising my Cruyff turn!'

Mum let me get on with it and I ended up using that skill so many times during my career. It was special because nobody had seen it before. And not many players have a move named after them.

The odd thing, though, was talk of Cruyff planning to man-mark me before the first leg at White Hart Lane. I thought that was weird. Some of the lads spoke about it in the dressing room and I was sure it was just paper talk. 'Why would they put Johan Cruyff on me?' I thought.

Yet it was in the back of my mind when I saw him during the warm-up and I couldn't believe it when he picked me up once the game was under way. 'This is strange,' I thought. 'One of the world's greatest players marking me. Surely he's so good you let him play. Why wouldn't you put a defender on me?'

I'm not sure if Cruyff or someone else came up with the plan. Either way it was a bad one. It gave me a huge lift and I had one of my best games for Tottenham. I wanted to show Cruyff that he couldn't stop me. I was on fire and created four goals in the first half.

Four–nil down at half-time, Feyenoord had to chuck the plan out of the window. They won the second half 2–0 and Cruyff started playing. The real Cruyff turned up. He was playing one-twos and scored a good goal from the edge of the area. He showed his talent and he was classy after the game, shaking my hand and giving me his shirt.

Cruyff knew we were the better side and we made sure in the second leg, winning 2–0 in Rotterdam to set up a tie with Bayern. The pressure was on again. We had bad memories of Bayern from the year before and we were up against it after losing the first leg 1–0 in Munich.

But we backed ourselves at home. We levelled on aggregate when I sent in a free-kick and Robbo nodded it down for Archie to score in the 50th minute. Bayern chased an away goal but I was in the mood, creating the winner when I chipped a reverse pass through for Mark Falco to score.

Mark was always good for an important goal and we had momentum after beating Bayern. Yet my Achilles injury was weighing me down. I went under the knife after we won our semi-final against Hajduk Split, giving me a month to recover for the two-legged final against Anderlecht.

I was desperate to make it back in time. I tried to rush it and the coaching staff were prepared to take a chance. But I wasn't doing myself any favours. I missed the final and spent a lot of time wondering if I'd long-term damage to my Achilles.

Not that I wasn't delighted when we beat Anderlecht on penalties after two 1–1 draws. It was a great effort from the lads given that we had so many injuries. Stevie P was out, and Ray, Ossie and Crooksy were all carrying knocks. Tony Parks played in goal and was huge in the shootout, while Gary Stevens and Micky Hazard were fantastic in midfield.

All the same it was a difficult time for me. I thought my career was over when I hurt my Achilles during the summer. I was messing around at home and I forgot about the injury when I jumped in the pool, using my injured right foot to take off.

I wasn't thinking. I felt it go immediately and I was in tears when I hobbled upstairs to bed. I was distraught. I called Mike Varney, the physio, who arranged to meet me at the ground. I could hardly walk. 'I've really done something bad, Mike,' I said. 'I think my career could be threatened here.'

Mike calmed me down and had a look at it. 'You know what, Glenn?' he said. 'Don't get too down. I think we'll just send you to a specialist when you can walk a bit better. I think you might have done yourself a favour and torn a load of the scar tissue.'

It was strange. I'd had an operation because of the scar tissue but more had formed, and I didn't feel different after the procedure. It took this explosion at the back of the ankle to clear everything up.

'I think you've broken all the scar tissue down, Glenn,' Mike said.

'You're just saying that to keep me positive,' I said.

'No, I think it's a good chance that that's happened. But we'll send you to this specialist in two or three days' time. Just rest it, let it settle down.'

I went away and three days later the Achilles felt looser. Mike told me to keep icing and stretching it, and I started to feel better. The dark cloud hanging over my head disappeared. I began to think positively again. I was optimistic and believed my career wasn't over after all. It's amazing how the mind works. It's such a powerful tool.

I was in a good place by the time I visited the specialist. Although the scar tissue was still there, he told me I had probably broken a lot of it. 'Mike's right,' he said. 'I think you've done yourself a favour in many ways. You might've done a month's work in one fell swoop.'

I was so lucky. I thought that jumping in the pool had ended my career. Instead I had managed to heal myself.

There are so many what-if moments in life. I've had a few near misses. I had my eye injury when I was 13, and I wonder what would have happened if Keith had stayed at Tottenham after winning the UEFA Cup. For all our success, our failure to win the league during that period was a disappointment.

Keith deserved better. He built a strong side after struggling in his first season but football was changing. Tottenham became a limited company and Irving Scholar, the chairman, wanted more of a say in signings. Looking back, perhaps Scholar was right. He wanted the best for Tottenham and we were the first English club to operate in a more continental way. But Keith wasn't having it after winning the UEFA Cup. 'I'd rather not be manager if you're going to do this,' he said.

Scholar inevitably came out on top. We couldn't believe it. We were devastated for Keith. 'There used to be a great football club there,' he said as he walked away from the ground.

Keith was a man of principle, an honest man, and Tottenham haven't won much of note since he left. He deserved more time. He deserved a chance to build again. It was an injustice. Tottenham were building corporate boxes and improving the stadium but events on the pitch determine whether a club is successful. That should never be touched.

Keith should have been allowed to continue, and leaving hit him hard. I used Keith as a scout when I moved to Swindon as player-manager in 1991 and told him my feelings about his departure. I think he struggled to get over the hurt. He went to manage Bahrain after leaving Tottenham and had spells with Sporting Lisbon, Gillingham and West Brom. He even spent time in Malaysia. Yet it was never the same for him after Tottenham. I was gutted when he left.

Nevertheless the team had to get on with it. We couldn't change it and we were happy when Peter Shreeves, Keith's assistant, stepped up as manager. Peter did a good job straight away and we should have won the league in 1985. Everybody thought it was our year when we won at Arsenal on New Year's Day. But we just couldn't get over the line. It was our fault. Losing at home to Everton in April killed us. I think we would have finished top if we had beaten them. It was in our hands, but Neville Southall had a world-class game in goal and Everton went on to become champions.

It was frustrating. We had the players and we kept making good signings. I loved playing with Chris Waddle after he arrived. Paul Allen and Steve Hodge bolstered the midfield, Richard Gough joined Gary Mabbutt at the back and I had a good relationship with Clive Allen after he signed in 1984. I made plenty of goals for Clive, who was a dangerous forward. He scored 49 goals in the 1986–87 season.

Yet while Scholar liked me, I was beginning to feel unfulfilled and the thought of trying something new entered my mind. When David Pleat replaced Peter as manager in 1986 I promised to give him one more year. I didn't have anything against David, even though I was sad when Peter left. I just needed a fresh start, and was thinking more and more about playing abroad.

People in England always misunderstood me, dismissing me as a luxury player. I yearned for the freedom creative foreign players enjoyed. I marvelled at Dutch football and felt envious of Romania's Gheorghe Hagi. I loved to create. I scored some unbelievable goals and some of them made me feel amazing. Yet I got as much satisfaction from assists. That was my forte: making chances for forwards. My real art was catching defenders out with a clever pass.

Yet it was tough to be a creative player in England. The No10 position never really existed for me. For most of my career I had to defend deep, often playing on the right side of a diamond for Tottenham or in right midfield for England. If I were playing today I would be a No10.

It's an interesting role and there are different types of No10s. There are players like Dennis Bergkamp, Eric Cantona, Gianfranco Zola and Teddy Sheringham, who are strikers that drop back to create, while Zinedine Zidane, Cruyff and Michel Platini are creative midfielders who played as No10s.

Frank Lampard, David Platt and Dele Alli are No10s who are box threats and second strikers.

I fell into the category that included Cruyff, Platini and Zidane. In England, though, our eyes weren't yet open. Although Tottenham played an expansive game, most of the teams were physical. Foreign players scoffed at our long-ball tactics. I despaired when talented players like Alan Hudson and Tony Currie were shoved aside by England in the 1970s. It was an outrage that Hudson only won two caps.

In my opinion it goes back to England winning the World Cup in 1966. Sir Alf Ramsey built a fine side, but we never moved on from that summer. We became stuck in our ways, arrogantly and blindly clinging to 4–4–2. While Germany reinvented themselves, we stood still.

5

OUTSIDE THE BOX

I laughed when I heard opposition players telling each other to hit the channel when they had the ball. 'What "channel?"' I said. 'The "English Channel?"'

I often think about the stretch of water separating us from the rest of Europe. Although both the Channel and the North Sea kept us safe from the Germans during the Second World War, they made us insular in other ways. When it came to football we had our head in the sand after becoming world champions in 1966. Sir Alf Ramsey played a mode of football that worked at the time, but we didn't evolve. We didn't have vision and coaching ability. We didn't think creatively. The British bulldog spirit helped win the war but it kept us repressed and isolated in other walks of life.

Of course, none of that occurred to me when England beat West Germany in the final in 1966. I always loved watching England. I was desperate for us to win and cried my eyes out when Germany equalised in the last minute of normal time. I was happier after Geoff Hurst completed his hat-trick in extra time.

Watching England was emotional. I was even more obsessed during the 1970 World Cup, taking in every game. I couldn't take my eyes off that special Brazil side. Pelé, Tostão, Jairzinho and Rivelino – what a team. I was purring when I watched their football. 'This is beautiful,' I thought. 'This is how I want to play.'

Although England were good in 1970, we couldn't play like the Brazilians. But we could have won it. We were 2–0 up against West Germany in the quarter-final, only for the game to change when Sir Alf's concerns about the Mexican heat saw him decide to take Bobby Charlton off and save him for the next game. It was the right decision in those conditions but it backfired. England weren't the same without Charlton and Germany went through, winning 3–2 after extra time.

That's the cruelty of football. I've played in those games. It's like you've dropped a bar of soap in the bath and it keeps slipping out of your grasp. England hadn't done much wrong against a very strong side and there was no reason to be alarmed. I broke down in tears but I wasn't crying because I was worried about the future of English football. I was just a 12-year-old boy who didn't like losing.

Yet if someone had tapped me on the shoulder that day and told me that I would be in the squad the next time England reached a major tournament, I'd have laughed. 'Don't be so stupid,' I'd have said, wiping my tears away.

And what happened? England were outcasts in 1972, 1974, 1976 and 1978. We went from world champions to no-hopers in no time at all. We didn't qualify for another tournament until the European Championship in 1980.

Lazy coaching was to blame. Creative football was frowned upon – we didn't understand it. We had great players during that period but we didn't use them. Germany used their great players, but we didn't know what to do with ours.

1966, our greatest moment, should have been the springboard for future generations. Instead it became our nemesis. It dragged us back in time because the people at the top were fixated with 4–4–2 and couldn't find room for talents like Rodney Marsh, Alan Hudson, Frank Worthington and Tony Currie.

I often wonder if George Best would have started for England in 1966 given that Sir Alf didn't play with wingers. If Best had been English, would Sir Alf have made room for him or would he have trusted in his system and ignored one of the greatest British players of all time? I don't think there's any guarantee whatsoever that Best would have played, which sums it all up in my view.

I loved watching Best. I adored him when he played for Manchester United, although Bobby Charlton had the greater influence on me. Charlton could play with both feet. He could score from distance. He had a lovely body swerve. He could create. He was probably the best player in the world when England won the World Cup – and we didn't use him as a template for future players.

What happened when I was a kid? We were so stagnant. The style of play was so sad. I yearned for Hudson and Currie to be given a chance. Hudson ran the show on his debut, helping England beat West Germany in a friendly in 1975. He was given one more cap. I couldn't believe it.

I was so frustrated when I watched England play. The blood and thunder wasn't for me. Yet it wasn't easy for players who wanted to get the ball down and play. Stevie Perryman once told me that he was a technical player when he came through at Tottenham. A passer. 'When Bill Nicholson put me in the side I suddenly got moulded into being a ball-winner and I played like that,' Stevie P continued. 'But you've stuck to your guns, Glenn. You weren't going to change.'

'Steve, I couldn't change,' I said. 'I couldn't become a ball-winner because that isn't my game. I can put my foot in, and I'll get back and do my defensive duties, but I'm not a ball-winner.'

I was prepared to stand my ground. I wasn't daft when it came to football. It meant the world to me, and if people wanted to criticise they were free to do so. I paid more attention when the great Danny Blanchflower, who was superb when Tottenham won the Double in 1961, sought me out after I bent a free-kick into the top corner during a win over Ipswich in 1980.

An astonishingly gifted player in his day, Danny was covering the game for a newspaper and I'd never met him before. Danny was a footballing romantic. He played the game the right way and we had similar views on football, although I was like a little kid when he came up to me.

'I just want a word with you,' he said.

Danny was a gentleman, a lovely guy, and I enjoyed talking to him about football. He told me that he enjoyed our game against Ipswich and I asked him about winning the Double. But he also wanted to get something off his chest.

'Glenn,' Danny said, 'don't ever, ever, ever listen to people saying you're a luxury player. The luxury player is the one that gives the ball away, is the one that can't see a pass, is the one that can't score a goal, is the one who can't create for his team.'

His point hit home. My eyes were completely opened. Driving home that night, I realised that Danny was right. 'That's the luxury player,' I thought. 'The one that runs around and can't see a picture, can't score a goal. He tries his best but there's loads of them. They're two a penny.'

It stayed with me and it helped that I was at Tottenham. But in England it was mainly about grafting and winning your headers and moving the ball forward quickly. The game was so physical in the 1970s. Ossie and Ricky told me that they wouldn't have come to Tottenham had they known what the football would be like. There were also rumours about Tottenham trying to sign Michel Platini, who probably never would have had the ball at his feet if he'd come to England.

Most of my possession came from the ball spilling free from headed duels. It was only the teams who got the ball down – teams like Liverpool, Tottenham and Nottingham Forest – who won European trophies.

I roll my eyes when people criticise me and downplay my achievements because I didn't win a league title with Tottenham. We proved ourselves in Europe by going up against teams like Barcelona, Bayern Munich and Real Madrid. We won the UEFA Cup, and people would have spoken about me differently if we'd won that title decider against Everton in 1985. In any case, the game isn't just about medals. It's also about creating indelible memories. There are players who have won loads of Premier League titles who weren't as technically gifted as me.

Yet some people called me 'Glenda', which sums up the mentality of fans and journalists at the time. Maybe it was because I didn't stick my foot in, even though I didn't hold back if I needed to send a message. Or perhaps it was because I let my shirt hang out. It was my punishment for daring to be different.

To be honest, I have no idea why I had that nickname. I just played naturally, even though it was always a battle for creative players. I saw great talents who played before me never get a chance for England, who never seemed to wonder why they weren't qualifying for tournaments. There was a culture war at play. I believe the Football Association at the time were on the opposite side, the long-ball game being down to the FA's director of coaching Charles Hughes, who promoted a direct style. It was all about scoring within three passes.

It wasn't that I refused to hit a long ball. I just preferred to have a theory behind one rather than punting a hopeful pass into the channels for a striker to chase. I preferred to be free.

I found the emphasis on physicality frustrating and there was no escape from the rigid thinking after I made my debut for England in a qualifier for Euro 1980 against Bulgaria in November 1979. My start at international level was deceptively good. Ron Greenwood brought me into the squad, which was heavy on Liverpool players. I didn't expect to play. But just as we were about to get off the bus at our training base on the day before the game, Ron decided to name the team. He went down the list and I was shocked to hear my name. I couldn't believe it. A couple of the more experienced players congratulated me and I couldn't wait to tell my parents.

Yet as we approached Wembley on the day of the game I realised that I couldn't see the stadium's twin towers. Fog was descending and I was fretting about the game being called off. My family had tickets but I couldn't see the pitch when we walked down the tunnel. I got to the halfway line and could just about make out the goal at the other end. 'Just my bloody luck,' I thought. 'My England debut and it's going to be off.'

The other lads were cracking up, calling it the debut that never was, and it wasn't long before it was indeed called off. Back in the dressing room, however, we found out that we were going to come back 24 hours later. 'Bloody hell, I've got to go through that again tomorrow,' I thought. That nervous feeling in my stomach was back.

Yet I settled into the game quickly. I knew Ray Wilkins and Viv Anderson from England youth games and I played well. I crossed for Dave Watson to score the opener and started to feel really calm, popping the ball around, beating players and almost scoring.

The second half was tougher. We went through a bitty spell where I wasn't getting on the ball. These weren't my normal team-mates and I felt odd demanding the ball. But I found my voice. Trevor Francis picked up possession on the edge of their area and I shouted for him to pull the ball back.

Trevor saw me and laid it back. The ball was bouncing and I opened my body, using the inside of my right foot to aim a half-volley towards goal. I could have laced it but I knew that a side-footer was the right choice. The ball flew off my foot, much like my goal against Stoke on my debut for Tottenham, and the Bulgaria goalkeeper didn't have a chance of saving it.

It was the most exhilarating feeling to score on my debut for my country. I ran but I didn't know where I was going. Wembley's a big place. In the end I embraced Trevor and thanked him for the assist. I had goosebumps. The win ensured we were one of the eight countries going to the tournament and I didn't want the game to end, even though I was knackered by full-time.

Yet while I couldn't have done much more to impress Ron, it was a while before he played me again. It was baffling. There was no explanation. No communication. I didn't understand it because when I returned to Tottenham after my debut I felt like I could jump over the moon. Ron didn't sit me down to explain why I wasn't playing and my shyness stopped me from asking him. I turned up to squads and found myself on the bench, wondering what I was doing wrong, and it sapped my confidence.

At least I went to the Euros, where the format saw the teams split into two groups of four. Yet I wasn't trusted to start a game until our hopes of reaching the final were already over. We were placed with Belgium, Spain and Italy, the hosts, and we didn't start well. We drew 1–1 with Belgium in our opening game and were on the brink after losing late on against Italy.

Beating Spain 2–1 in our final game wasn't enough to prevent an early flight home. I started, and Ron played an attacking midfield four, using me alongside Ray Wilkins, Trevor Brooking and Terry McDermott. 'We've just got to work hard together,' Ray said. 'That's how we win the game. We've all got to work as a unit.'

Ray played slightly deeper and our formation was comparable in a way to the diamond we used at Tottenham. I felt good. We played well and won, giving us hope of reaching a third-place play-off against Czechoslovakia, only for Italy to take our place by drawing 0–0 with Belgium later in the evening.

The scheduling left much to be desired. It was strange that Belgium's game against Italy didn't kick off at the same time as ours against Spain. It meant that Belgium knew they would reach the final by drawing with Italy, who only needed a point to end our hopes. That doesn't happen anymore: the final group games always start at the same time now.

Tournaments were structured in odd ways during that era. Two years later we went out of the World Cup without losing a single game. We finished top of our first group, beating France, Czechoslovakia and Kuwait, and progressed to a second group with West Germany and Spain.

After playing against Czechoslovakia and Kuwait, I found myself out in the cold against West Germany and Spain. We needed a win against Spain to go through after we drew 0–0 West Germany. Yet time wore on, with no sign of a break-through. I was itching to get on, convinced that I could put the ball on a plate for someone in the final 20 minutes, and it hurt when Ron brought Kevin Keegan and Trevor Brooking on instead. Although Trevor and Kevin were big players, they were injury doubts before the game. It was hard to take, and we were on our way home after another 0–0 draw.

I never clicked with Ron. He was a lovely guy and I thought that I had a chance with him because of how he approached the game. He played an attractive style when he managed West Ham and I thought he would have me in his team. Yet it didn't pan out that way. I don't think we had enough of a strategy. The message was that we were good enough to sort it out ourselves on the pitch. We had one 11 versus 11 training game at the World Cup but there was no big focus on shape or pattern of play. Ron didn't tell the centre-backs that their first thought with the ball should always be to play it into midfield. No, it was a case of 'Go out there and play like you do for your clubs'.

We needed more than that because we were coming up against teams who were playing five in midfield and we were exposed against teams with better structures. They outnumbered us and we ended up chasing shadows. Although Don Howe did a lot of work on shape with the defenders, the front players were left to fend for themselves. We didn't spend enough time concentrating on tactics and didn't need to train hard after a long, draining season for our clubs. It felt as if our bodies were ready, but it was our minds that needed fine-tuning. Yet we didn't talk about what we were going to do with and without the ball. It was 4–4–2 and very off the cuff.

It was different for club sides. Liverpool dominated with British players in Europe but they were working on patterns of play every day. Their players knew each other inside out. It was more spasmodic with England. In defence of Ron the camps weren't long and he had limited time with us. Surely, though, that meant there should have been an even greater focus on tactics.

It didn't change much when Bobby Robson replaced Ron after the World Cup. We loved Bobby and played for him because he was so endearing, but we didn't receive the same level of coaching as Holland, Italy and Germany. The Dutch had theories, and Cruyff learnt so much from Rinus Michels at Ajax.

Perhaps there was a feeling that we could play like Liverpool if we used a few of their players. However, while we had some great performances at times, our opponents tended to outsmart us more often than not. We had nowhere to go when we had the ball. Our defenders looked to the forwards and bypassed the midfield. It got on my nerves and I had battles with the centre-backs at times. International football needed more thought. Our defenders could focus on heading crosses away and getting the ball forward quickly when they played for their clubs, but with England they were coming up against players like Hagi, Spain's Emilio Butragueño and Mexico's Hugo Sánchez, who were totally different. We hit it long and the ball just kept coming back at us.

We wasted so much energy chasing good players who were playing in clever systems. I used to wonder why I was more knackered after playing for England. At first I thought it was just down to mentality. Eventually I realised it was because technically gifted players were passing around us all the time.

I'm pleased that English football has progressed in recent years. The academies have improved and we have defenders who can pass. In the 1970s and 1980s, though, creative players were frowned upon. We were painfully small-minded and it took us an eternity to change how we coached the youngsters. When I was 10 I played on full-sized pitches, whereas our European rivals had their young players working on smaller pitches. It was straightforward logic. Dutch, French and German kids were playing with smaller goals and they were touching the ball more. It's little wonder that their technique was better than ours.

Yet it took a long time for the penny to drop, and we didn't qualify for Euro 84 under Bobby, putting him under pressure. I often felt suffocated playing for England, stuck on the right flank most of the time. It baffled me. It wasn't my position. Steve Coppell was a better right winger than me when I first broke into the side, and Trevor Steven did a great job getting up and down the line for Everton in later years.

I tried to drift inside at times and play like I did for Tottenham, who were flexible and smart. Yet it was hard in a rigid 4–4–2. We only used a diamond once, away to Hungary in 1983. It was the only time I played as a No10. I scored the opener and made two goals. I was called on to perform and I responded well. Yet we never did it again. It was weird.

I always fought against the tide when I played for England. There was never a coach who truly trusted me. Perhaps it could have been Don Revie, who built a great footballing side at Leeds in the 1970s, although my biggest regret is that Brian Clough was always overlooked by the FA.

Clough said that he would have built his England team around me. He even tried to sign me once for Forest, although I didn't believe it was him when he called me out of the blue one day to talk about a transfer. I thought it was my mate Sean and I told him to eff off. Imagine my panic when the phone rang again.

'Young man, it's Brian Clough,' said the man at the other end of the line. 'I'd like you to come and play for Nottingham Forest.'

But I couldn't bring myself to leave Tottenham at the time. 'OK, young man,' he said. 'It's pretty obvious you're going to stay at Tottenham. Good luck to you.'

There were no hard feelings and I would have loved Clough to manage England. He would have been fantastic. He understood what made players tick and knew how to build a balanced side. Look at John McGovern. Clough took McGovern everywhere. He thought the world of him but he also made it clear to him that he couldn't play. 'You're a journeyman,' he'd say, telling him to give the ball to Trevor Francis or John Robertson.

Some players would have retreated into their shell. But Clough went on to tell McGovern that nobody could tackle like him. He understood how to communicate and make players feel 10 feet tall. He could get away with calling Robertson 'the little chubby one on the wing' at the same time as calling him a world-class player. It worked because he was praising Robertson.

Clough would have changed England. He might have been tested by not spending as much time with players, but he was a one-off. The problem, ultimately, was that he wasn't an FA blazer. I was gutted he didn't manage me. He thought outside the box and I played outside the box. Yet the timing wasn't right in so many ways.

A big part of my frustration was that we were perfectly capable of producing good players. We weren't a team of no-hopers, and although we were annoyed to watch Euro 84 from afar, we were optimistic when we qualified for the World Cup in 1986. We had threats: Gary Lineker was one of the best strikers around; Chris Waddle and John Barnes had broken onto the scene; and Peter Beardsley, a deep-lying striker, gave us something different in a 4–4–2, dropping behind Gary to become that No10.

Our forwards could hurt opposition defences and, wary of how hot it was going to be in Mexico, we prepared well by going there to play in a tournament in the summer of 1985. It was an important trip, even though it wasn't enjoyable playing at altitude and in scorching conditions. We found out what we were going to be up against and Bobby learnt a lot about the players.

I did well in the games against Mexico, Italy and West Germany. But the conditions were tough and the Aztec Stadium in Mexico City was 7,280 feet above sea level. Before we played Mexico Kenny Sansom and I tried carrying our bags up three flights of stairs because the lifts were occupied. We had to stop twice because we were gasping for air, but there was no respite during the games. I realised that we weren't going to be able to play the English way, so we stopped trying to press during that tournament and looked to contain our energy. After losing to Italy and Mexico we finished on a high, beating West Germany 3–0.

Yet we didn't take the lesson on board. When we returned to Mexico for the World Cup the following year we tried to press in our first game in Monterrey. It was a ludicrous decision. Portugal picked us off and won 1–0 thanks to a late goal.

It was a terrible way to start and we were really up against it when we faced Morocco in our second game. We lost Bryan Robson to a shoulder injury in the first half and things became worse when Ray Wilkins was sent off just before half-time, leaving us to play with 10 men in searing heat. All we could do was survive and hold on for a 0–0 draw. But it was horrible. We were losing five kilos a game in that heat, and the last five minutes against Morocco were frightening. I was hallucinating. I was running along, with Gary Stevens taking a throw-in, and I was asking myself which way we were going.

Utterly shattered after holding Morocco, we ended up having a day off training and visiting a monastery in Monterrey. It was a beautiful place – they set up a marquee for us and the barbecue was going. After a while we walked away from the marquee, wandered over to the side of a hill and started talking about how to approach the Poland game. The debate lasted for 90 minutes. We sat out in the sun, getting burnt, and talked about when to press the ball. Bobby Robson and Don Howe thought that we needed to harry the Poles despite the heat, adding that 'We're straying from the real strengths of English football.'

The debate continued in training the next day, with Bobby and Don trying to convince us to push higher. But it was the only time where player power reared its head. We decided to drop off. Although we were going to try and block them in if they had a throw, we didn't want to press in open play. The midfielders were determined to drop to the halfway line and press from there.

Our ploy worked. Gary Lineker scored a hat-trick to send us through to the second round and I laughed when I thought about that debate on the hill. It was the biggest match of our lives and we prepared for it by getting burnt to smithereens. Yet it worked, and we were on the right track. We played well when we beat Paraguay 3–0 in the second round and found ourselves in a quarter-final with Diego Maradona's Argentina, who were desperate to beat us because of the Falklands War.

The political situation between Britain and Argentina didn't really cross our minds before the game. Although I thought back to Ossie and Ricky missing the FA Cup final in 1982, we had moved on. Argentina took the opposite view. It was bigger than football for them. They had an extra emotional edge, a deep yearning to beat us, and it was like their players were the medium for a nation yearning for revenge. The footballers were the only ones who could get one over on the English, and it gave them extra motivation on the day. They were able to tap into something deeper, something more visceral.

We couldn't fool ourselves into feeling those emotions. They simply didn't exist. Our motivation was more straight-forward. We were simply desperate to reach the last four of the World Cup and we felt that we were good enough to beat Argentina – as long as we found a way to stop Maradona.

It was a month since I played with Maradona in Ossie's Tottenham testimonial at White Hart Lane. It was a wonderful night, and although we didn't know each other we gelled on the pitch. We had a fabulous time and we shared a nod when we were lining up in the tunnel in Mexico City. It was just a little nod – a sign of respect before we went out to compete.

There was no sign of the drama to come during the first half. It was an even game on a horrible pitch and there was nothing in it at half-time. We were tired and didn't create much. Maradona put a free-kick over the bar. He wasn't fantastic and wasn't doing much to unsettle our defence.

We weren't even that concerned when Argentina raised their tempo at the start of the second half. But the temperature was about to rise. I saw it happen. I saw the ball looping in the air and I saw Maradona punch it past Peter Shilton with his hand before running off towards the corner flag to celebrate putting Argentina 1–0 up. My stomach was churning when I saw the linesman running back to the halfway line. I felt sick as I ran after the referee with Terry Fenwick and Shilts to protest. 'It's handball,' I said. 'Handball!' The feeling of injustice burned inside me but I knew that the referee wasn't going to change his mind.

I didn't blame Shilts. Without the handball Shilts would have punched the ball away and taken Maradona out. Maradona's instinct worked for him because he realised in that split second that he wasn't going to reach the ball without using his hand. We later found out that he'd done it before. But the whole controversy would have been avoided if Shilts had arrived first.

Maradona was smart to celebrate and beckon his teammates over to make it look more genuine. I've never blamed him. I blame the officials for not spotting it and although we have always viewed Maradona as a cheat, it's fair for people to point out that Terry Fenwick was lucky not to be sent off for fouling him in the first half.

It's the difference between the British and the South American mentality. There were plenty of times at international level where our opponents won cheap free-kicks by going down easily. They were artists. We had no idea how to do it, so we looked stupid when we tried to con the referee. I used to despair when referees penalised us. The closer they got to our goal, the more theatrical they became. It was like they played with an extended penalty area.

The South Americans were taught how to do it, just as Italian defenders were taught how to tug a striker's shirt at set-pieces or knock him off balance when the referee wasn't watching. It was clever and we kept having the wool pulled over our eyes. We were naive by comparison and Maradona made the officials look like suckers.

As for his second goal, there was nothing we could do to stop him. It was an incredible goal, especially on that dismal pitch. The grass was really long because of the ruts on the turf and the ball was bouncing around all over the place but he kept it under control. It was a footballing miracle, although we gave Terry some stick for not flattening him at the start of the dribble. We told Terry, who was on a booking after the earlier foul, that he should have taken one for the team. He told us that he would have been sent off. We joked that it would have been worth it if Maradona had gone off on a stretcher. Terry hesitated when he came out to confront Maradona, who used that slight pause to slip by.

The rest is history, although our response after going 2–0 was impressive. I went close with a free-kick and we gave ourselves hope when Gary scored. We pushed hard for a second goal and Gary came within a whisker of equalising, but Argentina went through, before beating West Germany in the final. We went home to lick our wounds and nurse our sense of indignation. It was another case of close but not close enough, summing up my England career.

I have heard esteemed thinkers of the game like Ruud Gullit, Michel Platini and Arsène Wenger say that England wasted my talent. Platini said that I would have had 100 caps if I'd been French and Ruud told me that I was born in the wrong country.

People often ask me if I agree with Ruud. 'No,' I say. 'I was born in England and I'm proud of the 53 caps I got.' I play it down when they say I should have had more.

But when I spoke to my family about my experiences with England, I didn't hide my emotion. I was truthful and told them that I felt bad. I watched Brazil win the World Cup when I was a kid and I came up against wonderful teams when I was a player. The Romanians bowled me over at times and I loved how the Dutch played. Those countries built their teams around players like me. I had two feet, I could use the outside of my foot and I had skill. But people in England called me 'Glenda', mistaking style for softness. Of course it would have suited me to be Dutch or French, yet I'm proud of my achievements and I cherished all of my caps. But the time has come for me to be open. Ruud was right: I was born in the wrong country.

I wasn't a luxury player. I never abused my talent. I never took the game for granted. When I scored that individual goal for Dad's team as a 15-year-old, it was the right thing for the team in the circumstances. I wanted to make my team-mates happy by maximising my talent and being effective with it. I could have been selfish, I could have done tricks for the sake of showing off to the crowd, I could have flicked the ball up a million times. But I was always focused on producing an end product. If I did a flick, it was for a reason. If I hit a 60-yard pass, it was because I wanted to send Steve Archibald through on goal.

I was from the Bobby Charlton school, the Alan Hudson and Tony Currie school. Although Johan Cruyff affected the game with his skill and I could have been much more flash when I was at school, I didn't play for the buzz of the crowd.

I think that stems from my upbringing, how Mum and Dad taught me, and my shyness as a child. Entertaining the fans was a by-product of my skill. I didn't set out to do it. I just wanted to help the team, and even though every pass or piece of skill didn't come off, I was brave enough to keep trying. My team-mates understood that I was looking to affect the game with my imagination.

There was only one time when I played for myself. When Tottenham were relegated at Manchester City in 1977, we still had to close out the season with a home game against Leicester. There was a bit of excitement in the crowd, and with 10 minutes to go I received a throw near the Leicester box. I was being marked from behind and could have played the ball back to the thrower. Instead I caught it on my chest, controlled it on my chest and held it on my toe, turned and showed my marker the ball. When the defender moved towards me I flicked the ball over his head before half-volleying a cross to the back post, where it was headed behind for a corner.

I could do that in training all the time, and this was the only time I decided to do it in a game. I never did it again. It wasn't me. The crowd loved it, but when I thought about it later I realised that I'd gone against my natural instincts. My brand of creativity wasn't self-indulgent.

Yet England didn't harness my talent, and the more I saw foreign sides, the more I wanted to play for them. Playing for Holland would have been as simple as getting up to have my breakfast. But I just got on with it. I wasn't a rebel. I got my head when I played for England. 'I'll just keep playing the way I am,' I thought. 'If it's good enough, it's good enough. If it's not, it's not.'

I won my 53rd and final cap when we exited Euro 88 in the group stage after losing 3–1 to the USSR. I'd moved to Monaco two years earlier and was playing for Arsène Wenger at club level. Arsène was baffled by England's style. He scratched his head when he watched our games. He came to one game at Wembley and got straight to the point with me. 'They play so rigid,' he said. 'There's no flexibility in their play. It doesn't suit how you play, Glenn.'

I think having me and Mark Hateley at Monaco meant that he was ready for English football when he moved to Arsenal. Arsène knew what to expect because whenever I returned to Monaco after an England game he asked how it went. 'The same,' I said. 'The usual.'

I was frustrated. Bobby Robson rarely came to watch me when I moved to Monaco. It was a case of out of sight, out of mind. Yet so many people I respect in football have told me that I was a misunderstood talent.

It was a struggle if you were a creative player in England during that era and so much talent slipped through the net. Many skilful players became disillusioned because they couldn't catch a break, and they were soon lost to the game. It took strength to survive when a lot of coaches just wanted the ball in the air. Terry Venables, who coached me when I played for England at Under-21 level, was among the few forward-thinking ones in those days. Dave Sexton was interesting as well and England missed out by not giving Clough a chance.

Ultimately I come back to what Danny Blanchflower said to me after that game against Ipswich. We were insular and closed off. Our island mentality stood in the way of progress. If you didn't conform, you were treated with suspicion. 'The average player puts in the work rate, is athletic,' Danny said. 'You never, ever hear people go, "Yeah, but he can't put a ball on a plate for a striker."'

Why wasn't that seen as a weakness? Nobody ever pointed out that the tacklers couldn't pass or shoot. Yet there were always question marks about creative players. It was always about what he couldn't do; it was always about when he'd let you down, when he'd go missing.

But Danny summed it up brilliantly. The luxury players are the ones who can't pass. The game isn't called chaseball, it isn't called headball, it's called football. The clue's in the name.

6

MONACO

I craved the challenge of playing abroad. Although I wasn't fed up at Tottenham when David Pleat replaced Peter Shreeves as manager in 1986, I couldn't shake that feeling while I was away with England at the World Cup. Opportunities had come and gone in the past. I'd had a dalliance with Cologne when I was 21, and thought that I was going to Napoli after the World Cup in 1982. Tottenham knew nothing about it. Napoli laid out the welcome mat, even paying for us to have a 10-day holiday in Positano. My first wife, Anne, was pregnant with our first daughter, Zoe, at the time, and they put us up in a fabulous hotel. Napoli's interest was serious and I had a good look around the place.

Fate intervened in the end. Dennis Roach, my agent, didn't sound optimistic when he called me after the holiday. 'Look, it's about Napoli,' Dennis said. 'We have a problem.'

There were several issues threatening to derail the move. Not only were Napoli chaotic off the pitch and had problems to sort out at board level, but we hadn't told Tottenham that I wanted to leave. Convincing them to sell me wasn't going to be easy.

The timing wasn't right for all parties. Perhaps it was a blessing in disguise. Naples looked like a manic place when we drove around the city and I assumed that living there would be a challenge for a young family. 'This is going to be full-on,' I thought.

I had to bide my time. Two years later, when I was being courted by several clubs, I again thought about leaving. Tottenham were worried. The chairman Irving Scholar, one of my biggest fans, was determined to keep me, so much so that he even offered me a new five-year contract.

It was hard to turn down given that I was worried about my career after having surgery on my Achilles. The contract offered security at a time when I was full of doubts about my future, so I decided to be pragmatic, putting pen to paper and telling myself that I would still be young enough to move abroad once the deal expired.

My desire to test myself in another country never faltered, and the right time came at the end of the 1985–86 season. David Pleat was doing some work in Mexico during the World Cup, and I was honest with him when we met. 'It's nothing to do with you,' I said. 'I just need to play abroad.' My mind was made up. I needed to broaden my horizons personally and professionally – to experience a new culture and improve as a player. I had no particular destination in mind and was open to playing in France, West Germany, Italy or Spain. I just wanted to get away from England.

When I returned from Mexico, though, David asked me to give him one more year. I agreed, and although at first I found it hard to motivate myself, it wasn't long before I was enjoying my football. 'Let's give it my best,' I thought. 'Let's hope we win something and I go out on a great note.'

We played some good football that season. We were in transition – Steve Perryman and Graham Roberts had both left – but I didn't feel stagnant because I knew that I was going to leave. It was a long farewell and I couldn't have scripted my last goal at White Hart Lane any better. I picked up the ball in our half against Oxford, dribbled past three defenders, went round the goalkeeper and blew the crowd a kiss after scoring. It was a lovely way to end, especially as it was so different to my first goal for Tottenham – that 25-yard rocket against Stoke on my full debut.

Of course, saying goodbye wasn't easy and it was disappointing to finish the season empty-handed. We came third in the league, finishing 15 points below Everton, and losing the FA Cup final to Coventry City was a bitter blow. Coventry were massive underdogs but they played so well on the day. Cup finals are weird. Strange things happen at Wembley. We went 1–0 up through Clive Allen and led 2–1 at half-time, but Coventry pegged us back through Keith Houchen's incredible diving header and won it in extra time when Gary Mabbutt scored a freak own-goal.

I was gutted when the ball deflected off Mabbsy and spun over Ray Clemence. I was desperate to leave on a high and win one more trophy, so it was tough to take and my emotions were all over the place. Although losing to Coventry made me even sadder to be parting company with Tottenham, I was excited about the prospect of starting a new adventure. Paris Saint-Germain had made their move and I assumed that I was going to join them.

I enjoyed meeting Gérard Houllier, PSG's manager. Gérard was a gentleman and living in France appealed to me. Anne spoke a bit of French and our two little girls were at an age where it wouldn't take them long to adjust to living in a new country.

I was due to sign after visiting Paris to look at schools and houses. But something wasn't right. Irving still didn't want me to leave, and negotiations between Tottenham and PSG weren't easy. Three weeks went by without the clubs reaching an agreement over a transfer fee. I wasn't sure about the PSG board when I met them and Irving became elusive, avoiding Dennis and me when we tried to track him down in Paris to discuss the deal. It seemed that Irving, who was staying in the Ritz as negotiations dragged on, wasn't prepared to sell me to PSG.

Something had to change but it wasn't down to me. Although Irving was being strange, I still expected to join PSG after returning to England. The French team were even preparing to hold a press conference to unveil me as their new signing.

The night before our flight back to France, however, Dennis called me with surprising news.

'I'll pick you up at 8am and we'll go to Heathrow,' he said.

'That's early,' I said. 'You said it was a 2pm flight. Why are we going at 8?'

Dennis had been cooking something up in secret.

'We're not going to Paris,' he said. 'We're going to Monaco. There's a guy who's just gone to Monaco – Arsène Wenger. He desperately wants you. He's just signed Mark Hateley and now he wants a No10. We should go down and talk.'

I was nonplussed. I had never heard of Arsène Wenger, I knew nothing about Monaco and PSG were expecting me. It was a lot to absorb. PSG wanted me to do a press conference, even though they still hadn't struck a deal with Tottenham. I had enough on my plate without Arsène Wenger and Monaco coming in to make the situation even more complicated.

Despite all this I decided it was worth speaking to them. It was cloak and dagger stuff, all very secret, and I wasn't sure what to expect. I knew Mark from playing for England, however, and he was pleased when I said I was heading over to speak to Monaco. He gave it the usual sales pitch, making sure to tell me that the manager was really good. 'I'll see what they have to say,' I said. 'This thing with PSG has dragged on for ever.'

I was still a little sceptical, but my doubts began to fade when we arrived in Monte Carlo. The place was astonishing to an outsider. 'I didn't know it was like this,' I thought as a helicopter took us to a spot near the ground to meet various dignitaries. I was starting to warm to the idea. We spent the evening in the Loews Hotel, where we had a lovely meal, and I was fully convinced when I met Arsène the next day. It was like trying to find a new house. You can see 100 houses before you find the right one or you can find it straight away. It wasn't long before I knew that Arsène was the perfect manager for me.

Monaco were taking a risk appointing Arsène, who was an inexperienced and unproven manager. They were brave to give him the job after his final season with Nancy ended with relegation to Ligue 2. It took impressive foresight from Jean-Louis Campora, Monaco's president, to look past that setback and focus on how Arsène had made an unfancied club like Nancy punch above their weight in the first place. Campora must have seen something special in this urbane and intelligent footballing obsessive.

Even so it was a big season for Arsène, who was under pressure to prove that Monaco had made the right choice. It was an experienced squad with plenty of strong characters, and winning silverware was the aim. Campora was ready to back Arsène, who brought in Patrick Battiston and Rémy Vogel to strengthen his defence, and Mark to play up front. I was to be the next piece in the jigsaw, and I didn't take much convincing once I sat down with Arsène to talk football.

I felt at ease as I listened to Arsène's ideas. I knew that I could play for him and I wasn't concerned about the lifestyle in Monaco. I had two young girls and so did Mark, which meant that we weren't going to be alone in a foreign country. After the drama with PSG, I sensed a synergy. Everything appealed to me: the beach, the weather, the manager. It felt right. The international school for the kids was on the third floor of the stadium, which is above a car park, and it was amazing to think of living in a place like Monte Carlo after growing up in a council house in Harlow.

My gut was telling me to sign for Monaco. I often make decisions in that way. My belief is that there's no point trying to force the door open when things are out of our hands. If you keep pushing, you end up making a mistake. I believe we have to trust our instincts. PSG wasn't happening. The deal wasn't moving. Irving would not budge.

Sometimes the universe is telling us which way to go. Tottenham's stance relaxed when it came to Monaco. Irving met Campora over breakfast one morning and thrashed out a deal worth £800,000 in the space of 15 minutes. The negotiations were a breeze after the fuss with PSG. Part of me wonders if Irving, who spent a lot of time in Monte Carlo, was happy because he would still be able to watch me play for Monaco. Either way, the door to Paris was shut and the path to Monaco was open.

It wasn't a difficult choice when I looked at it that way, although I felt dreadfully guilty about letting Gérard Houllier down. I wanted to call him, even though Dennis thought it wasn't necessary. I wanted to make sure there were no hard feelings, and the best way to do that was by telling the truth.

'Look,' I told Gérard, 'if the clubs had agreed what they should have done three or four weeks ago, I would have signed.'

Although it was one of the most awkward phone calls I've ever made, Gérard took it like a gentleman. We smiled about it in later years, and he eventually became close with Arsène, who used to joke about the time he nicked me from under PSG's nose.

It's interesting to compare their managerial styles. They had different approaches when they moved to England. While Arsenal played fantastic attacking football under Arsène, Liverpool were more pragmatic under Gérard. So although Liverpool won plenty of trophies under his tenure, they were regarded as quite a defensive side. In that context I understand why people would assume that I might not have been able to play with as much freedom if I'd joined PSG.

It's impossible to know. My suspicion is that Gérard proceeded with more caution at Liverpool because he thought it was the best way to succeed in England. Although PSG were slightly more constrained than Monaco, I thought they played on the front foot when we came up against them and they didn't strike me as a negative team. They were in the hunt to win the league. It was a competitive division, with no obvious favourite. PSG were up there, Bordeaux were massive, Marseille couldn't be ruled out of contention and Monaco, who'd been off the pace for a few years, were ready to challenge with Arsène in charge.

I loved how Arsène set us up. It was so different to anything I'd experienced before. The drive up to La Turbie, Monaco's training ground, was astonishing. It's actually in France and is reached via a winding, dangerous road. The training ground was built out of the side of a cliff and the view south across the Mediterranean was incredible. I felt a long way from

Cheshunt. I couldn't believe this was where I was going to be playing football every day.

I also had to adjust to Arsène's training methods, and I'd never previously experienced such a difficult pre-season. We went to Switzerland and trained three times a day. The schedule for the first five days floored me. We woke up at 5am, had a coffee and then got a bus to the forest for a really hard run. When it was over we came back for breakfast, a massage and a sleep before jumping on the bus at 11 to go to the training ground for a two-hour session.

On it went. After lunch we had another sleep before another two-hour session at 7pm. We finished with a late meal before going to bed, conscious that we were going to be up at 5am to do it all over again.

Those first five days were a shock to the system. It was so different to Tottenham. Everything was highly organised. The cones were always perfectly laid out when we arrived at training and Arsène was big on timing. He refused to budge if Mark and I asked him to extend an eight-a-side game, even if it was 2–2 at full-time. We played next goal wins in England, but Arsène stuck to the clock. He wasn't prepared to deviate from his strict timekeeping.

Arsène knew what he wanted and I had to adjust to him. At the end of the first session I was about to walk off the pitch with Mark when we saw the other players walking in the opposite direction.

'We do a warm-down,' Arsène shouted.

I was entering a brave new world, as we were lucky to even do a warm-up at Tottenham. Another surprise was in store when we wandered over to find a ballet barre at the far end of the training ground. We had to hook our feet underneath two bars before stretching for 45 minutes, and the other guys were laughing at the two novices trying and failing not to fall over. We got better at the exercises, eventually.

The whole approach felt more scientific and I was ready to embrace cultural change. I would have been laughed out of the treatment room at Tottenham if I'd asked for a massage during the week, but Arsène made sure that we had one before leaving the training ground on certain days. He was a trailblazer. Although the daily warm-downs were tough at first, it was all part of experiencing a different environment and getting a new outlook on life.

This was why I left Tottenham. I enjoyed every minute of it and was quickly on board with Arsène's methods. I didn't mind changing my diet. I tried to drink three litres of water every day, ate more fruit because of the heat, and gave up meat for footballing and spiritual reasons.

I could feel the change in my body, and I was fitter at 28 than I'd been at 21. Arsène was always working out how to give us an edge. Training the day after games kept us fresh. At Tottenham we had a day off after playing, which allowed the lactic acid to build up, making us stiffer. Under Arsène we played on Saturday, trained on Sunday and had Monday off if there was no midweek game. Everything was so organised, even when the balls came out. Everything he introduced – the nutrition, the stretching, the massages – was there for a reason and made us focus on winning football matches. Arsène innovated; he was the ultimate professional. No wonder Arsenal fans ended up calling him 'Le Professeur'.

Arsène also had an eye for a player. Jean-Luc Ettori was a dependable goalkeeper, Battiston was a class centre-back, Luc Sonor was brilliantly adventurous at right-back and Manuel Amoros, who helped France win Euro 84, was an excellent left-back despite being right-footed. We were tough to breach, especially with Vogel going man for man with the opposition striker and Battiston operating as a sweeper.

The shape reminded me of how Arsène set up his Double-winning Arsenal side in 1997–98. Jean-Marc Ferratge tucked inside from right midfield, playing the Ray Parlour role, and Youssouf Fofana was a speedy left-winger like Marc Overmars. The two holding players, Marcel Dib and Jean-Philippe Rohr, were the original Petit and Vieira. We had a lovely balance in midfield. Marcel and Jean-Philippe were strong, tough in the tackle and could pass, while Claude Puel was a smart player. I was free to play as a No10, dropping back like Dennis Bergkamp to create behind Mark, who played up front.

We had such a strong team. We played attractive football and we knew how to stand up for ourselves in away games, especially with Mark in attack. He was quick, good with his feet and unstoppable in the air.

It was a great system, although I struggled at first. Our first pre-season game was against Red Star Belgrade, and I was dropping too deep because Keith always asked me to track back at Tottenham. Old habits die hard. I kept doing it during the first half, and Arsène had to intervene at half-time.

'Glenn, you're coming too deep,' he said. 'We have two players in midfield. I want you to defend, but defend with Mark up there. Press in the other half and then when we win the ball, you get into position so you can be fed.'

It was music to my ears. I ended up scoring after listening to Arsène's advice. I realised that I should have been playing with that freedom since I was 17. The No10 role didn't exist in England but it was so important in France. It was like being a quarter-back in an NFL team. There was a status attached to the position, perhaps because of Platini's importance to the national team, and it suited me down to the ground. I thrived under Arsène, who wanted me to focus on creating in the opposition's half. He didn't want me to drop deep; he simply trusted that my team-mates would be able to find me with their passes.

I became a bigger goal threat. I began to score more inside the box and even threatened in the air. It was an exciting time and it helped that I felt good off the pitch. I was fitter than ever and my family life was good, which is important when you move to a new country.

I did, however, encounter difficulties during the first two months of the season. Settling into a new team isn't easy. At the end of that first training session I'd embarrassed myself by standing on the ball and falling over during an eight-a-side game. It wasn't the best way to introduce myself, not least because I was critical with myself whenever I miscontrolled a pass. Everyone fell into one of those awkward silences apart from Mark, who was cracking up laughing. The players must have been looking at Arsène and wondering why he'd bought me.

It's amazing how nerves affect us. I was like the new kid at school who was covered in food after tripping over my shoe-laces in the canteen at lunch. It wasn't a fun experience. I've seen young players shrink in those situations.

Starting over is challenging. After having had such an important role at Tottenham, I needed to prove myself to my new colleagues. But I was experienced enough to handle humiliation and avoid doubting myself. I knew how to respond when I wasn't happy with my early performances. They were fine, but I knew that I could produce more. I knew that the others were waiting to see what Arsène had seen in me. I had to battle to find my best form and I was being held back by a terrible pain in my stomach.

I assumed it was the hernia that Dr Gilmore, the surgeon who'd given his name to Gilmore's groin, had diagnosed during my final year at Tottenham. 'You probably need an operation,' he'd said at the time. 'But you don't need it now.'

Knowing that I was about to leave England, I was keen not to put the move in doubt by going under the knife. Yet the problem didn't go away. It worsened during pre-season at Monaco and made it hard for me to kick a dead ball. I was fine if the ball was rolling towards me, but I was the set-piece taker and was in agony when I took corners and free-kicks, as the weight of the ball was too much in those situations.

It was frustrating, and nothing changed until Arsène sent me to see Dr Zimmerman, a specialist in Strasbourg, just before Christmas. I didn't have an appointment – Arsène grew up in Strasbourg and was friends with the doctor, and said I could just show up on the day. Dr Zimmerman performed a miracle. I would have had an operation in England, but he just manipulated my back and found the source of the pain. He laid a block of wood on the base of my spine before straddling my legs either side of the end of a bed and telling me to exhale.

I didn't know what was coming next. Out of nowhere Dr Zimmerman pressed his knee into the wood. I heard a crack and felt a release in the base of my back. 'Oh my God,' I thought.

But he seemed confident. I had to fly back to Monaco straight away, and he told me not to worry if my back started to feel sore. 'It's a good sign,' he said. 'Don't panic. Over the next two days you'll probably have to stay in bed.'

He was warning me. I got on the plane and assumed everything was fine until I felt a sudden pain – as agonising as toothache – in my back. I managed to make it home and collapsed on to my bed for two days before speaking to Arsène.

'I don't know what this guy's done but I'm in agony,' I said.

Arsène promised to speak to the doctor. When he did, though, he received the same message: please don't worry. If there's pain it means the procedure has worked.

There was nothing I could do, and I still wasn't sure if it had been a success or not when I went into training for a massage on the third day. The next day, though, I was doing a swimming-pool workout and running around in water when I felt a change. I immediately knew I could kick a dead ball. I went out, found a ball, smashed it into the net and felt no pain in my stomach. I was so relieved. I finally felt free. My form improved and my team-mates' initial doubts faded away when they watched me shine in training. They began to give me the ball in games even though I was being man-marked the whole time. And everything was starting to fall into place in the league: it was between us and Bordeaux for the title, and we were playing good football. With Arsène in charge, we felt confident that we were going to outlast them.

Monaco had gone six years without winning the league. Bordeaux had dominated French football before my arrival and they were our rivals in my first season with Arsène. The race was tight and my mind often drifted back to big moments at Tottenham. I thought of my free-kick deflecting off Tommy Hutchison when we were on the brink of losing the FA Cup final to Manchester City in 1981, Ricky Villa's errant pass against Liverpool in the 1982 League Cup final and Neville Southall performing wonders in goal when we lost that pivotal title decider to Everton.

That defeat to Everton in 1985 stuck with me. The title was there for us that season and we let it slip from our grasp. It was my one regret at Tottenham. We were an excellent cup team, capable of beating anyone on our day, but a league season requires something else. It's a different challenge on a Saturday afternoon. Cup games are one-offs: it's jubilation or devastation. If you lose, that's it. It's over. In the league, though, you have to be consistent. You have to be steady. You have to stay motivated.

It wasn't easy to stay focused at Monaco. The lifestyle on offer was a potential distraction and our home games were often played in front of small crowds. While the fans were happy to come during the early months of the season when the weather was still pleasant, I noticed that numbers dwindled when winter arrived.

It would have been difficult to succeed in that environment had our team been full of players who didn't love the game. It's probably been a problem for certain Monaco sides. But we had pride. We motivated ourselves when we saw rows of empty seats in the stands. We knew that the fans weren't going to intimidate the opposition. It was down to us to make them suffer by playing them off the pitch.

The key was that we all loved football. Mark and I were desperate to prove ourselves and players who'd been there for a long time wanted to bring the title back to Monaco. We set the bar high early on and refused to let standards dip. We had a professional attitude under Arsène, who kept us focused, and we didn't allow ourselves to get carried away. If we came from behind to win a game, we didn't get too excited. Cup football was an emotional rollercoaster, whereas this was a straight line to the finish. It was more of a grind.

I welcomed the respite of my first ever winter break. It gave me a chance to recuperate mentally and physically. It was a proper rest and it was lovely to be able to spend Christmas with Anne and the kids.

The winter break is a good idea, but I was slightly concerned that it would halt our momentum in the league. I cast my mind back to how heavy snowfall in England disrupted Tottenham's hopes of winning the league in 1985. Fixtures were called off so we ended up with a massive backlog, cramming the schedule in the run-in, and it played a big part in us falling short. Although the break in France was scheduled, I didn't want anything to get in the way of Monaco's charge.

Arsène being Arsène, though, he made sure that we didn't take our eye off the ball. His philosophy was that we needed another mini-pre-season after putting our feet up for a bit. Tongue in cheek, I used to tell him that we almost wasted the break because of his demands in training. It made me laugh. One year we went to Morocco for a friendly tournament, and the strangest thing was coming back to England to play a friendly against Tottenham during my first season.

It was part of the deal that took me to Tottenham. We beat Aston Villa, drew with Newcastle, and then I had to run out at White Hart Lane in a red and white shirt. It was surreal. It felt like coming home, only I wasn't a Tottenham player anymore. We were there to put on a show and we played well against a good side. I thumped a shot against the bar and we surprised the crowd with the quality of our football, winning 4–0.

We went back to Monaco in good spirits. Yet we couldn't get ahead ourselves, even though we did start to think it was going to be our year when we dropped points away from home on a couple of occasions and returned to the dressing room to find that Bordeaux hadn't taken advantage of us slipping up.

That gave us a boost as we approached the finishing line. I yearned to become a league champion after missing out at Tottenham. Although I didn't feel that I had anything to prove to people back in England, I was hungry for success and I was playing great football under Arsène. My game changed in that more advanced role and I didn't object to being told to reserve my best work for when the ball reached the final third. 'I don't mind you coming back and hitting passes,' Arsène said. 'But once we progress up the pitch, you've got to become available.'

The shape of the team required me to come alive around the area. I was driving into the box to score, even bagging some with my head, which was probably because defenders were so focused on Mark that they forgot to pay attention to me. I had fun pulling Mark's leg and asking him when he planned to score some headers.

Bordeaux, the defending champions, couldn't keep up with us and the race was all but over when they lost 1–0 to Nantes on a Thursday night. But we stayed professional. I didn't watch the Bordeaux game. We visited Metz the following day and they flew at us in front of a passionate crowd in the first half. We had to dig deep to earn a 2–2 draw, Rohr and Amoros scoring our goals.

The title was ours and the celebrations started in the dressing room. The champagne flowed and even Arsène had a glass. He was a happy bunny on the plane back to Monaco. He didn't mind us having a beer on that flight.

It was a huge moment for Arsène. Monaco had placed a lot of faith in him and he went on to have a fantastic career. More importantly, he was a decent man. He trusted us and we respected him.

Arsène didn't want us to take our foot off the gas. We prepared as normal before facing Auxerre at home. There was no hangover. We put on a show for our fans and I scored one of my favourite ever goals in a 3–2 win, catching out the goal-keeper by whipping a disguised shot inside his near post from the left flank.

It was time to get the party started. The champagne flowed back in the dressing room. Arsène was delighted and it was one of the proudest moments of my career. We celebrated with the lads at Jimmy's, one of the most expensive nightclubs in the world. The weather was incredible and I think most of our bonuses went on the drinks that night. I didn't care. Winning the league meant so much to me. It was proof that I could do it after falling short at Tottenham.

I could puff my chest out now that I owned a Ligue 1 winner's medal. We were in the European Cup and had shown that we were a proper team. The next challenge was doing it all over again. We knew that defending our title and competing in Europe at the same time was going to be a tall order.

The need for more depth was not lost on Arsène. One morning Mark and I arrived at La Turbie to find a tall African guy waiting outside the dressing room. He was wearing a long robe and sandals, and was carrying a brown paper bag under his arm. We shook his hand, went to our lockers and thought nothing more of it until he walked in with Arsène five minutes later.

'This is George,' Arsène said. 'He speaks English and is from Liberia. I'll put you in between Mark and Glenn so you can speak English.'

The penny dropped. This George character was having a two-week trial with us. We quickly introduced ourselves and made him welcome. He took his robe off, revealing a fantastic physique, and pulled a pair of tatty old boots out of the brown bag. He didn't have anything else with him. Louis, the kit man, handed him a spare kit and we went out to train.

I was paying close attention to George, who looked like he had some decent skills when we were warming up. There was something unusual about the whole situation. It was a Tuesday and Arsène decided that we were going to have a match between the first team and the reserves, which wasn't the normal routine. George played for the reserves and he looked lost at first. We were running rings around them and I felt sorry for the newcomer. 'Wow, the poor kid can't get a touch of the ball,' I thought.

After another 10 minutes without a kick George drifted out to the right wing to collect possession. And then my jaw fell to the floor. He dummied to go to the right before dragging the ball inside, leaving Amoros for dead, then went past Battiston as if he wasn't there. He moved into the box and spanked a venomous shot against the bar before the other centre-back could get across.

'Whoa!' There was nothing else to say, although I made sure to wind up our centre-forward. 'Mark, you better get your arse in gear,' I shouted.

It was astonishing. Another ten minutes went by before the ball dropped at George's feet again. He didn't hesitate, immediately beating a couple of defenders with ease before sending a dangerous cross into the box.

I was seriously impressed and asked Arsène where he'd found this guy. He just chuckled. 'We have our spies,' he said.

Arsène would go on to show how good he was at spotting unpolished gems when he joined Arsenal. He bought Nicolas Anelka for £500,000 and transformed Thierry Henry from a winger into one of the best strikers in the world. But I saw him work his magic first hand. The stranger outside the dressing room was George Weah, a future winner of the Ballon d'Or.

George was out of this world and he quickly became our No9 after Mark got injured. I played behind him and needed to guide him at times, telling him where to move when we didn't have the ball. He was raw and leant on me for advice.

'Glenn, you have to tell me where to go,' he said.

'George, I don't have to tell you what to do,' I said.

'No, defensively,' he replied.

Happy to help, I said yes and basically played George's defensive game for him, telling him when to press and when to stand off. Although he was sensational with the ball, he needed coaching and he was extremely anxious when I missed one game because of an ingrown toenail. 'I am worried,' he said. 'I cannot play. Glenn is not playing. What am I going to do? How am I going to defend?'

Arsène was laughing. I wasn't worried. 'He's fine,' I said. 'Give him the ball and just let him go out and play.'

George had so much ability. He did things on the pitch that left you scratching your head. He could have two defenders surrounding him in the corner and still twist away from them with ease. He had so much pace and this long, powerful stride. He was a brilliant player and a lovely guy.

Yet that second season was frustrating. We didn't have enough depth and finished third in Ligue 1. Marseille, Arsène's nemesis, won the league and we lost 2–1 on aggregate to Galatasaray in the last eight of the European Cup. It was a frustrating defeat. I had a knee problem before the first leg and was only fit enough to come off the bench in the second half. We lost 1–0 and couldn't turn it around in the second leg, which took place in Cologne because of crowd trouble at Galatasaray's previous home game.

A late goal from George wasn't enough to prevent our exit and there was more disappointment when we lost the French Cup final 4–3 to Marseille, who won thanks to a hat-trick from Jean-Pierre Papin. My family all came over to Paris for the game, which was special, but we couldn't get the better of Marseille that season.

Arsène despised Marseille. Their president, Bernard Tapie, wanted to topple us and Arsène almost came to blows with him in the tunnel after one game. It was a bitter rivalry. Marseille signed a few of our players, infuriating Arsène, and they tried to buy me as well. I politely declined, making it clear that I was happy at Monaco.

It was the truth. I was content at Monaco even after losing that cup final. We had to go to a posh do round the corner from our hotel and we were all feeling sorry for ourselves after losing. There was a show on stage, but nobody was paying much attention. The mood was sombre.

But as I looked across the table, I saw the Monaco royal family. Prince Rainier III was there, and his children – Princess Caroline, Prince Albert and Princess Stephanie – were with him. I felt odd. I had come a long way from that council house in Harlow and I was even more surprised when I saw Prince Rainier pick up a piece of bread before throwing it at his son.

'Did I just see that?' I thought.

It was bizarre. It didn't stop. Prince Albert picked up a piece and threw it back at his father. We watched this scene unfold and couldn't help but laugh. Prince Rainier must have done it on purpose. He must have done it to break the ice and lighten the mood after our defeat. It was the kind of thing we would have done in Harlow after a game and it turned into a fantastic night in the end. 'Harlow or Paris?' I thought. 'It doesn't matter if you're having fun with your mates, does it?'

I loved my time in Monaco, even though I didn't win anything after my first season. It was fantastic off the pitch. Although the other players didn't drink, Mark and I sometimes went out if we got back late on a Saturday after an away game. There was a pub round the corner from our apartments and we just went down there in our tracksuits to have a couple of pints. We were English and we liked a beer, even though Arsène didn't approve.

There was no way to keep Arsène in the dark. Monaco was such a small place and he had his spies. He knew what was going on and pulled us in for a chat one day.

'It's not the best thing to be drinking,' he said, which started a little battle.

'Look, you've got to understand, we're not staying up until six in the morning going to nightclubs,' I said. 'I don't know what the other players do. I don't know whether they go straight home, I don't know if they have a glass of wine, I don't know if they have a beer. But Mark and I, we're experienced players. This is what we do. This is where we relax. We always come in on the Sunday morning, we would never be drunk. We've got to do something.'

'No, it's not good for your body,' Arsène said. 'Do you understand that?'

'But we've got to relax,' I replied. 'This is what we've done, this is the English.'

'I don't like it, it's not correct.'

'Well, it might not be correct, but our mentality is correct,' I said. 'And if we're out of order, you'll get to find out.'

Arsène relented in the end. I had never been so fit before in my life, and although Mark had a few injuries here and there, I don't think we were abusing our privilege. We won that battle, although I'm sure that Arsène would have clamped down on it if the results hadn't been good enough.

I like to think that we were preparing him for when he moved to England. I had a wonderful relationship with Arsène and didn't mind recommending him to Arsenal in 1996, even though I'm a Tottenham man. David Dein, the board member driving Arsène's appointment at Arsenal, was putting his neck on the line by pushing for him. Nobody in England had heard of Arsène, and David called me a few times for advice.

'Go and get him,' I said. 'You'll be successful.'

I wasn't going to stand in Arsène's way. He was my friend. I was managing England at the time and I didn't want to stop him going to Tottenham's biggest rivals. It's just a shame that he ended up winning so much with the red half of north London.

Few people thought it would be possible when Arsène arrived in London. 'Arsène who?' was the headline on one back page, and Ian Wright told me that he was baffled by the appointment. Even I wondered how Arsène was going to cope with the culture at Arsenal. They had a top side but they didn't mind a night out.

Arsène silenced the sceptics, however, winning the Double in his first full season in England. Although I didn't like seeing Arsenal winning trophies, I was pleased for him on a personal level. He's much more than a football manager; despite being obsessed with the game, he can talk to you about anything. He's extremely astute and his dignity sets him apart. I didn't like how Arsenal treated him when he left in 2018. They should have put him on the board after everything he did for that club.

Arsène has so much to give the game, so he was a great appointment as FIFA's chief of global football development. I learnt so much from him at Monaco, the two of us gelling straight away. We spent a lot of time talking about politics, religion and philosophy. Arsène is a very intelligent man, although I was surprised to discover from Tony Adams, Lee Dixon and Wrighty that he never raised his voice with them at Arsenal. 'He must have learnt how to be patient,' I said. 'In France, in the early days, he used to go nuts at times.'

It was all in French, and Mark and I would have been none the wiser if he was saying things about us. Arsène certainly knew how to put on a show. Sometimes he kicked bottles, sometimes he threw them, and then he was off. Obviously I knew the French swear words. I understood the general message.

Monaco was a big job for Arsène. He was only 38 and inexperienced, yet he was eager to succeed and desperate to win. But he always had our support. I think that he respected the fact that I understood the game. He liked how I talked in training and organised people on the pitch. We connected. We respected each other. Sometimes you just have that with people in life. We were on the same wavelength.

It was a shame that we didn't win more trophies. Losing our European Cup Winners' Cup semi-final to Sampdoria during my third season stung. We were missing key players – I was out with a serious knee injury – and our squad wasn't big enough.

I was starting to worry about my career at that stage. I had spent almost an entire season on the treatment table and was wondering if I would ever play again. But it was then that

Arsène planted the first seed of going into management in my head. I hadn't thought about coaching until he came over one day to talk about it.

'I hope you don't mean that because I'm going to finish my career with this knee problem,' I said.

'I just see things,' he said.

Arsène was so astute. He understood people. I missed a year with my knee injury and started to think about the game differently. It was like an early apprenticeship. I pretended that I was a manager when I watched games. I studied opponents. A new door was open thanks to Arsène. It was up to me to decide whether to walk through it. Or more appropriately, bearing in mind the discomfort in my knee at the time, hobble through it.

7

BAPTISM OF FIRE

The pain was excruciating and it arrived out of nowhere, catching me by surprise. Nobody anticipated it. I was still happy at Monaco and was ready to fight Marseille after our failed title defence. We were in the European Cup Winners' Cup, Arsène still had a good team and we made a fairly encouraging start to the 1989–90 season. I played three consecutive games in August and scored in a 1–1 draw with SM Caen. Nobody could have imagined it would be my last game for Monaco.

I wasn't worried when one of Caen's players caught my left knee. It wasn't a serious injury and I assumed that I would be back in no time at all after having an operation to repair some minor cartilage damage. It was a routine procedure and there was no reason to suspect that anything was wrong afterwards. I made good progress with my rehab and felt ready to play again five weeks later. Even Arsène was encouraged when he saw me at training during the week. 'You look fit,' he said. 'Let's see how you go. It looks like you could be in the squad on Saturday.'

My worries evaporated. I was hitting balls, sprinting and jumping. I was on my way back and felt optimistic when I went outside to train. I was oblivious about what was really going on until I collapsed after suddenly feeling the most horrendous pain inside my knee. It was like someone was jabbing me with a hot needle over and over again. I had never felt anything like it before. 'This is wrong,' I thought, panicking. 'This is wrong.'

I couldn't believe it. One moment I was running with the ball, the next I was sprawled on the ground in agony. This wasn't how it was supposed to go. This wasn't part of the plan. And I certainly I didn't expect to pull my tracksuit bottoms down to find that my knee had turned completely purple.

I limped over to the treatment room, aware that I was in trouble, and a specialist doctor found the problem. Hidden from view, an infection had caused untold damage, eating away at the bone and leaving a little hole inside my knee. The assumption was the infection has happened while I was in the operating theatre. It was pure misfortune and there were no warning signs until my fall, as everything looked all right and I felt fine. The shape was back to normal, I was working on strengthening the muscles and the knee wasn't hot. Although there had been a bit of inflammation at first – some water that needed to be drained away – there was no cause for concern.

As I lay there in pain, however, I realised that I was going to have a tough time getting back. My knee blew up horribly and I had loads of treatment on it. I went to Munich to see Dr Hans-Wilhelm Müller-Wohlfahrt, who treated a lot of footballers with knee problems, and spent two weeks in a hospital in Lyon.

It was a testing time, to put it mildly. In Germany I spent three days on a drip having cow's blood pumped into my body, which I found scary, and when I was in Lyon they treated the infection by giving me three knee washouts in ten days. The challenges came thick and fast. An hour before I was due to fly home from Lyon it became clear that an infection had seeped into my bloodstream. I started shaking and had to spend another few days recuperating in hospital.

My knee took such a pounding. It was a long, hard road to recovery, and I struggled to imagine myself reaching the end of it at times. I missed the rest of the season and was nowhere near the training ground. I was on the treatment table and was only doing some leg weights by the time I wrapped things up at Monaco.

However, while more than a year passed without any sign of real improvement, I wasn't fearful about the prospect of my career drawing to a close. My mindset was different to when I hurt my eye when I was 13 and my knee when I was 14. I was wiser, calmer and more philosophical. That brief conversation with Arsène ignited something inside me. I began to look at the game in a different way. I started to think about coaching.

I was going down a new path. Monaco had talked about offering me a new contract after my cartilage operation, but the infection changed everything. They released me in November 1990 and I returned to England, although I didn't want to settle back into the old routine. Moving back to Essex after living in Monte Carlo would have been too big a shift. Keen for a change of scenery, we decided to move to the west of London and bought a house in Ascot.

Although I knew that I faced an uphill battle to save my career, I still wasn't ready to throw in the towel. I wanted to do everything in my power to give it one last shot before entering the world of management. Word of my desire for a comeback soon got out. It wasn't long before my agent Dennis Roach was telling me about receiving a call from Bobby Campbell, Chelsea's manager. 'You can use the facilities at Chelsea and do a bit of scouting for Bobby,' Dennis said. 'And there might be some work you can do with the youth teams if your knee doesn't get better.'

There was no hint of a contract. Although I suspect that Bobby thought that he would be in pole position to sign me if I returned to full fitness, I wasn't optimistic. My knee was still extremely sore – it still swells up now – and I knew that I was coming back on a wing and a prayer. I couldn't give Bobby any guarantees. I was starting from scratch when I went to Chelsea. I was limited to running and muscle work at first. I didn't know where it would lead.

Yet the hunger still burned within. I was desperate to make it back and pushed myself so hard, tirelessly slogging away and playing in practice matches at training until I was finally in a position to turn out in a reserve game against Watford at Stamford Bridge in March 1991.

I felt quietly optimistic on the day of the game. Although I was nervous, I was excited about playing again for the first time in almost two years. I thought about that first tackle and wondered how I would cope. I thought about how good it would feel to kick the ball again. I was getting myself in the zone, so it wasn't the best timing when the phone rang just as I was about to leave for the ground.

It was one of those sliding doors moments. I was almost out of the door when I decided to take the call. I had no idea who it was and certainly wasn't expecting to hear from Peter Day, who had left his job as Tottenham's club secretary to become Swindon Town's chief executive.

'Glenn, can I speak to you?' he said.

'Well, I'm literally about to head out,' I said, explaining that it was my first game in two years.

But it was a matter of urgency as far as Peter was concerned. 'Look, we want you to be manager,' he said. 'Ossie Ardiles has gone to Newcastle.'

I wasn't expecting Peter to say that and I didn't want to give him any false hope. 'Peter, I trust you're not just trying to get me as player-manager,' I said. 'I'm not sure if the knee is going to be good enough, mate. How it reacts after this match is really going to be the key.'

Peter wasn't swayed. He insisted that Swindon wanted me and I promised to speak to him again later that evening. I was in a daze. I drove to Stamford Bridge with my head in a spin, somehow trying to forget about the job offer and concentrate on my comeback game.

Peter wanted to know how the game went when we spoke again. Although I understood why he was asking, I didn't want to give him any false assurances. I was at home with an ice pack on my knee, relieved to have made it through the 90 minutes unscathed, and needed to make it clear that I probably wasn't going to be able to play for Swindon. 'Pete, no,' I said. 'Take it as if I'm not going to be able to play.'

If Peter was disappointed he certainly hid it well. He wasn't put off by the prospect of me hanging up my boots. His line was the same: Swindon wanted me to be their manager.

It was a big decision. I was only 33, a total novice, and had no coaching experience at all. I knew nothing about dealing with players or sorting out contracts and I'd never taken any coaching sessions. Although I had a connection with Peter from my Tottenham days, I didn't know why Swindon wanted me. It was a gamble, and I could have said that I was too young to take the job. I could have gone down a different path, perhaps by coaching in an academy or by becoming the assistant to a more experienced manager.

Yet those months on the sidelines at Monaco stayed with me. Arsène had planted the seed when he told me to think about coaching. Listening to him helped. It can be hard to get enthusiastic about watching games when your career's on the line, but I was almost using that period as an apprenticeship. The thought of management intrigued me and I didn't need long to come to a decision after mulling over Swindon's offer.

I told Peter that I wanted to give it a go and arranged to meet him and the board. Negotiations went well and my appointment was confirmed at the start of April.

I was excited. Everything was moving so quickly. I had jumped straight in at the deep end and realised that I was going to be learning on the job. It was a daunting challenge and I knew that I needed support. Picking the right assistant was important, and it didn't take me long to think of John Gorman, who was the youth team manager at Leyton Orient.

John was a mate. I'd played with him at Tottenham and we had similar views on football. We understood each other and I knew that I wanted him by my side. It was a straightforward deal. Orient didn't want compensation and their manager Frank Clark was happy to see John move up the coaching ladder. 'This is great for him,' Frank said. 'You two have been friends for a long time.'

Having John on board was a boost. A plan started to fall into place. There was only one thing left: finding out who I was going to be managing.

Everything happened too quickly for me to do any research about Swindon as I was just focused on signing the contract. Here I was naive. Although I was looking forward to seeing what the players were like, my lack of knowledge about the overall situation at the club didn't hit me until we were driving down the motorway for our introductory press conference.

'John,' I said, 'where are Swindon in the league?'

Flummoxed, we had to stop off at a service station in Newbury to buy the local paper. Turning to the sport section, we scanned down the table until we found Swindon languishing in 17th place in Division Two, five points above the relegation zone with eight games left.

'Crikey,' I thought. 'My first managerial job and I'm already in a relegation battle.'

Talk about a baptism of fire. It was a difficult time for Swindon. They were in the doldrums after winning promotion to Division One under Ossie during the 1989–90 season, only to have the achievement wiped out after an investigation by the Football League revealed financial wrongdoing by the club's previous board. The scandal forced them to go back to square one and inevitably had a negative impact on the team's performances. Although Ossie had them playing good football, the wins weren't coming.

Yet there were reasons to be positive. Peter had reassured me that I was inheriting a capable squad and I was rational about the situation, telling myself that it must have been difficult for Ossie to pick the players off the floor after the blow of having promotion snatched away.

Anyway, there was no time to worry. I survived the press conference – it was just as well that the paper hadn't been sold out – and returned the next day for my first training session. We didn't have long to prepare before welcoming struggling Watford to the County Ground for my opening game.

I had to think on my feet. I was buzzing when I arrived in the morning and went to my office to talk to John. I was improvising and making it up as I went along. I made plans to hold a meeting with the players in the dressing room before heading outside to train. I thought about having individual talks with players. I looked ahead to Watford. I couldn't wait to get out on the grass and have some sessions with the ball, but the reality of managing a club like Swindon was yet to dawn on me. I thought that I wouldn't have to think about anything other than football and assumed that a player had come to speak to me about his contract when I heard someone knock on the door at 9am.

I couldn't have been more wrong. It wasn't a disgruntled player at the door, it was a little old lady.

'I'm Jeanie,' she said in her Wiltshire accent.

'Jeanie,' I thought, ushering her inside. 'You look like you popped out of a bottle.'

Jeanie looked worried when we sat down at my desk. She was nervous and I had no idea what she could possibly want from me.

'Well, Mr Hoddle,' she said, 'I'm the laundry lady. Mr Ardiles and his directors, they promised me two new massive washing machines just before he left. I'm worried – will I still get them now you've become manager?'

It was the last thing I expected to hear. I thought I was at Swindon to manage a football team, not to take care of the washing machines. Yet it was like that at Swindon. There were so many different areas to worry about and it was people like Jeanie who made it a family club.

I could tell that it was a big deal for Jeanie to come and speak to me. John, who was in a little office to the side, came in to see what was going on and we made a fuss of her. 'Jeanie, I'm pretty sure that you'll still get your washing machines and everything will be fine,' I said. 'It's lovely to meet you.'

Jeanie's face lifted straight away and she looked like a weight was off her shoulders when she left my office. As for me, I was trying to make sense of the conversation. I didn't remember this being in the brochure when Swindon approached me. 'I thought I was here to be a football manager,' I said, turning to John. 'I didn't realise my first buy was going to be washing machines.'

Yet I couldn't separate myself from the people working behind the scenes, the people without whom the club would fall apart. I was driving home later that evening when I realised that so many departments depended on me. I remembered Louie, the kit man at Monaco. I remembered the physios who helped me when I was injured. Everybody had a job to do, and although I had to spend most of my time thinking about the directors above me, I realised that I wasn't just in control of a group of players. There was more to the club than the team. There were so many hopes, so many fears, so many anxieties, so many people depending on me to keep them happy.

I learnt so much from Jeanie on that first day. Although results were the main focus, I realised that it was going to be easier to win if we were working in a positive environment. If Jeanie was happy, she would do a better job in the laundry room. If she was in a good mood, she would be able to cheer up one of my strikers and make sure that he was relaxed before the weekend.

It was such a steep learning curve. John was the only person I brought into the club, but everybody else was worried about the prospect of change. Later that week Andy Rowland, the reserve team manager, came to ask me if he was going to keep his job. 'They've all got families and I'm the decision-maker,' I thought. 'I've got to give them time.' It was hard to take it all in.

With the Spinney Dynamos team of 1969. I'm at the front,
third from left, with the ball.

An early photo of me turning out for Tottenham's
youth team in 1975. Look at that fresh face!

I was delighted to make my England debut against Bulgaria in 1979.
Scoring was the icing on the cake.

Representing England at the European Championship in Italy in 1980.
I'm in the back row, fourth from left.

The glory years – the moment of victory in the 1981 FA Cup final
replay against Manchester City.

Celebrating with my old friend Ossie Ardiles.

It was amazing to win the FA Cup again a year later. I scored
the winner in the replay against Queens Park Rangers.

More celebrating, this time with Steve Archibald.

Taking on Johan Cruyff when Spurs met Feyenoord in the UEFA Cup in 1983 was a great experience. We managed to see off the Dutch great, winning 6–2 on aggregate.

With Arsène Wenger, my new coach and mentor, at AS Monaco in 1987.

Representing England at the 1986 World Cup was an honour. I'm in the front row, third from left.

I've coached some wonderful players during my career. I was delighted to bring in Ruud Gullit while I was managing Chelsea in 1995.

Coaching Paul Gascoigne when I managed England was also a pleasure.

I experienced the ups and downs of managing England. Here I am alongside Terry Venables as I begin the job in 1996.

I can only watch on as David Beckham is sent off for fouling Diego Simeone when we lost to Argentina in the last 16 of the 1998 World Cup.

I was thrilled to come home and manage Spurs
between 2001 and 2003.

Extra time for me! Here I am performing on
The Masked Singer in 2021.

I needed wins but my opening game, a 2–1 defeat at home to Watford in torrential rain, was a disappointment. Watford were managed by my old mate Steve Perryman, who had another former Tottenham player, Peter Taylor, as his assistant, but I quickly discovered that there's no room for sentiment on the touchline. We had a beer after the game, but it was dog eat dog during the 90 minutes. It was all about getting points on the board. Our survival was on the line and I was already under pressure.

The crowd gave me a bit of leeway when we lost to Watford, but I was under no illusions. I knew that the fans weren't going to be happy if we kept losing. The buck stopped with me and it was a level of responsibility I had never previously experienced.

It's different for players. When you're a footballer you put yourself first. You think about keeping your place in the team and playing well. This was something else. Now I had to do post-match press conferences and speak to journalists after defeats. I had no media training and had to pick my words carefully. Although I knew why we had lost, I couldn't be specific and pick out individuals. I needed everybody on board. I was wet behind the ears and felt my inexperience when I met opposition managers for a glass of wine after the final whistle, especially when another game early in my reign ended in a 2–1 defeat at home to Neil Warnock's Notts County, who bullied us physically.

Those first few days were a whirlwind. I learnt so much about myself. I was a novice who was trying to find out which methods worked. I had no idea if my message would reach the players when, shortly after my chat about washing machines with Jeanie, I walked into the dressing room to meet them on my first day. It was a nerve-wracking experience. I could feel their anxiety when they looked at me. They were looking at me for guidance and I knew that some of them were worried.

It was up to me to put everyone at ease. I needed to relax and show authority, although this was easier said than done. John Syer, our psychologist at Tottenham, had made us stand up and speak in front of our team-mates when I was a player, but it was different as a manager. It's easy to talk about a game after the event, but it's far from straightforward when it's half-time and you have to make quick adjustments. I was the leader and people were waiting for me to tell them what to do. Although I eventually learnt how to delegate, every decision comes back to the manager – even little things like when we were going to leave the hotel for a game.

The bus driver wanted answers. Everyone wanted answers. Yet it was no use making the challenge seem bigger than it was, and I left that first meeting fairly optimistic. 'Bloody hell, I think I did all right in there,' I thought. 'I coped. It wasn't as bad as I thought it was going to be.'

I realised that I needed time to grow. Although I was shy when I was growing up, I couldn't afford to be reserved in this role. I had to puff out my chest. While I was always going over decisions in my head, to the extent that my family probably wondered if I was truly present when I wasn't working, I couldn't afford to let the players know if I had doubts. Managers put on a face sometimes. It can be lonely at the top and I needed people in whom I could confide.

It helped that John Gorman was on the same wavelength. When I reflected on early mistakes, I was relieved to find out that he was thinking the same thing as me. I had someone I could lean on after making an inconsistent start. I didn't taste victory until my third game, winning 2–1 at Wolves, and I came to realise that it was too early to ask the team to play the expansive style that I liked after a 2–0 defeat at West Ham. Although we played some lovely stuff at Upton Park, our naivety cost us. Some players weren't ready to carry out certain roles.

It was a learning process. It helped that I was at a small club and had room to make errors. I fear for former players when they walk straight into jobs at a Premier League side. Although they don't have to worry about what time the bus should leave for the ground, they still have to find their coaching identity, only under a much harsher spotlight. Starting at Swindon allowed me to develop. I was discovering so much all the time, even finding out that methods I planned to use would be more effective if they were implemented in a different way. I learnt when things worked, such as a piece of positive reinforcement bringing the best out of a player, and when they didn't.

Management is tough. Games can turn on the tiniest of details, as I discovered during my second game, a 3–3 draw away to Plymouth. Trailing 2–1 after a difficult first half, I was thinking about substituting our striker, Duncan Shearer. He was a goalscorer with a good record, but I wasn't overly impressed with his touch after looking at him in training and I felt that the ball wasn't running for him against Plymouth. I was going to take him off, but John told me to give him five more minutes.

It was a valuable lesson. We kept Duncan on and he paid us back immediately, equalising with a smart header. I'd been lucky, and I realised that I couldn't make such quick assessments on my players.

Confidence was key. At first my focus was more on results than performances. I had a long-term vision but I told John that the short-term goal was staying up. 'We've got to get the points,' I said. 'The points are more important than how we play. We've got some good players here, but we've got to try and get that little bit of freedom into them.'

It was difficult to be expansive when we were fighting for survival. Yet I could see the basis of a promising team. Micky Hazard, my old Tottenham team-mate, was a superb midfielder. I soon discovered that Duncan was a fine striker and I reckoned that Dave Kerslake could play as a right wing-back.

I was determined to play a 3–5–2 system. I knew how effective it was after coming up against it in an England Under-21 game against Yugoslavia. They swamped us in midfield and we couldn't get the ball off them. It felt like they had an extra player on the pitch and I couldn't understand why nobody in England was playing that way. I knew it would give our players time on the ball and unsettle our opponents. I pulled Ross MacLaren, who was a fine passer, back from midfield to play as a sweeper, and I felt that Colin Calderwood, who went on to play for Tottenham and Scotland, was a capable centre-back. I could see a way forward, although I still needed to find out if these players were good enough on the ball. Some players don't know how to use time and space. They become frantic when they have too much time to think.

Fortunately I had smart players. I saw our belief grow after we beat Wolves and I found out more about my squad. One lad, Martin Ling, had arrived on trial from Southend before Ossie's departure. Lingy was a little winger who stayed out wide in a 4–4–2, and I felt he was restricted in that position. He didn't see enough of the ball and I decided to try him out elsewhere in the reserves, playing him off the front two.

It suited Lingy perfectly. He broke into the box, he went out wide and he was clever in his movement. I was convinced. We threw Lingy in and I saw signs of the team developing an identity. Although we only won one more game before the end of the season, smashing Leicester 5–2 at home, we stayed up after finishing in 20th place. We had passed the first test. Now it was time to build.

I quickly realised that I wasn't going to get much of a break during pre-season. I could see a team coming together and I couldn't stop visualising what it would look like. I was thinking about bringing in players even when I went on holiday, and I was running round Ascot racecourse to keep myself fit. I knew that it would be a bonus if I could play. I planned to play sweeper and move Ross back into midfield.

My knee was beginning to improve. I think that I had a breakthrough during my first 10 days in the job. I wasn't pounding it as much as I had been at Chelsea, and although I wanted to see if I was fit enough for pre-season, I had so much on my plate after taking the job that I forgot all about it.

I felt better by the summer. My knee was holding up thanks to plenty of icing and my role changed. As a player-manager I had to make sure that I trained well, although I also needed to focus on picking the team. But I embraced the challenge. I looked at how we could make tweaks behind the scenes. I was in the treatment room a lot and learnt about the medical side. I found out more about the kit man's job. Using my experience from Tottenham and Monaco, I brought a masseur in. I wanted the best for Swindon.

It wasn't easy. With funds tight, I ended up loaning the club £200,000 to buy Shaun Taylor from Exeter. We needed someone to head the ball and Shaun was a tough defender. I didn't mind paying for Shaun. Promotion was our aim and we were developing, although Shaun struggled with my demands at first. We needed to make him confident enough to play out from the back. 'Simplify your game,' I told him.

It was a case of remodelling the players. I wanted Colin Calderwood to go wide when we had possession. I wanted us to take three touches with the ball and move it quickly into the final third, at which point they were allowed to have as many touches as they liked. I saw positive signs when we won a pre-season tournament in Holland, beating a couple of decent Turkish sides. The players grew in confidence.

Later in life a scout came up to me and said that he loved my Swindon team so much that a few scouts sometimes pretended that they wanted to look at one of our players just so they could see our games. He said that no one else played like us, with three at the back, wing-backs bombing on and a spirit of adventure that made us great to watch. It was a lovely thing to hear. We had good players, our football was scintillating at times and the crowd lapped it up. At the same time, though, I knew that the fans demanded winning football. I had to make sure that we had an end product, and I was always thinking of ways to get the upper hand on our opponents.

Call it marginal gains. In those days there wasn't one ball used by the whole league. You could pick your own one for home games, and I knew that the Adidas Tango was light and lively. I brought these in, but the lads weren't happy at first. The balls were flying all over the place and the goalkeepers were struggling.

The lads soon became more accomplished and I realised that we could surprise our opponents when they came to the County Ground. We gave them heavy old Mitre balls to train with before games, leaving them completely unprepared for the unpredictable Tango. 'Get ready,' I said to our defenders at goal-kicks, aware that their goalkeeper was going to punt the ball straight out of play.

It gave us a huge advantage because we were a footballing side. It removed part of the physical aspect and we started the season well, hurting teams with our system. We had so many options on the ball, and it wasn't until we hosted Derby in October that anyone came up with a way to stop us. Arthur Cox, Derby's manager, was clever. He changed to a 4–3–3, pushed his wingers high and left one striker up against our three centre-backs. We were confused, our wing-backs weren't sure how to react and we lost 2–1.

But this was a rare off day. Most teams couldn't handle us. John Moncur, a good midfielder, joined from Tottenham, and Paul Bodin, who had left the club just before I joined, returned to play at left wing-back. We were on course to earn a place in the play-offs, and maybe more, until Blackburn came in for Duncan Shearer at the end of March.

Duncan was scoring for fun and had formed a great partnership with Steve White. He was key to our promotion hopes, so I couldn't believe it when I heard that the board were thinking of accepting Blackburn's offer. 'We cannot sell the striker who's going to get us up,' I said. 'He finishes all our moves off. Why would we sell him now? I know £850,000 is a lot of money, but how much are we going to get if we go up?'

It turned into a four-hour meeting. I was trying to explain the situation to the board and the conversation was pretty heated at times. It went on and on until someone finally stuck their neck out and told the truth, revealing that the club were in a dire financial situation. Some board members had put personal guarantees up and the bank was asking for payment.

'Guys, we've just wasted four hours of our lives here,' I said. 'If you'd told me that in the first minute of the meeting of course I'd have agreed. You have to sell him.'

There was nothing left to say. Duncan left and we lost momentum during the run-in. The goals dried up and we missed out on a play-off place after losing to Derby on the final day. Blackburn finished sixth, won the play-offs, found another Shearer to play up front and won the Premier League three years later.

It was a crucial lesson for me as a young manager. It was another reminder that the club was about more than the 11 players on the pitch. There were so many people working behind the scenes, so many people giving everything to the cause, and I was desperate to make them happy. I wasn't ready to give up after one setback.

The thought of quitting because of Duncan's departure never crossed my mind. I wanted to take Swindon up and I focused on improving the team during the summer. Kevin Horlock was a good signing. He could cross, he could head the ball, he got stuck in and he was on a free transfer. I saw Kevin providing support for Paul Bodin at left wing-back and fancied that he would stretch teams with his pace, creating space for Lingy and allowing us to play our football.

We had a lovely balance. John Moncur, Ross MacLaren and Micky Hazard were two-footed midfielders, which created plenty of passing angles. I could play with two feet and Lingy wasn't bad at it. It gave us another dimension. I think we played Total Football at times, playing a very Dutch style that gave us great flexibility up front. I thought back to my spell at Chelsea and remembered seeing Dave Mitchell in the reserves. I had no qualms about snapping him up. Mitch could run behind defences, Steve White came alive in the box and Craig Maskell, who had a lethal left foot, was a top finisher, and added guile after joining from Reading.

We were smart in the transfer market too. I didn't have a lot of money and relied on free transfers. I signed Moncur for £70,000, which was peanuts at the time. We were punching above our weight.

We earned respect by staying true to our beliefs, even when we were up against it. Everyone pulled together. Swindon were such a lovely club and nothing summed up our camaraderie more than our trip to Brentford at the end of March.

I had it all mapped after telling Peter Day that I wanted to take the players to La Manga for a training camp. I thought that they needed to recharge their batteries, soak up some sun and forget about the pressure of the promotion race. The club agreed and everything was ready on the day of the game. We were going to head to Heathrow to catch our flight to Spain after playing Brentford, and I was feeling excited as I made my way to a hotel off the M4 to meet the players before kick-off. But the day was to take a turn for the worse when I got out my car and saw the team bus arrive.

The door opened and I saw Eddie Buckley, our kit man, standing there. Eddie was Swindon through and through, and a lovely man. He was a popular character who never swore, but something was bugging him.

'Fed up, gaffer,' Eddie said.

I knew it was serious at that point because that was Eddie's substitute for using the 'F' word.

'What's the matter, Ed?' I said.

'I've left the kit at the County Ground,' he replied. 'But I've got the boots and I've got the slips.'

I couldn't help but laugh as I imagined us running round Brentford's pitch wearing nothing more than boots and jock-straps. But it wasn't an ideal situation. John arrived soon after and we decided to call Peter, hoping that someone could bail us out.

It soon transpired that the supporters' bus hadn't left Swindon yet. They picked up the kit from the ground, hoping it was the right one, leaving us fretting as we had our pre-match meal. 'You've got one job, Ed,' I said. 'One job.'

Eddie was so relieved when the supporters finally arrived. Crisis averted, we set off for the ground and arrived slightly late, before heading off to find the tiny away dressing room. It wasn't the best way to prepare for a vital game. The Brentford fans were out in force and we were in even more trouble when Steve White, playing alongside Dave Mitchell up front, got sent off for a bad tackle after 10 minutes.

Playing at the back, I steeled myself. We needed to stay composed. We needed to be calm. We didn't need Dave to start putting himself about when he challenged for headers. I saw him stick an elbow into a defender at one stage and knew that I had to intervene.

'Mitch, what are you doing? What *are* you doing? We're down to 10 men. Calm down.'

It was in one ear and out the other. Moments later Mitch steamed into their left-back. He got away with it, but I was starting to lose my rag. I could see only one outcome and, sure enough, we were down to nine men when Mitch elbowed one of their centre-backs shortly before half-time.

I couldn't believe it. We started the day without a kit and now we had no strikers. I was so angry with Mitch that I booted him up the backside when he walked past me. Utterly livid, I was waiting for Brentford to score. Yet I couldn't feel sorry for myself. I looked at John, and although we had Shaun Close as an option to come on up front, I decided not to change anything until half-time.

Somehow, it was still 0–0 at the break and I was feeling strangely optimistic when I spoke to John. 'They're not that great a team technically,' I said. 'I don't think they'll open us up. Let's play with no strikers. We'll keep our three at the back. Maybe five if they push us back. Let's defend like Trojans and keep the score down. If we keep it to 0–0 we can put Shaun on in the last 10 minutes, although we'll need to put him on earlier if they score.'

I had no idea if it was going to work and John asked if I was absolutely sure about not putting a striker on. Yet my hunch was right. Brentford just lumped the ball into the box, we headed it away and we went for it in the final 10 minutes. Shaun came on and Paul Bodin should have scored.

It was an incredible effort. But I was fuming when we got back into the dressing room. 'You,' I said, pointing at Mitch, 'you ain't effing well going to La Manga.'

I was livid and wasn't ready to listen to the lads when they stuck up for Mitch. I marched off for a shower and stood there on my own until John came in. The lads knew that John was the good cop. They had won him over and although I wanted to stick to my guns at first, I realised that I had an opportunity to make myself popular.

The players were waiting when I came out of the shower. They knew. 'OK,' I said. 'You can go – but you can't sunbathe.'

It was like we had won the cup. I had decided I didn't want to ruin the spirit and potentially lose a couple of players by being too tough on Mitch. The lads were cheering and laughing, and we ended up having a great trip. Going to Spain helped us. We were in a good mood when we came home and beat Peterborough 1–0, setting ourselves up nicely for the run-in.

I hoped that we were building momentum. On Easter Monday we went to Birmingham, which is always a tough game, and found ourselves 4–1 down early in the second half. I decided to go for broke. I told Micky Hazard to play with freedom and I told my fellow centre-backs that I was going into midfield. I was demob happy. I just wanted to throw caution to the wind and I couldn't claim that it was a tactical masterstroke when Craig Maskell pulled a goal back.

All the same I could sense a change in the atmosphere. Mitch scored to make it 4–3 and our supporters were going mad. Everybody looked at me, wondering if we were going to revert to three at the back. I could hear Colin Calderwood asking John for more support. 'No,' I said. 'Leave it as it is.'

Birmingham were shellshocked. I told Micky to keep pushing forward, and we ended up winning 6–4. Mitch, the villain at Brentford, ended up as our hat-trick hero. It was incredible. The dressing room was in a state of shock after the game and I didn't really know what to say when I met Birmingham's manager Terry Cooper for a drink. We looked at each other in silence until I broke the ice. 'That's football, innit?' I said.

There was no logical explanation, although I think that it showed the advantage of being a player-manager. I was in the thick of the action and could tell which way the wind was blowing when we started to push Birmingham back. It was how I knew that we had to keep going in the second half. I could deliver instructions quickly and I was also part of the comeback. I was still capable of affecting the game. I wasn't playing simply to prolong my career. It wouldn't have been fair on anyone if I was hanging around just for the sake of it.

Yet while I knew that I could help us win promotion, we were going to have to do it the hard way. We didn't win any of our final four games, and Newcastle and West Ham went up automatically. I felt a sense of apprehension around the club. The supporters were worried after having promotion snatched away under Ossie and I think it fed through to the players, who looked weighed down by anxiety.

We needed to push against the tide. We had to relax after finishing fifth and setting up a play-off semi-final with Tranmere. I reminded the players how good they were and focused on making them believe again. We knew that our system worked and we came flying out of the traps when we hosted Tranmere in the first leg. The nerves evaporated. We played like Brazil and were delighted to win 3–1, although we knew that Tranmere were going to throw the kitchen sink at us in the second leg.

So it proved. Although Johnny Moncs gave us an early lead, Tranmere refused to give up. John Aldridge was a wily old fox up front and they were a goal away from levelling the tie on aggregate when they swept into a 2–1 lead in the second half. We weren't safe even when Craig Maskell made it 2–2. Tranmere immediately scored again and my heart was in my mouth when I mistimed a tackle in our area. I was on my knees, pleading with the referee not to point to the spot. I knew it was a foul. Their players were going mad and I was convinced that the referee was going to blow.

I was the most relieved man on the pitch when he waved play on. The margins were so fine. We survived and made it over the line. After a draining season, we were one game from reaching the Premier League. All eyes were on our trip to

Wembley to play Leicester. We just needed one last push, and it was down to me to make sure that the players were ready for the game of their lives.

8

PROMOTION

I wanted to take the pressure off before meeting Leicester in the final. We had 12 days to prepare and I decided to take the players to the Dormy Hotel in Bournemouth for a quick break. It was important to train in a different environment. There was a nervous energy around the club and although the players were excited after beating Tranmere, I was quick to remind them that we still had one more game.

We had to focus. Behind the scenes, though, my head was spinning. Along with preparing for the biggest game of my short managerial career, I was also mulling over an offer to leave Swindon for Chelsea.

I knew that I was going to play at Wembley and my emotions were all over the place with this bubbling away in the background. It started when Colin Hutchinson, Chelsea's chief executive, sounded me out at the end of the league campaign. I went to see Ken Bates, Chelsea's chairman, at his house and found myself in a bind. Although I was flattered by Chelsea's interest and knew that I needed to move if I wanted to progress as a manager, my heart was telling me to stay. I had achieved so much at Swindon and part of me was attracted to the idea of trying to keep them in the Premier League.

It was a conundrum. Although John Gorman and both of our families knew what was going on, I spent a lot of time in my head while we were at the Dormy. It was hard to gather my thoughts. I worried about ruining Swindon's big moment. I still had to plan our training sessions, prepare for Leicester and make sure that I was ready to play, even though I knew that my agent Dennis Roach was talking to Ken and Colin about Chelsea's offer at the same time.

Word inevitably began to seep out after the semi-final. The rumours swirled, creating a potential distraction, but I stayed quiet. I didn't want to add fuel to the fire. I had enough on my plate without creating a media circus. I had given my word to Chelsea and they wanted me to sign a contract immediately. Although I wanted to wait, they were worried that I would walk away, so I arranged to meet Colin at my house in Ascot to talk through the final details a couple of days before the game.

First I had to take training. I was on my way down from Ascot in the morning when I took a phone call from Tony Berry, who was on the board at Tottenham. I hadn't spoken to Tony for a while but he quickly got to the point.

'We've heard on the grapevine that you're going to Chelsea,' he said. 'Is it true?'

'It could be,' I said. 'I've not made any decisions yet.'

That wasn't strictly true. Colin was due to come over in the evening and I was going to join Chelsea. I wasn't expecting any curveballs and I was shocked when Tony told me that Alan Sugar wanted me to become Tottenham's manager.

'Terry Venables is your manager,' I said.

'There's a problem here with Terry and Alan Sugar,' Tony replied. 'I want to talk to you face-to-face. I'll come to your home.'

It wasn't ideal. I told Tony to come over in the afternoon, took training, rushed through my press duties and returned home five minutes before he arrived. We had coffee and reminisced about the old days at Tottenham before Tony put Alan on the phone.

'Terry's out,' Alan said. 'I can't explain why we can't do it now, but I'm changing the manager. Whatever Bates is offering you, I'll give you treble.'

Roachy's ears must have pricked up when he heard Alan's offer but I looked past the money. I wandered around my garden, deliberating for ages, and struggled to make up my mind. Tottenham were my boyhood club and I couldn't fathom turning them down. Yet the timing wasn't right. I had given my word to Chelsea and although my heart was telling me to go to Tottenham, returning to White Hart Lane at that stage felt wrong. After all they still had a manager. For all I knew Alan could have ended up keeping Terry. I had to decline when I went back inside to join Tony. 'I'm sorry, but I'm going to Chelsea,' I said.

It took a lot of willpower to turn Tottenham down. Tony called shortly after leaving my house but I think he knew that I was going to Chelsea when I said that Colin was coming over.

I felt like I was in a washing machine. Aware that I was at risk of becoming distracted, I decided not to sign anything with Chelsea before the game. I knew that I would feel responsible if we lost and I was determined to refocus. I remembered the guidance of John Syer, my sports psychologist at Tottenham, and how he taught me to compartmentalise. I visualised shutting the drama over my job in a drawer and switched my attention to the game. I needed to be fit and I needed to prepare a team to play Leicester. Although my days at Swindon were coming to an end, I couldn't let them down now.

The problem was that the whispers became louder as the big day drew closer. Someone in London must have let the cat out of the bag. There were some questions about my future from journalists and I tried to play it down, insisting that I was concentrating on winning promotion.

Thankfully the story didn't get too much traction. People understood that we had a huge game and although the players could sense that something was up, it didn't affect them. Our bond was strong and I looked to motivate the team by talking about injustice, reminding them of how promotion had been snatched away from Swindon before. I wanted them champing at the bit when we walked out at Wembley.

I reminded them that they might never get another opportunity like this and I drew on my experience of playing at Wembley. 'We've got to normalise this game,' I said. 'It's a special game, but when we get out on that pitch we've got to play like we have all season. We've played some wonderful football, but we're going to win this as a team. Leicester are a strong, physical side. We have got to get the ball down, be brave, pass the ball and play our style, but don't play as individuals.'

I explained that Tottenham almost froze in our first FA Cup final in 1981. 'I don't want you looking for your parents and your wives in the stands,' I said. 'We made a mistake like that years ago. Get your head on the game. It's 90 minutes plus of football and it's probably the biggest game you're ever going to play. You don't want that regret after the game. If you lose the play-offs, the season is done. Don't be individuals. We are winning this as a team.'

My message hit home. The Wembley surface was beautiful, better than anything we'd played on all season, and we were fantastic in the first half. It was a pitch for the purists and we controlled the game, passing beautifully.

Leicester couldn't cope with our system. Playing at sweeper, my first concern was making sure not to leave myself isolated against Julian Joachim, their speedy forward, and I kept catching him offside. We nullified Leicester's pace and I was able to advance into midfield at times, safe in the knowledge that Ross MacLaren would drop back to cover for me in the back three.

This was the beauty of that system. With three minutes to go before half-time I decided to have another saunter, and I was in the right place to give us the lead, latching on to a back-heel from Craig Maskell and caressing a low shot inside the left post from 18 yards.

We were halfway there. We went in ahead at half-time and I managed to have a few minutes away from the team with John. 'We've just got to keep it going,' I said. 'We have to keep the passing. They can't handle us.'

My only concern was that the lads were too giddy. They were deep in conversation about the game, which I usually liked to see, but I needed to bring them back down to earth before the second half. 'Look, by the time we get up the top of that tunnel for second half let's be nice and concentrated,' I said. 'Let's get the job done.'

The positive for me was that I had a good group. I could trust them to listen and I knew that nobody was going to hide. We had players who wanted the ball and we continued to dominate at the start of the second half, extending our lead when Craig smashed a beautiful left-footer into the top corner.

The place went mad when the ball flew in off the post. We were all over Leicester and were pinching ourselves when

Johnny Moncs nodded a loose ball back into the area for big Shaun Taylor to attack. Shaun was brave as a lion. He was a defender who gave everything to the cause and he didn't flinch when Kevin Poole, Leicester's goalkeeper, came flying out to punch clear. Shaun was too strong for Poole and we looked certain winners after taking a 3–0 lead with 53 minutes on the clock.

Yet that giddiness hadn't gone away and Leicester flew back at us. Joachim pulled one back and Leicester subjected us to an aerial barrage. We lost our composure and were rocking when Steve Walsh made it 3–2. It was turning into our worst nightmare. After 69 minutes I made a bad decision, stepping into midfield, and was out of position when Leicester countered, sending their fans delirious after Steve Thompson completed the comeback.

'For fuck's sake,' I thought. 'What was I doing up there?' I was kicking myself. Our 3–0 lead was gone, wiped out in the space of 12 mad minutes, and at that stage most people must have been backing Leicester. Our fans were in despair. We looked like we had nothing left to give.

Yet it was another moment when being a player-manager worked in my favour. Instead of trying to restore order from the touchline, I was able to lift the players on the pitch.

'We're going to win this,' I said to Martin Ling at a throw-in.

Lingy's head was down and he wasn't convinced.

'No, Lingy, look me in the eyes,' I said. 'We're going to win this game.'

'Yes, gaffer!'

After 84 minutes I stepped into midfield with the ball and waited for someone to make a run.

It could have gone either way when Steve White went down. Spotting him making a run, I lifted a pass over the top and

Leicester panicked. Steve tumbled and, although it was a tight call, luck was on our side. David Elleray pointed to the spot and Paul Bodin stepped up.

Paul was great under pressure. He was brave, he had a lovely technique and he struck the ball so cleanly. There was no one I trusted more in that situation, and the game was ours to lose again when Paul smashed his penalty down the middle, making it 4–3.

What a rollercoaster! Leicester threw the kitchen sink at us in the closing stages and it took a titanic effort to hold them off. I almost smacked myself in the face, telling myself not to do anything stupid. 'Don't you dare go into midfield,' I thought. 'Stay back. Do your job.'

We dug deep. The lads were brilliant. Nicky Summerbee gave us an outlet with his energy on the right, while Lingy and Johnny Moncs ran themselves into the ground. The fans roared us on and it was pure ecstasy when the final whistle blew. It was fantastic watching the lads go up the stairs to collect the trophy. Those lingering feelings of injustice faded away when we did our lap of honour. It was wonderful for the players who were there when Swindon had promotion taken away from them three years earlier. They must have thought their chance had gone. Now they were Premier League players. I couldn't have been happier for them.

Watching those jubilant scenes at Wembley, I could have been swept away by the romance of it all. I could have given in to sentiment and decided to stay at Swindon for one more year.

It would have been the wrong way to think. I told myself before the game that I couldn't allow myself to become swept away by emotion. Whatever happened on the day, I didn't want to think about leaving. I didn't want to feel like I had to stick around if we lost and I kept Chelsea out of my mind when we were cavorting around the pitch with the trophy. My head was in the sky and I didn't want my heart to take over. I needed to stay on an even keel. I had already made my decision. The final didn't change anything.

I was exhausted. The journey back from Wembley took ages because the Swindon fans were all driving back down the M4. The scenes were special – we saw celebratory banners hanging off bridges and it took for ever for us to crawl off the junction taking us back into the town.

It was time to celebrate. We had a big do, everyone had a few drinks and we partied until the early hours. Johnny Moncs had his tie around his head and the music was still going at 6am. There was no room for formalities. The players found some Dutch courage after having a few beers and it was the first time they addressed the rumours about Chelsea. 'Come on, gaffer!' they shouted. 'You've got to stay!'

I couldn't help but feel a tinge of sadness. We had gone through so much together and I would have loved to continue with them on their journey. It was a difficult time. I struggled to enjoy myself when we had an open-top bus tour through the town the following day. The players were celebrating with the fans but every interview was about my future. The journalists kept telling me that the fans wanted to know if I was staying.

I couldn't be truthful in that situation. It would have put a huge dampener on the party if I had admitted that I was going to Chelsea. I didn't want to ruin it for the players. I tried to bat everything away, even with thousands of people cheering in the streets and asking me to stay. It was suffocating and I felt worse than I did before the game.

I had nothing left in the tank when I got home. I still had to deal with Swindon's board. They weren't aware of Chelsea's interest before the play-offs, but this changed when Ken Bates contacted them shortly after the final. They were disappointed and tried to persuade me to reject Chelsea's offer, but there wasn't much to discuss. I knew that I wouldn't have huge finances at Swindon, even after winning promotion. It was time to move on and I didn't need long to sign my contract at Chelsea.

'I won't be the first person to leave a club,' I said to John, who shared my view on the move. He was my confidant. He knew about Chelsea from the start and I kept him in the loop when Tottenham asked me to replace Venables. 'Well, John,' I said, 'just to throw another spanner in the words, Tottenham have offered me the job.'

John was shocked when I rejected Tottenham. We were so close, mates rather than colleagues. We clicked on the pitch when John, who was a good full-back, left Celtic for Tottenham, and we were on the same wavelength when it came to coaching. We both wanted to play attractive football and our families spent a lot of time together.

The chemistry was right and John was with me on my final day at Swindon. The air felt heavy – it was a wrench to leave a place where I had made so many memories, but it had to be done. We were almost out of the door when the chairman Ray Hardman asked John if he could have a quick word.

John glanced at me. 'Go and have a chat with him,' I said, fully aware of what was about to happen. I wasn't surprised when Ray asked John to stay and replace me. I had repeatedly asked John over the previous 10 days if he would take the job if they offered it to him, but he insisted that he was coming with me. I was disappointed when he changed his mind at the very end.

Yet it was a great opportunity and I didn't begrudge John for jumping at the chance to manage in the Premier League, even if it meant that I was heading to Chelsea without my mate.

I didn't have time to worry about John staying behind. I wished him the best, hoping that he would keep Swindon up, and turned my thoughts to the King's Road. The move had taken place in such a rush, giving me little opportunity to analyse Chelsea's finances, facilities and players before accepting their offer.

My first task was to find an assistant, so I turned to another ally, asking Peter Shreeves to come with me. I felt that Peter's experience would come in handy, especially as lifting Chelsea out of the doldrums wasn't going to be easy. I wasn't walking into the finished article. Chelsea weren't the all-conquering giant we know today. Roman Abramovich's arrival was still 10 years away and the club were crying out for a change of culture after finishing 11th in the newly formed Premier League.

Although I found the challenge exciting, I knew that it was going to be hard. The players were stronger, fitter and quicker at Chelsea, but I had better technicians at Swindon. The squad wasn't anywhere near ready to win something. It was going to be a rebuild across the board. I wanted to change the way we played, introducing the style and formation that brought me success at Swindon, and I didn't need long to decide that Harlington, our training ground, had to improve.

To put it into context, Swindon had better facilities. It was an eye-opener, and I knew that something had to be done while I was doing a deal with Ron Atkinson, Aston Villa's manager, to sell my captain, Andy Townsend, during pre-season.

It was a blow when Andy told me that he wanted to join Villa, who had just finished second. Andy was my best player and I didn't want to sell him, but he was adamant that he needed a fresh start after three years at Chelsea. Although I tried to persuade him to stay, I had to move on. Standing in Andy's way might have soured his mood and affected the dressing room. I reluctantly gave in and prepared to call Ron to speak about the deal.

Keen for some privacy, I realised that I needed to find my office at Harlington. I asked one of my coaches for directions and was taken to the staff changing room before being shown a BT pay phone with the bottom missing by the entrance. 'You put 50p in,' he said. 'When you hear the pips on the phone it will drop through and you'll need to put 50p in again.'

It was ridiculous. While I was trying to complete a £2.1m deal to sell Andy to Villa, apprentices were walking through to put dirty kits in the laundry, my staff were getting changed behind me and the pips kept going on the phone when my 50p began to run out. It was embarrassing when Ron asked why he kept hearing odd noises at my end. 'I'll tell you what, I'm going to phone you this afternoon,' I said. 'I'm going to Stamford Bridge.'

I was exasperated when I put the phone down. I went to the stadium later that day and didn't hold back when I met Ken Bates. 'The training ground's a disgrace,' I said. 'It's not even ours. I've tried to plan my pre-season, and when I was trying to schedule in some running for Wednesday afternoon I was told that we can't do it then because Imperial College use the place for hockey.'

I couldn't believe it when I found out a university hockey team had priority over a Premier League side. But it didn't stop there. I wasn't finished with Ken. 'The pitches are poor,' I said. 'There's not even a bath, there's no gym, there's nothing. No wonder the players always have flu.'

The place wasn't fit for purpose. Players were crammed inside tiny changing rooms. They walked down cold corridors and had to bring their own biscuits in because there was no food. If they went into the boot room to use the one available leg weight, they had to pause when an apprentice squeezed past them with the dirty boots.

There was no sense of care, no sense of pride. We were setting ourselves up for failure and I wasn't having it. 'Ken, this is Chelsea Football Club,' I said. 'We need to stay in better hotels when we go away before a game. The mentality of the players has to rise.'

We were acting like a Sunday League side. Although we had good, experienced players like Nigel Spackman, Dave Beasant and Dennis Wise, they were coasting because of the club's parsimonious attitude. People didn't know any better and it was up to me to stand up to Ken, who was a tough character.

'You need to spend some money,' I said. 'You need to ask the university to put six individual baths in this area here. I need an office. The treatment room needs to be here. The gym needs to be here. Go and get the plumber.'

Ken wasn't happy, but he accepted that we had to modernise. And it wasn't just Harlington. Anybody could see that Stamford Bridge itself fell well short of the required standard. The pitch was poor and the atmosphere was lacking during home games because a greyhound track around the pitch meant the fans were far away from the action. We had to do more for the players and change the philosophy of the club. Although results were important, we had to start by opening our minds and revolutionising our approach off the pitch. It was the only way forward. And I needed people to believe in my vision.

9

TO THE BRIDGE

Chelsea were in transition when I arrived in west London. The squad wasn't up to scratch and although I wanted to hang up my boots, the team needed me to keep playing. My time at Swindon demonstrated that I could still have a positive impact on players and I felt a responsibility to keep playing, even though it was starting to take a heavy toll, physically and mentally.

Those early months were tough. Although Ken Bates was ready to spend on the club's infrastructure, the team weren't ready for the brand of football I wanted to play. I wanted to continue with three at the back, with me as a sweeper, but some of the defenders were uncomfortable with my demands. There was no hiding place in the Premier League and there were times when I had to switch to a back four.

I couldn't be dogmatic. I needed to keep an open mind and make sure that I wasn't asking too much from the players. I didn't have all the ingredients to hand and sometimes was forced to play Craig Burley, a midfielder, as a wing-back. After arriving in such a blur, I had to shuffle people around as I found out more about the group. Erland Johnsen was a good defender and I saw that Steve Clarke could play well in a back four or as a wing-back. Yet Frank Sinclair and Michael Duberry, two promising young defenders, were nervous about playing out from the back and needed plenty of reassurance.

It was a slow process. I moved Dennis Wise, who was a very good player, inside from the wing and had a lot of battles with him about his habit of taking too many touches on the ball during the first year. I think that Dennis was reluctant to pass to certain players because he didn't trust them to keep possession, but he sometimes played himself into trouble and I needed him to realise that he had less time in the middle of the park. He improved when I told him that he couldn't take more than three touches during training.

Although there were games in which the system functioned quite well, there were others in which we gave too many chances away. It wasn't running as smoothly as at Swindon and I had to be patient. Money was tight. I bought a Danish defender, Jakob Kjeldbjerg, for £400,000 during pre-season and also signed Gavin Peacock for £1.25m from Newcastle. I liked Gavin a lot. I saw him playing off the front two and linking in the final third with Dennis, John Spencer and Mark Stein, a striker who joined from Stoke in October.

The snag was that Dennis, John, Gavin and Mark all lacked height. We were a small team and struggled physically. The ball often came back at us from goal-kicks and we toiled at set-pieces. We couldn't go long and play in the traditional English way. We had no option but to play on the floor and take risks on dodgy pitches.

I saw encouraging flashes at times. Although I had to wait until my fourth game for a win, I felt that we were on the right track when we hosted Manchester United in September. We showed tremendous spirit to beat the champions 1–0 thanks to a goal from Gavin, and it was encouraging when we closed the month with another big win against Liverpool.

But it all soon came crashing back down to earth. Confidence evaporated and we went on a horrible run, picking up two points from our next 11 league games. The defeats piled up and I was under huge pressure when we lost 3–1 at Southampton on Boxing Day. We were second from bottom and the fans were livid. They were waiting for me when I walked out of the away dressing room and they didn't hold back, telling me in no uncertain terms to 'piss off back to Tottenham'.

I was lucky that that Matthew Harding, a Chelsea obsessive who had just become a director at the club, saw what was happening. Matthew used to watch games in the stands before he burst on to the scene, and he still went to the pub with his mates before putting his suit on and heading up to the directors' box to watch the game. He had so much clout with the fans and he didn't hesitate when he spotted that I was under fire, jumping off the team bus to give the people who were abusing me an absolute roasting.

I appreciated that support from Matthew and I felt even better when Ken, who always went away over Christmas and New Year, called me from wherever he was on holiday. 'Glenn, you're our man,' he said. 'Don't panic.'

Although part of me wondered whether I'd just received the dreaded vote of confidence, I knew in my heart that Ken was being genuine. Colin Hutchinson laughed when I relayed the conversation to him, telling me that Ken hadn't said that to any of his other managers.

It helped that I had an immediate chance to repay Ken's faith in me. There was no respite over the festive period in those days. We had to host Newcastle a day after losing to

Southampton and we dug in against a good side on a cold, misty day at Stamford Bridge. It was a horrible game and we won it thanks to a scrappy goal from Mark Stein.

I was delighted for Steino, who had struggled after joining us. He seemed to suffer from a mental block. It happens to strikers sometimes, and although the players could see his finishing prowess in training, nothing quite ran for him in games. He just needed one to go in and he went through a purple patch after scoring against Newcastle, finishing the season with 13 goals.

Steino's journey summed us up. We only needed a couple of good results to turn our fortunes around and we improved as the season wore on, rallying and finishing 14th. I sensed more positivity in the team and the crowd. Chelsea weren't expecting miracles. Ken was prepared to look past results. He wanted to see progress on the pitch and I appreciated his words of encouragement before Newcastle.

It was over to me to show the players that I wasn't giving up, and I benefited from having Peter by my side. He was a different type of assistant to John, but he was experienced and was great at lifting my spirits and picking the players up when they were low. Football is about belief, even if you're a great side. So much is possible when you're feeling confident in your mind and body. Sometimes teams are waiting for someone to give them that push and it's a wonderful feeling when momentum starts to build.

The hard part is getting to that point. I was under the cosh during those difficult winter months. The fans weren't sure about me because of my links with Tottenham and it was tough when results went against us. There were times when I drove home from training wondering what was going to happen. I was consumed with doubts about my team selections and I was beginning to wonder if my player-manager role was proving to be a hindrance. I kept pulling my calf muscle and I questioned if I could balance keeping fit with scouting, organising training and everything else that came with management.

I had to fight myself to keep negative thoughts at bay. Managers are stuffed when doubts weigh them down. It's an easy job when you're winning all the time. The challenge for managers is coping when results turn. I was on a steep learning curve but I refused to hide. Adversity made me stronger. I was desperate to prove that Chelsea were right to stand by me.

Winning a trophy in my first season would have been an unexpected bonus, and we had a chance in the FA Cup. Our belief grew as we progressed through the early rounds and I had another date at Wembley in the diary when we won our semi-final against Luton 2–0.

It was a major step for Chelsea, who were in the final for the first time since beating Leeds in 1970. We were massive underdogs going into the game, with Manchester United, the league champions, our opponents after they survived a scare against Oldham in their semi-final. United were seconds away from losing before Mark Hughes scored a brilliant volley, and they had too much for Oldham in the replay. We were up against it, although I still felt that we had players who could cause them problems.

United had good reason to fear an upset. We had done the double over them in the league, and the first half was even. We almost went ahead when Gavin, who scored the only goal in both league games against United, smacked a volley against the bar. But it wasn't to be. United were a terrific side and we couldn't handle it when they upped the tempo in the second half. Eric Cantona put them in control with two penalties – the second, given for a barge by Frank Sinclair on Andrei Kanchelskis, was a very controversial decision by David Elleray – and they ended up winning 4–0. Weirdly, Elleray was the referee who gave Swindon the winning penalty in the play-off final. Sometimes it goes for you, sometimes it doesn't.

I couldn't be too disappointed. Although every defeat hurts, we were beaten by a better side and I wanted to turn the experience of playing in a major final into a positive. It was a big day for the club. Ken enjoyed being at Wembley in his suit and sitting in the royal box. The directors loved the experience and I wanted to use it to my advantage, especially with Matthew on the scene. 'There's more to come,' I said. 'If we can spend a bit of money, we can do this. We're building towards something.'

We needed to invest. We were in Europe for the first time since 1971, qualifying for the European Cup Winners' Cup via the back door. But our squad wasn't equipped for European football. We were adding sprinklings of talent, but I was frustrated at times. I had to be careful with my budget and was restricted to three signings, buying Scott Minto, David 'Rocky' Rocastle and Paul Furlong for a combined £4.3m. We also struggled to settle in to a back three, and I was often forced to move into midfield and play a back four. The balance was never quite right. Success wasn't going to arrive overnight, although I was excited about the prospect of managing in Europe for the first time.

It gave the club reason to believe there was light at the end of the tunnel. I was desperate not to lose in the first round, although I was worried about UEFA's ridiculous rule stipulating that teams could field only three foreign players in Europe.

It made life even harder for us because they classed Scottish, Welsh, Northern Irish and Irish players as foreigners. Our options were limited. My calf kept going, ruling me out of the first leg of our first-round tie against Viktoria Žižkov, and Nigel Spackman was battling through back pain. Numbers were tight and I had to tell Graham Rix, who had moved down from Dundee to become the youth team coach, to keep himself fit on the off chance we needed him to play.

Graham had to sign on as a player. He was reluctant at first but he soon came round to the idea of playing again. He even came off the bench when we beat Viktoria 4–2 in the first leg at Stamford Bridge, with goals from Frank Sinclair, Paul Furlong, Rocky and Wisey giving us a commanding lead. It was one of those special European nights under the lights. Stamford Bridge was at the start of its redevelopment, but the atmosphere was terrific and the players rose to the occasion before going through thanks to a 0–0 draw in the second leg. The adventure had begun. We didn't know where it was going to end.

The players embraced the challenge. They wanted to test themselves, so the mood in the dressing room was downbeat after Austria Vienna held us to a goalless draw in the first leg of our second-round tie at Stamford Bridge. The reaction spoke volumes, underlining how much the players were out of their element at this level. 'Guys, this ain't a bad result,' I said, reminding them it was still all to play for. 'They haven't got an away goal. We go to their place, we've got to score. If we get a goal we're in a really strong position.'

We had a clear target when we travelled to Vienna in the second leg. They put us under pressure but we had an opportunity when John Spencer broke when we cleared a corner just before half-time. Spenny was such a clever little player. He was a great character, a very funny guy, and he only needed half a yard to hurt a side. He had pace, and although he had passed a fitness test on his hamstring injury, he showed no sign of slowing down as he went past the halfway line.

Sitting on the bench, I was worried about Spenny's hamstring going. 'Careful!' I shouted. Yet there was no stopping him. I forgot about his hamstring once he was up against the last defender. I urged him on and he finished expertly after going through, giving us that vital away goal. It didn't matter when they equalised in the second half. We were through and it was great seeing the Chelsea fans celebrating behind the goal.

We were giving them some special memories. It was like Chelsea were back, but we realised how far we still had to go after beating Club Brugge and setting up a semi-final with Real Zaragoza. The first leg in Spain was a disaster. It all went wrong when Zaragoza won a corner after eight minutes. I had a bad feeling when I realised that Paul Furlong had forgotten who he was meant to pick up. I could see him asking us for directions from the bench, but he couldn't hear us. Paul went to their No5 when he was meant to be picking up the No6, and he realised his mistake too late.

I went berserk when the ball ended up in our net. We were 2–0 down at half-time and I made my feelings clear in the dressing room. Although Paul did well for me with his pace and hold-up play, he lacked discipline at times and I was furious with him. Sometimes managers lose it. I took a risk, dragging him to a board with instructions for defensive set-pieces.

'Tell me what it says there!' I said. 'It says 6! Why the hell have you gone at the 5?'

Paul was so apologetic, but it was a tough moment for the team. We would have forgotten about it if Zaragoza hadn't scored, but they were ruthless. Our naivety cost us, and this is why players have to remember their jobs. There has to be discipline. We weren't a Sunday League side; this was a massive European semi-final.

We had given ourselves a mountain to climb and although we chased an away goal in the second half, it ended 3–0 to Zaragoza. They were better than us technically and we came up short in the second leg. Despite Paul putting us on the front foot with an early goal, they took the wind out of our sails with an away goal. Our fans were up for it but the job was too big. The last 10 minutes were agonising. We had chances after going 3–1 up but Zaragoza defended well, and they ended up beating Arsenal in the final.

The journey was over in more ways than one. While the defeat was hard to accept, it was also the night when I decided that my playing days were over. I couldn't push myself any further. Although I came off the bench, I knew that I needed to call it quits at the end of the season. It was instinct. I was warming up during the second half and could feel the pressure from the fans, who were urging me to put myself on.

'I'm going to have to go on,' I thought. 'I might do something.' Yet I wasn't feeling it when I was on the pitch. The expectation from the crowd was too much. The strain of being a player-manager had finally taken its toll. One thought kept running through my head during those final 20 minutes: 'It's time.'

If acceptance made the end of my playing career easier to take, having a big job on my hands made it all the more important to focus. I could not spend too long dwelling on the pain of losing to Zaragoza. Managers have to move on quickly after defeats, and the positive way to look at the end of our European adventure was that it showed how far Chelsea had come as a club.

I saw further evidence of progress after we finished the 1994–95 season in 11th place. The next challenge was to keep building. One-off wins over United were welcome but I wanted us to go toe-to-toe with the big sides on a regular basis. I wasn't satisfied with mid-table finishes and the odd cup run; I wanted to create a team capable of challenging at the highest level.

It was, however, going to take money to make my vision a reality. The club needed financial backing and I was grateful that Matthew Harding wanted to help. Matthew had so much passion for Chelsea, although there were times when it was awkward between him and Ken.

I didn't relish being stuck between the pair of them. I think Matthew wanted to become chairman one day and I got on well with him, which made Ken think that I wasn't on his side. It wasn't easy. Ken was a different character to Matthew, but he was the boss and he was in control. He still had the final say and he did a lot for Chelsea.

Matthew was a dreamer, a real character. He used to call me after I finished training and insist I meet him in central London for lunch. His reason? 'I want to tell you about my dreams for Chelsea.'

It was genuine when Matthew told me about his plans to build a new stand at the stadium. Yet there was always a sense that he was holding back. If he'd been the chairman I knew he would have spent the money straight away. But until that day arrived I had to keep watching the pennies.

All the same it was wonderful listening to him. He asked me which players I wanted to buy during my second season and I said Matt Le Tissier, who was playing superbly for Southampton.

'Right,' Matthew said. 'I'll write you out a cheque for £6m.'

'That's too much,' I said. 'We don't need …'

I don't know why I bothered protesting. Matthew was off. 'If I write you a £6m cheque, let's go and get him,' he said. 'Let's go.'

Matthew was so excited that day. Le Tissier could change a game in an instant and we did try to find out if he was available. Yet the move fell apart when our interest made it into the papers. I'm not sure if Ken had blocked it.

Ken operated in a shrewder way than Matthew. He was passionate but he was more cautious. He didn't act on whims, which made me immensely grateful when he gave me that message of support after we lost to Southampton on Boxing Day in 1993. It made me confident that I had Ken's backing, so with Matthew willing to invest his money, we had a chance to make our presence felt in the transfer market in the summer of 1995.

My focus was on finding someone capable of operating as a sweeper in a three-man system after my retirement. I wanted to make a statement and I was excited when I told Colin Hutchinson about a tip I'd received from an agent.

'Look, you might think I'm mad,' I said, 'but I've heard that Ruud Gullit is available on a free transfer. Can we go for him?'

I was convinced we'd found our man. Although Ruud was 32 and had been suffering with a knee injury, there was no doubt about his quality. I remembered him playing as sweeper for Feyenoord when they lost to Tottenham in the UEFA Cup in 1983 and I reckoned that he would like playing there again if we could convince him to join us from Sampdoria.

We needed to sell it to Ruud. His agent invited us to Italy and I flew out to Milan with Colin in an attempt to make the deal happen. I just wanted to talk to Ruud about football when we met. 'I haven't quite got the players yet,' I said. 'I'm getting them. I'm building this team to go with a back three and I want you to play as the sweeper.'

Ruud, who remembered me from our battles when England played Holland, was intrigued. I was encouraged, although I knew that the deal could still fall down on a couple of details. The first was whether we could afford him – his wages weren't going to be cheap; the second was whether he would remain interested if he found out more about Chelsea. I certainly didn't want to tell him too much about the training ground so I kept the conversation to football and went back to the hotel feeling cautiously optimistic.

It wasn't a pipe dream. I was relieved when we heard that Ruud was impressed and wanted to come to London for further talks. We were in with a genuine chance of signing a true great. There was only one problem: making sure not to find myself giving Ruud a tour of Harlington.

Although we had spruced it up a bit, adding a few baths in the shower area, putting a new gym in place and building me a better office, it still fell well below the luxury Ruud would have experienced when he was at AC Milan. I was worried that everything would fall apart if this Dutch superstar had a look at our modest surroundings, particularly when he started telling me about his Milan days. 'The training camp is so important,' Ruud said. 'We virtually lived there in Milan. It was like a second home.'

I had to think on my feet. The training ground was off limits and Stamford Bridge was also out of the question because construction had started on the new Matthew

Harding Stand. 'The thing is, Ruud, we've got a problem,' I said. 'There's building going on at both places and we'd have to put these hard hats on. If someone takes a photo of us in those we really wouldn't want that getting out. How about we go and have some lunch down the Fulham Road?'

Panic over. We went to a good restaurant and I laid on the charm, wining and dining Ruud and telling him more about my plans for the team. 'You won't be a deep sweeper, where you're going to be the spare man,' I said. 'You're going to have to mark. But when we get the ball, you can pull off and we'll start out from the back.'

Ruud was happy. He needed a fresh challenge after his time in Italy. He couldn't go anywhere in Milan without people stopping him in the street, and I promised him that he would have a calmer lifestyle in London. 'You'll be recognised, but you'll have a better life,' I said.

It was meant to be. I was anxious about the medical, but it turned out that Ruud was still extremely fit. He passed it with flying colours, and it was such a big moment in Chelsea's history when we announced the signing of Ruud Gullit. It changed the perception of the club. People were starting to take notice of us.

Ruud lifted Chelsea to another level. Although I needed to give him days off here and there because of his knee, he still had so much to offer and his attitude was first class. He was strong-minded but didn't have a big ego. 'It is what it is,' he said after finally seeing the training ground. 'It's not perfect, but we get on with it.'

Ruud was that kind of guy. He hit it off with the lads straight away, going on nights out with them and bantering with Wisey and Spenny, and he was a big fan of Paul Furlong when he first saw him in training. 'Wow, what a good centre-forward he is,' Ruud said.

'He is,' I said. 'But maybe you can help him as well on the pitch. We have to give him a lot of confidence to reach his best.'

That summed up Chelsea's challenge. We were building a good team but we weren't the finished article. I wanted us to show ambition and I tried to sign Dennis Bergkamp after hearing that he was available for £8m from Inter while we were negotiating with Ruud in Milan. We spoke to Bergkamp's agent and Colin called Ken to test the water, but the finances were too much and we had to stand aside when Arsenal met Inter's asking price.

Bergkamp wasn't the only one who got away. I also scouted Gianfranco Zola, who ended up joining Chelsea after I left, but the money wasn't quite there during my time. We had to be careful after handing Ruud a big contract; I couldn't break the bank on new signings and I had to choose wisely that summer. Mark Hughes was an important signing from United. Although Mark wasn't at his peak, he increased our threat up front and he was up for the challenge. He could see that Chelsea were improving and I added another important piece to the jigsaw a few months into the season, buying Dan Petrescu from Sheffield Wednesday and making him my new right wing-back.

We were moving in the right direction but it wasn't easy at first. We made a mediocre start to the season and I decided that something had to change after a 3–0 defeat at the champions Blackburn in October. Ruud was a terrific footballer, but it wasn't working with him in defence. The blend wasn't right and we couldn't play out from the back properly. Ruud was giving the ball to people in positions where he thought they could deal with it, but they were finding it difficult to manage the pressure and we were giving away too many easy chances.

Some of the players were itching to tell me that they were struggling to cope. In the end I had to pull Ruud aside at training one day. 'We'll have to push you forward,' I said. 'I'm going to try and play you in a little bit of a free role. You go and play. We'll get you the ball.'

Ruud took it like a man. He was a team player and he was great when he moved forward. Watching him during the first five minutes of games was fascinating. Whether he was playing at the back or as a No10, he used to spend that time on the fringes of the action, almost as though he were getting the measure of the opposition and working out their weak points. I think it was his experience kicking in. He kept it very simple during the early stages, but he wasn't coasting. His mind gave him the upper hand and I could always tell when he suddenly lifted the handbrake, increasing the tempo of our play and taking the game by the scruff of the neck.

With Ruud setting the tone, I was getting closer to where I wanted to be. Mark was great at holding the ball up, Dan was a clever player and Gavin Peacock made good runs from midfield. Yet I still didn't have centre-backs who were confident playing my way. It worked at Swindon, but the pace of the Premier League made it tougher to build from the back. I had to keep changing the system and I didn't manage to find the right formula before the season was over.

We were still a cup team, and we were a good one. I wasn't intimidated when we drew Newcastle in the third round of the FA Cup, even though they were miles clear at the top of the league. We drew the first game at home and Dan was brilliant in the replay at St James' Park, where I backed him to get the better of David Ginola.

'If you do the job on him defensively, you know how to make the right runs in our system,' I said. 'I don't need to tell you that. We'll get you in all day long.' I turned to Ruud and emphasised the point. 'Ginola won't be able to stay with him.'

We played so well that night. We held our own against a top side, drawing 2–2, and deserved to go through on penalties. It gave us the belief that we could go all the way, and we were one step away from another trip to Wembley after reaching the semi-finals.

United stood in our way. They had eaten into Newcastle's lead by that stage and everybody was beginning to see why Ferguson had so much faith in the Class of 92. But I think we should have knocked them out at Villa Park. The pitch was a disgrace, which didn't suit either side, but we handled it better in the first half and were ahead at half-time thanks to a header from Ruud.

The second half was full of regrets. We gave them two poor goals, Andy Cole and David Beckham scoring, and we couldn't find an equaliser. United must have known it was going to be their day when Eric Cantona headed a volley from Spenny off the line.

We were almost there. We just needed another push. I was happy, and although Ken was suspicious about my bond with Matthew, my only focus was on making the team successful. The first building blocks were in place and the thought of leaving the club hadn't once crossed my mind as we approached the end of the season. Then a phone call came out of the blue, two days before we were due to face Blackburn in our final game. It changed everything.

* * *

It didn't feel real. I was alone in my car when I took the call, sitting outside Stamford Bridge on a Friday afternoon, and I couldn't believe what I was hearing. The voice at the other end of the line belonged to Jimmy Armfield, a consultant for the FA, and he caught me completely off guard. The words coming out of his mouth didn't really make sense. He told me that he was calling to sound me out about a job. Apparently my name was on a shortlist of potential candidates, and Jimmy wanted to know what I thought about replacing Terry Venables as England's manager.

I was in shock. There had been a bit of talk around about Terry potentially leaving when Euro 96 was over but I hadn't paid much attention to the noise. Terry was doing a good job and had a chance to win a trophy that summer. There seemed to be no need to make a change and I assumed that other managers had said no to the FA. I was inexperienced and would never have imagined that I'd be in with a chance of managing England at that stage.

I can't remember the drive back to Ascot from Chelsea, and when I got home I wondered whether the phone call had ever really taken place. I kept the conversation to myself for a few days, assuming it might have been a dead end. They probably still had to speak to six other people, so I had no desire to get ahead of myself. Chelsea had only finished the season in 11th place after losing 3–2 to Blackburn and I still had much to prove.

Yet the picture changed when I received another call informing me that the FA were down to the last three and I was still on the list. It was the first time I knew that I had a genuine chance of getting the job and I realised that I needed to have a proper conversation with Anne about the potential impact that managing England would have on our family. I would have only turned the job down for personal reasons. Our children, Zoe, Zara and Jamie, were still young, and there is so much pressure attached to the position.

Perhaps my family would have told me to steer clear of it had they known what lay in store off the pitch. Yet there was no way of predicting the future. We were all going into the unknown. None of us understood how big the job really was, and in any case I didn't feel that I could say no to my country. It was an incredible opportunity. My mind started to race when I thought about the team and managing the likes of Tony Adams, Paul Ince, Alan Shearer and Teddy Sheringham.

I was excited. I thought about the euphoria that would come with England hosting the Euros. As a fan I wanted us to win and as a manager I wanted my players to be full of confidence when I took over. My head was in the clouds. I was dreaming and I let myself get carried away until one evening I told myself to stop being so silly. Nothing was decided yet.

Jimmy didn't want our second meeting to take place at the FA's headquarters in Lancaster Gate since the FA didn't need news of Terry's potential replacement leaking out, especially with the tournament so close to starting. Everything was very cloak and dagger; it felt like we were in a spy film when I ended up meeting him in a parking lot in Hyde Park, and I was worried about someone sussing us out when I saw a long queue at a nearby ice cream van.

Yet nobody noticed us in the end. We sat in the car talking about football and the conversation went well. I didn't put on any airs and graces. I didn't ask about money. I just spoke about my style of play. I told Jimmy that I liked to use a back three and I took the chance to get to know him as a person. Jimmy was a great player in his day. He was part of England's squad at the 1966 World Cup, and I enjoyed listening to him talk about playing with Bobby Moore and Jimmy Greaves.

It was a pure football chat, which suited me perfectly. I knew that I was in with a chance of getting the job. It was Jimmy's role to go back to the FA with his recommendations, and I must have impressed him. I was confident. I wanted the job and I was thrilled when I found out that I was the last candidate standing.

Chelsea weren't going to stand in my way. Ken obviously wanted compensation from the FA but he didn't have to look far for my replacement. Ruud stepped up as player-manager to become my replacement, and Chelsea really began to put themselves about that summer. The Premier League was growing stronger because of the Sky money, and Chelsea, who were increasingly ready to spend, benefited from Ruud's Italian connections, signing Roberto Di Matteo and Gianluca Vialli.

The club were on the way up and they took another huge step forward in Ruud's first season in the dugout, beating Middlesbrough in the FA Cup final. It wouldn't be long before they were playing in the Champions League.

It might have been me bringing in those stars, but the universe took me down a different path. If the deal with the FA went through I was going to be leading my country into a qualifying campaign for the 1998 World Cup. I just needed to jump over one last hurdle: make it through a meeting with Graham Kelly, the FA's chief executive.

It had to be done in secret, and my agent Dennis Roach said that we should ask our friends Alec and Vicky, who lived in Hurley, if we could borrow their house for the day. As they would be in South Africa on holiday they were more than happy to help out, and Alec told us that he'd leave the front-door key under a plant pot.

Everything went to plan at first. The gardeners left the gate open and we made our way up the drive towards a lovely house, only to find that the key wasn't where Alec said it would be. Dennis was going berserk. Graham was 15 minutes away, it was a scorching day and we were locked outside.

We had to play for time when Graham arrived. Dennis was looking everywhere and we weren't sure if Alec had pranked us. It wasn't the best way to prepare for a huge meeting and although Dennis eventually found the key, our mood didn't improve when we rushed inside and discovered that Alec and Vicky had left the heating on before leaving the house.

We might as well have gone to a sauna to negotiate the contract. It was no time for formalities. I took my jacket off and Dennis removed his tie. Graham, however, was an FA man. He sat there with his England blazer on for an hour, getting hotter and redder as the talks progressed. He looked like he was going to explode. It didn't exactly give him the upper hand in negotiations. Eventually I had to pretend that I needed to go to the toilet just so I could burst out laughing.

I think Graham just wanted to get out of there. Eventually he left and I went into the garden with Dennis to discuss everything in the cool of the shade. It was clear that I was going to become the next England manager.

My parents were delighted when I told them the news. Although I sensed they were a bit concerned about the impact on my private life, their overriding emotion was pride at seeing their boy have the hopes and dreams of an entire nation resting on his shoulders.

Admittedly Mum was a bit confused at first, pointing out that Terry was still manager. She had a point. I respected Terry, who taught me a lot when he managed England's Under-21 side, and was a bit baffled to hear he was leaving. I wasn't privy to the reasons behind his departure. As far as I was concerned Terry was a good coach and had given England hope after a difficult few years.

It was awkward. For some reason the FA wanted us to do a press conference together to announce that I was replacing Terry, who wasn't best pleased with the request. We filled up a huge room and the journalists kept firing questions at us. It wasn't fun. It was fortunate that Terry and I respected each other, but I'm not sure if it was a good idea. I felt for Terry, who could have done without the distraction before a major tournament. He didn't want to say too much and it became very stilted.

There was another tricky moment for both of us after the FA asked me to come in to meet the players at training one day. Again, it was nothing to do with me. The FA wanted it to happen but it wasn't an easy day. The players were focused on the Euros and I don't think that they needed me around at that stage. There would have been individuals wondering if I was going to have them in my squad. It felt unnecessary and I tried to keep it low key. I watched them train, had some lunch with the staff and made my exit.

I can understand why Terry wasn't that happy about it all. Although I couldn't wait to get going and test myself against the best in the world, I didn't want to affect his preparations. I was an England fan and I wanted to inherit a winning side, especially as we were in a World Cup qualifying group with Italy.

It was an odd time. In normal circumstances the announcement of a new England manager comes after a tournament. Yet I was out of sight and out of mind, even though I got straight down to business, cancelling a holiday to Spain and using the time to scout some of our qualifying opponents with my assistant John Gorman, who, despite being a Scot, had agreed to work alongside me again following his spell at Swindon. There was barely time to pause for breath as we flew to Romania to have a look at Moldova in their friendly before heading up to Russia to analyse Poland.

We were the only ones thinking about the World Cup, with the FA inevitably focusing on hosting the Euros. Michelle Farrer, who was wonderful at looking after the manager's diary, was a huge help, making sure that our flights and hotels were booked, but we were basically on our own. It was hard not to feel that we were viewed as something of an inconvenience.

I couldn't complain, though. It was an unforgettable summer. The atmosphere at Wembley for England's games was amazing and the team went so close. I enjoyed my watching brief. Although I made sure that my punditry work during the tournament didn't involve any England games, I paid close attention when they were in action.

They didn't start well and there was a bit of pressure before Paul Gascoigne's incredible goal sealed victory over Scotland in their second group game. Gazza's volley dissolved the tension and England hit the heights in their next game, thrashing Holland 4–1. It was a truly outstanding performance and it was special to be inside Wembley that night. I made sure to drink in the moment, allowing myself to sit back and just enjoy the thrill of being a fan again during the final 20 minutes.

That was the pinnacle. England squeezed past Spain in the last eight and were desperately unlucky to lose their semi-final to Germany. If only Gazza's studs had been longer when he had that chance to win it in extra time.

I was in the stands, watching as Gareth Southgate's penalty was saved in the shootout. It was a strange feeling. In that moment of despair for the country, I realised that the torch had passed to me. It was my job to lift the mood. 'Wow,' I thought, 'I'm England manager.'

10

THE ROAD TO FRANCE

It was incredible to think that my tenure as England's manager began amid such heartbreak. Terry's reign was over the moment Andreas Möller sent Germany through to the final with an emphatic penalty, and although I struggled to make sense of my emotions at first, I quickly realised that I had to get my head in the game. My time had come and I could feel that the eyes of the nation were now on me, waiting to see how I was going to lift their devastated team off the floor.

I simply had to step up. There was no hiding place, no chance to ease myself gently into the job. Failing to qualify for the World Cup wasn't an option. The pressure was on straight away and I didn't have long before the start of our qualifying campaign for France 98, which started with a trip to Moldova at the start of September.

It was a new experience for a lot of the players. England didn't have to qualify for Euro 96 because they were hosts, and the vast majority of their games under Terry were at Wembley. They were never really out of their comfort zone. For all the excitement about football coming home, the squad had little understanding of what it meant to go away to a hostile place, stay in a mediocre hotel and play on a bad pitch.

As a team, Moldova didn't scare us. Yet the trip was going to be a test of our character. I was going to find out a lot about the squad's mentality, and I felt better after spending a few days watching the players train. It was my first chance to have a proper look at them and I was excited when I saw close up how much quality they had. It was different to managing a club side. With England, every player had talent, pride and a burning desire to succeed. The standard was so high and the team did well to calm my nerves, coping with an awkward pitch and ensuring that my first game ended in a comfortable 3–0 win.

I was pleased with the scoreline too. A 1–0 win would have led to a few grumbles, while a thrashing would have sent expectations through the roof. I was fine with goals from Nicky Barmby, Gazza and Alan Shearer, who had never scored away from Wembley before, and happy that the players handled my switch to a back three. It didn't matter that we had a couple of key injuries. Gary Pallister slotted in to central defence, Andy Hinchcliffe had a good debut at left wing-back and the big story was the first appearance in an England shirt for David Beckham, who was on his way to becoming a superstar after scoring from the halfway line against Wimbledon on the opening day of the season.

I had no worries about starting David. Although he was only 21, he was talented enough to handle anything that came his way. David had so much quality. He oozed class when I first saw him play against my Chelsea team. He already looked the part and I tried my luck with Alex Ferguson after the game, cheekily asking if there was any chance we could have David on loan. He'd just been loaned out to Preston but Alex made it clear in no uncertain terms that David was already set to be a regular in United's first team. I wasn't surprised. His technique was second to none and I had no doubt that I was going to call him up after seeing his extraordinary goal at Selhurst Park.

I was ready to make changes. Although Tony Adams captained the side at Euro 96, I wanted Alan to wear the armband. At club level I would have gone for Tony or Incey, but I felt that the international game called for someone who would command instant respect with opponents and referees. The armband needed to be worn by a player with global status. Cruyff, Maradona and Platini did it for their teams, and while Alan was a good captain off the pitch, the main reason I chose him was for his aura. Alan was a world-class striker who could hurt any team and it made sense to capitalise on his reputation, not least because he had just become the most expensive player in the world after joining Newcastle for £15m.

Tony understood the logic behind my decision. He was a top defender but was struggling with a few injuries and needed time to adjust to playing in a back three as he was used to playing in a back four at club level. That Arsenal defence was so organised, and it wasn't easy for Tony to settle into a new rhythm at international level. I wanted him playing in the middle at the back, dropping deeper at times, and it was a work in progress during training. I had a lot of discussions with Tony about the nuances of the role and I felt that it helped him not to have to focus on captaining his country.

Tony's reaction was perfect. He embraced the tactical challenge, got on with the job and listened when I explained my reasoning to him. 'I've got three captains,' I said. 'I've got you at the back, Incey in midfield and Alan up front.'

I had leaders who could take control of their units on the pitch and I was spoilt for choice up front, giving me a tough decision to make when we hosted Poland a month later. I had so many strikers at my disposal and although I could have gone with the subtlety of Teddy Sheringham, I decided to scare Poland with the pace and power of Alan and his Newcastle team-mate Les Ferdinand.

It was my first time managing England at Wembley and, knowing that it was important to pick up the points, I wanted to be bold. I felt proud to be leading my country out and even a little nostalgic as I took a few moments to drink in my surroundings, despite being slightly concerned about the night ahead.

Returning to Wembley for the first time since losing to Germany felt a bit like after the Lord Mayor's Show. I sensed an emotional hangover in the crowd and I told John Gorman that I was worried before the game, saying that I thought it was going to be tough.

It wasn't as exciting as a semi-final against Germany. Expectation levels were high and the fans were waiting for us to excite them. It was an odd occasion in many ways and we looked inhibited at first, starting slowly and gifting Poland a sloppy early goal.

At that point my mind went back to Poland qualifying for the 1974 World Cup at our expense. We felt sorry for ourselves and it was a relief when Alan equalised with a good header. The equaliser freed our minds and Alan popped up again before half-time, smashing in a shot from the edge of the area to make it 2–1.

Alan's goals seemed to cleanse the place of memories of the Germany defeat. They were crucial. We didn't play particularly well, but it didn't matter. Victory is all that counts during qualifying.

* * *

The group challenged us. In November we travelled to Georgia for another test of character and skill. They were a dangerous side. We watched a video of them destroying Wales 5–0 two years earlier and realised that we shouldn't underestimate their creativity. They had Georgi Kinkladze in midfield, plus about five others like him, and I ensured that our players knew that it was going to be a difficult game.

'Listen, guys, I want you to understand how good this team can be,' I said. 'But defensively they look weak, so we've got to pick a side that's going to make sure that we stop them playing. Then we'll be too good for them offensively.'

We had to be smart. I didn't want to scare my players, but they had to be aware that they couldn't take their eye off the ball and give Georgia's creators time to settle. It was vital not to assume we could be gung-ho and forget about their threats. International football is about finding the right balance.

Switching to 3–5–2 after Euro 96 gave us more security, although I don't think it was a defensive move. My first thought was always about how we were going to get the ball to our forwards. At the same time we had to make sure that both attacking and defensive sides of the game were covered. An extra man in midfield made us solid, the wing-backs gave us width and the formation ensured that we were still capable of starting two strikers.

Playing one up front wasn't an option. England were blessed with great strikers during the 1990s and it made no sense to consign a load of them to the bench. Leaving Alan to fend for himself would have been counter-productive when I had Teddy, Les, Ian Wright, Andy Cole and Robbie Fowler all pushing for selection.

Yet I wasn't going to play a bland 4–4–2. I hadn't forgotten about being outnumbered in midfield and not having options on the ball when I played for England. I remembered us desperately trying to win back possession for most of my international career and I was determined not to let history repeat itself now that I was manager, even if at times it meant having to make compromises in attack.

The shape didn't work for everyone. Steve McManaman was someone who ended up missing out because of my desire to have one attacking wing-back and one who played as more of a full-back. I couldn't take the cavalier option of playing Macca on the left and Becks or Darren Anderton on the right. I had to be cuter than that. Our tactics required someone to help the attacking wing-back; while it was easy for Gary Neville to play as a right-sided centre-back and drift wide to cover for Becks and Darren, the problem for Macca was that Stuart Pearce was coming towards the end of his England career, leaving us without a defender who was capable of performing a similar role on the left.

In the end Macca was unfortunate. He was a great player and I would have loved to have found space for him in the team. Yet I couldn't even justify playing him in the hole. Paul Scholes was coming through, Gazza was still an important player for us and I didn't want to make a habit of leaving Teddy out.

Teddy was such a clever player and he had an important role against Georgia. 'You're going to drop in there like a striker,' I said. 'But I really want you to play almost like a midfield player.'

It was a sign of our tactical flexibility. With Alan injured, we had Les playing on his own up front and Teddy pulling deep to make us more compact in midfield. It was a defensive move but he had freedom to move between the lines and combine with Gazza when we won possession. We worked on the system, dropped behind the ball and made ourselves really difficult to break down. It was a finely tuned plan and the lads played it to perfection, shutting Georgia's threats down and passing the ball with real authority.

There was no way through our midfield. I brought David Batty in as a partner for Incey and he was utterly magnificent. Batty was such an underrated player. He was a far better passer than people realise. He saw pictures and moved the ball crisply, but he also put his foot in and allowed us to take control of midfield. Georgia rarely got past Batty and Incey, our two midfield generals, and if they did we knew that our back three would be there to mop up.

Yet while I was focused on defending properly, our football wasn't reactive. I loved how Teddy and Gazza played as the two inside forwards. We had a lovely mix of control and flair, which is crucial at international level, and we deservedly won thanks to goals from Teddy and Les.

It was a big challenge for the team. All those friendlies at Wembley before Euro 96 were no preparation at all for these kinds of games. You can easily get turned over by teams like Georgia. The training ground was dour, the pitch wasn't great and we had to show plenty of character. The players were finding out what international football was really all about and I was delighted to see them making the step up.

I was also adjusting to the different rhythms of managing my country. It was tough no longer having daily interactions with the players. International breaks were short and sweet in those days, so I didn't have long to communicate my ideas to the team and there was barely any time for a post-match debrief. The players had to go back to their clubs straight away and injuries were a frustration, constantly forcing me to tweak my squad from one camp to the next.

The problem was that we were striving to reach a tournament, at which point we would become like a club side. Yet the qualifying process was a stop-start process and the slower pace was a challenge. I almost had too much time to prepare for games. There were three months before our crucial meeting with Italy at Wembley and I was able to devote hours to watching analysis videos, meaning that I had an intricate understanding of the opposition's style by the time the game eventually came around.

Yet the danger of having so much knowledge was the potential of overloading my players with information. I didn't want to make them fearful of Italy, and our meetings needed to be tight and focused. Otherwise there was a risk of confusing the players, who didn't want to spend hours watching videos of our opponents. Their concentration levels inevitably started to dip after half an hour and at times I simply had to pray that they were paying attention as we talked to them about taking on a very strong Italy side.

Italy were our biggest rivals in the group. Their back three was so organised and we needed a plan for Zola, who had taken the Premier League by storm after joining Chelsea, when we hosted Cesare Maldini's side in February 1997.

I wasn't worried about him turning us but our back three had to be aware of his movement. The middle centre-back couldn't afford to follow Zola if he dropped short. We had to be disciplined and ensure that the players on the left and right of the back three weren't split apart, leaving room for a runner to burst into space through the middle.

Sometimes, though, there's no plan that can stop a player as gifted as Zola. The game was predictably tight and we were in trouble when Zola gave Italy an early lead. Sol Campbell wasn't quite tight enough to him when a ball was played over the top of our defence, and Ian Walker, starting in goal in place of the injured David Seaman, was beaten at his near post by the little maestro.

It was just what Italy wanted: a lead to protect and an attack to smother. Their back three made it so tough for our forwards. They dropped back in perfect harmony and they were good on the ball. It was a defensive masterclass and we found it hard to create chances.

It didn't help that my plan to leave Les on the bench and start with Matt Le Tissier was leaked earlier in the day. I was frustrated to lose the element of surprise. We needed something special to pick the Italian lock and I didn't want us to charge at them right from the get-go. We had to be clever if we were going to pull Italy out of their shape and Matt's performances for Southampton had demonstrated that he was as good as anyone when it came to picking a clever pass or producing a piece of individual magic.

My view was that it would have played into Italy's hands if we had started Les in a front two with Alan and tried to be direct. Les and Alan would have walked straight into a trap, given that Italy had three superb man-markers in defence and were more than capable of handling themselves in a physical battle. We had to be more inventive than that and I felt that Matt's ability to drop deep would give us a different dimension, creating holes for others to exploit.

Yet the plan didn't come off. Italy were waiting for us and Matt received a lot of unfair criticism. But it wasn't his fault that we lost. Although we struggled to prise Italy open, Matt was one of our better players. He kept going and had one of our biggest moments, heading wide when I thought that he was going to equalise in the first half.

Perhaps it would have turned out differently for Matt had he converted that chance. As it was his England career ended up being defined by his eighth and final cap. Matt was a fantastic footballer and I had visions of playing him off the front, scheming behind Alan, but in the end I found it hard to get him into the side. I wasn't going to use him in a wide role and he was unfortunate to be competing for a spot in the centre with Gazza and Scholesy, who was emerging as a terrific young talent at United.

Even so it was too easy to blame Matt for our setback against Italy. I preferred to look at the bigger picture when I analysed our performance. Even though we played with too much excitement against streetwise opponents, it wasn't a disaster, nor was I overly downhearted after the game. Despite being in a difficult position, I was in a defiant mood when I held a briefing with a small group of journalists and insisted that we were still going to win the group, qualifying automatically.

Something told me that we were going to bounce back. An unshakeable confidence took over and nothing was going to make me change my mind, even though we were going to have to go to Rome and get a result in our final game. I trusted my instincts. I fancied Georgia to take points off Italy and I knew that I wasn't merely relying on blind faith after taking a closer look at our performance.

We had filmed the game from a diagonal position behind the goal, enabling us to see every position on the pitch from a wide angle, and we learnt a hell of a lot just from watching. The truth is that we hadn't done much wrong and it was more about giving ourselves a better chance by making a few minor tweaks. I was particularly fascinated when I studied Italy's back three, paying close attention to the way great defenders like Paolo Maldini and Alessandro Costacurta played the system.

It was an important lesson. Italy had used a back three for a long time and there was merit in going through an edited version of the tape with the players, even though they were reluctant to sit through it. It was a valuable exercise, particularly for the defenders. We showed them how Italy did it, pointing out when they dropped deep, when they pulled wide and how cleverly they used the ball.

Italy were simply more adept at it than us. They split wider than we did and their central man knew when to pull back. We were less sure of ourselves and ended up playing in straight lines. We were too shallow at times and there were moments when Sol, our central player, could have been deeper.

My intention wasn't to criticise. It was to make us stronger. We looked at ways in which we could play ourselves out of trouble more easily and we improved when we started to play with more width in the back three and midfield, giving ourselves opportunities to come at teams from different angles.

The back three isn't an easy system. Although Gary Neville and Gareth Southgate were happy playing as the right centre-back, Tony and Sol needed more convincing. Tony was uncertain about his position in the middle and Sol was initially apprehensive about his role on the left, particularly when we asked him to split and move wide.

Yet Sol loved it in the end. Eventually we hit upon a good rhythm and became a smart, flexible unit. We just had to trust in the process.

*　*　*

I was certain that we were on the right path. We kept the pressure on Italy when we beat Georgia at Wembley in April, Alan and Teddy scoring, and we were flawless when we visited Poland in May. It was another test of our mental strength and the team refused to roll over, dealing with a hostile crowd and producing a display of immense tactical maturity against opponents who had done us a favour by drawing 0–0 with Italy.

I couldn't have been happier when Alan gave us an early lead after a brilliant surge from Paul Ince. Although Incey was a holding midfielder, I didn't want to restrict him. You're easy to read if all you do is sit. Opponents know that you're never going to shift your position and I was keen to make the most of Incey's power and intelligence. I constantly told him that he had the freedom to maraud forward once or twice a game, and I made it clear that his partner had to be ready to sit if they saw him going on one of his charges.

I trusted Incey. He was my midfield general. He was a bossy player, the type who'd blame everyone else even when he was at fault, but he was wonderfully astute. He knew when to pick his moments to attack and he played it to perfection against Poland, taking them by surprise by bursting through midfield and releasing Alan, who finished well.

The points were ours when Teddy scored after good work from Rob Lee. We looked like a good team. I had strong, experienced players and plenty of depth. Two months earlier I had experimented in a friendly against Mexico, giving an opportunity to some youngsters. Nicky Butt made his international debut and Robbie Fowler scored his first goal for his country in a 2–0 win.

There was a lot of excitement about Robbie, who was in incredible form for Liverpool. Yet I had so many options in attack and I had to think about more than club form. Although Robbie was a cracking striker, Ian Wright was a better fit for our system. His movement was second to none. He was on a par with top strikers like Hernán Crespo and Pierluigi Casiraghi. He had developed an unstoppable partnership with Bergkamp at Arsenal and he used to give defenders night-mares, either by dropping short before spinning behind, or by moving across the line before making his movement when nobody was marking him.

It made Wrighty a huge threat at international level. I wanted to utilise his talent properly, and there was no chance of us taking our eye off the ball when we travelled to France to take part in Le Tournoi in June. Although it was only a warm-up tournament for the World Cup, we were determined to treat it seriously. Italy, France and Brazil were the other sides involved, and we saw it as an opportunity to show how far we had come as a team, especially as our opening game doubled as a rehearsal for our crucial qualifier in Rome, which was only four months away.

We were ready for Italy this time. I played Teddy and Scholesy as inside forwards behind Wrighty, and Italy couldn't handle the quality of our football. All those hours watching clips of our defeat to Cesare Maldini's side at Wembley were beginning to pay off. The players were clever enough to take the lessons on board and adapt, making our system so much more effective.

The improvement started with the back three gaining more belief. Tony, who was an underrated passer, was developing as a footballer under Arsène. He was dropping deeper to receive the ball when he played in a back four at Arsenal and he was showing it for us in training. Tony was a top defender. His communication was excellent and he knew how to organise a defence, which made life much easier for the players either side of him.

Sol was growing in stature as well. He had time on the ball when the centre-backs split and I told him that he had more options when he pulled wide. 'You ain't got to pull up trees in possession,' I said. 'Just keep the ball. The midfield player is there, the wing-back's there, and you can always play it back to Tony.'

I had other options back there as well. I shifted things around against Italy, using Gareth, Martin Keown and Pearcey at the back, playing Phil Neville at right wing-back and taking the opportunity to give Scholesy his first start for England.

I loved Scholesy. He was so versatile and could do anything. He could play as a second striker, behind the front two and as a No8. He understood the game. If I wanted our midfield to switch into a four when we were defending against a 4–3–3, Scholes was more than capable of moving to the left to help us keep our shape. It came naturally to him, and I could count on him sliding straight back into the middle and moving behind the attack as soon as we regained possession.

Scholesy's intelligence was unrivalled and he had a fantastic game against Italy. He picked out Wrighty for the opening goal with a raking 50-yard pass and finished emphatically to make it 2–0 on the stroke of half-time.

We could have won by four or five in the end. We totally outclassed Italy, and I could tell that the French fans were impressed with our play. We knocked the ball around beautifully, opened Italy up and played so well that Zola came up to me after full-time to say that I had a very good team.

Maldini was less generous than Zola. He had just seen us play his team off the park and I think he wanted to gain a psychological edge, saying 'Arrivederci, Roma' as we shook hands.

'Yes,' I replied. 'We'll see you there.'

I was confident. I liked how we played with two inside forwards and I planned to use that approach again in Rome. It was a massive victory, so I decided to show the game back to the players, reasoning that they it would help them to see just how well they played.

We were on a roll. It was a huge boost to beat a team like Italy and we impressed again when we met France. It was a tight game but we were resilient and strong. We went toe-to-toe with them and snatched another win when Alan scored near the end.

France didn't look like potential world champions that night. I didn't think they'd be a team we'd struggle to beat at the World Cup. In the event, though, they timed their run to perfection a year later.

That was my concern after winning Le Tournoi. Although it was great for England to lift a rare piece of silverware, I was worried about peaking too soon. In a way I was glad when we lost our final game 1–0 to Brazil. They made us defend and it was no disgrace to lose to a goal from Romário. The defeat brought us back down to earth and reminded me that the job was nowhere near complete. Maldini was right – we still had to go to Rome.

We were in a good place as that make-or-break game against Italy drew closer. When I reflected on Le Tournoi I realised that the manner of our performances mattered more than winning the tournament. We weren't lucky. We didn't nick wins through a mistake or a set-piece. We simply produced stylish football, and I came away from a briefing with the FA feeling optimistic about the future.

I didn't panic when Alan broke his ankle during pre-season

with Newcastle. Although we were gutted to hear that our captain and best striker was facing a long spell on the sidelines, we weren't a one-man team. We had plenty of strength in depth in attack and I was confident that I had strikers who were capable of shining in Alan's absence.

My philosophy was that there was no point feeling sorry for myself. I was concerned for Alan and prayed that he made a quick recovery, but I had to think about how to put the jigsaw together in his absence. After all we had already beaten Italy without him. It was hardly as though I had no other strikers available. Fowler was in great form for Liverpool, Les had done well for me and I had already seen that Italy didn't like playing against Wrighty.

England managers have to be ready to make quick adjustments. Although I had an idea of my best team, I needed back-up plans in case of injury. This was no different. I accepted the challenge and found my replacement for Alan when I saw Wrighty banging in the goals for Arsenal at the start of the season.

Wrighty was suited to playing as a lone striker, with support coming from deep, and he scored two excellent goals when we thrashed Moldova 4–0 at Wembley in September. Scholes and Gazza, who had a fine game, were also on the scoresheet, and we were delighted when we returned to the dressing room to find that my prediction about Georgia taking points off Italy had come true.

Italy's goalless draw in Tblisi meant that we only needed a point in Rome, although that was easier said than done. I could never understand why the FA had agreed to make that our final qualifier during negotiations over the schedule. We knew that it was going to be like walking into the Colosseum. With 90,000 Romans trying to intimidate us, it would certainly be a night for cool heads and strong characters.

Yet we had the upper hand after outplaying Italy in France. Our preparations for the game were thorough and the build-up was smooth. It was the only time when there were no withdrawals from the squad during my tenure and I was able to name my starting line-up well in advance of the game, allowing me to spend a few days working on shape and tactics before the moment of truth arrived.

The good thing was that we weren't under pressure. Although there was tension and excitement, the mood in our camp was light and airy. We didn't want the players thinking about Italy's long unbeaten run in Rome. We made sure that the players didn't look at the papers and continued to build a positive atmosphere. Everything was going to plan. We were relaxed, and it was amusing when Graham Kelly, the FA's chief executive, kept the ball after scoring a hat-trick in a staff game.

It was Italy who needed to chase the game. Our job was working out a plan to frustrate them. We needed to stay compact and I decided that it was a night for our experienced players. Leaving Gary Neville and Scholesy out was difficult, but I felt that we needed Gareth in defence and David Batty in midfield.

All the same we needed to have our wits about us when we travelled to Italy and set up at La Borghesiana, a complex on the outskirts of Rome. I was sure that the Italians would have a spy or two in our camp, hunting for clues, and I didn't want to give anything away about our line-up. I sent Becks and Gareth in from training early one day, just to keep the Italians guessing, and I kept swapping the bibs around when we had a little 20-minute shadow game at the end of one session.

Not that it really mattered. We had already done most of the work on our shape and one of my biggest points before we got on the bus to go to the game was about the importance of staying cool. The atmosphere at the Stadio Olimpico was intense and we couldn't afford to lose anyone to a red card.

A lot of it was aimed at Gazza. I was a bit worried about him doing something silly, especially as it was emotional for him to go back to Rome two years after leaving Lazio, so I asked Incey to keep a close eye on him. 'Keep talking to him,' I said. 'Make sure he's all right and don't let him lose it. If we stay 11 v 11, we're going to qualify.'

At the same time I fancied Gazza to have a good game if he was focused. Despite my concerns I sensed that he wasn't cowed by playing in Italy. Gazza knew what to expect and so did Incey, who had spent two years at Inter. Not a lot of English players had experience of playing abroad and tasting different cultures, but Gazza and Incey had taken the plunge and they were relishing the challenge of turning up in Italy's backyard.

These games so often come down to mentality. Although there was a lot of focus on our tactics and the importance of not allowing ourselves to become stretched, we also had to be brave, bold and resilient. The pressure was immense. The hopes and dreams of an entire nation depended on us, and I needed my players to drown out the noise and believe that they could do it.

So much is possible when you have a team of gladiators. You can move mountains when you have players with the substance to stand up to a team of Italy's class. The problem for a manager, though, is not knowing what's going to happen when the game begins. There's only so much you can affect from the touchline. If a player has an inspirational night, you win. If someone makes a mistake out of nothing, you lose. Sometimes it comes down to chance and, for all my confidence, the chance remained that one slip would send Italy through and us into a play-off against Russia.

Yet I was strong enough to handle the expectations that came with managing England.

People don't realise how driven I am until they get to know me. As a player, outsiders saw me as a luxury. A lightweight. Yet I battled to prove myself in the harshest of environments and ended up silencing the doubters. 'What people say doesn't matter to you,' Stevie Perryman told me when I was a youngster. 'If you give the ball away, you won't shirk your next pass. You won't shirk your next bit of skill. You've got to be brave to do that.'

It made sense. It was the right way to look at it. Management is about decision-making and it's impossible to get everything right. Football can be random. But I trusted in my selection. Influenced by our performances in Georgia and Poland, I had no hesitation picking Batty in midfield. Italy had Christian Vieri and Pippo Inzaghi up front, and Zola, their danger man, was in the hole. We needed Batty and Incey to shut down the space in front of our defence. We would have come unstuck if we had only played one holding midfield player against Zola, who was such a special player.

We couldn't be too adventurous. The atmosphere was ferocious and there were times when Italy flew at us. Yet we refused to roll over. Batty and Incey, who ended the game bloodied and bandaged after a nasty clash of heads with Demetrio Albertini, didn't just nullify Zola. They were good passers and we controlled the game for long spells. We ended up having more possession than I anticipated. We kept the ball crisply, with Gazza and Teddy doing well as the inside forwards, and Wrighty's movement up front once again troubled Italy.

In the end it was Italy who lost control, going down to 10 men in the second half. We had frustrated them brilliantly and even looked like we were going to steal the win when Wrighty went through on goal in added time. He went round the goalkeeper and looked certain to score, only to hit the post from an acute angle. Our emotions were all over the place on the touchline. The substitutes were all off the bench and we still thought that we were going to snatch victory when the ball came out to Teddy, but he couldn't get his shot away and, all of a sudden, we were watching in horror as Italy roared down the other end.

It was pure torture. Wrighty was still lying in a heap when Italy attacked down the left and I was convinced that we were finished when Vieiri rose at the far post. David Seaman looked beaten. He was motionless as Vieri's header went back across goal and looped towards the top corner. It looked like it was in from my angle on the touchline.

It gave me such a scare. My heart really felt like it had jumped out of my body when I saw the ball float past David before drifting inches wide. It all happened in a matter of seconds. My heart went boom, and then all I could feel was this overwhelming sense of relief. It was actually quite frightening. I should have got myself tested. I immediately broke out in a sweat after Vieri's miss – my hair was soaked and I knew that something strange had happened.

Yet I didn't see a doctor after returning home and it caught up with me when I was on holiday in Spain a few years later. I was doing too much. I played golf and tennis in the heat and felt awful. We had to call for an ambulance and the specialist gave me some pills before telling me to seek help when I got back to England.

It turned out that I had atrial fibrillation, an irregular and sometimes unusually fast heart rate. I was managing at Southampton and was fortunate that the League Managers' Association were able to refer me to a specialist. I went to hospital to have the rhythm restored, but the improvements after my treatment only lasted a week. The problem kept coming back and the doctor told me that I was going to have be on medication after the third attempt.

I was lucky that the doctors caught it when they did. 'You've probably had that for some time,' the doctor said when I ended up in hospital in Spain.

I immediately thought back to that night in Rome. It must have been the enormity of the occasion. I was fine until Vieri almost scuppered our plan. Yet the game was so intense and the emotion came pouring out of me when the referee blew for full-time, confirming that we were going to the World Cup. It was such a wonderful achievement and the excitement made me forget about that strange feeling in my heart. I just wanted to savour the moment.

11

ONLY A GAME

Something that has been suggested since my time with England is that the job came too soon for me. Our results suggest otherwise, and my youth didn't seem to matter when the press were pushing for the FA to give me a 10-year deal after Le Tournoi, but stories sometimes take on a life of their own in football.

I am intrigued by the focus on the way that I handled players. I have seen Gary Neville, for instance, say that my man-management skills didn't match up to my football intelligence. Perhaps some players misunderstood me. My main motivation was always about how to get the best out of them. I didn't have to be best friends with them. I needed them to respect what we were trying to achieve, and everything I did was designed to improve our chances of winning the World Cup.

There is no doubt that I would now have a different approach in terms of how I handle personal relationships with the players, but I would still use the same tactics. In my head a lot of man-management comes down to making sure that your team know what you want from them on the pitch.

Perhaps I could have spoken to players in greater depth, but time was of the essence. You're only leasing the car when you're an international manager. They aren't your players – they belong to their clubs, and international camps were very brief in those days. We didn't have long to sit down with players during the qualifiers, and the atmosphere was incredibly frenzied during the World Cup. There were multiple press conferences to attend and masses of opposition analysis to do, and the biggest challenge was ensuring that the players were well versed in our style.

I always made a big point of asking the players what was more important: the starting 11 or the team that finishes the game? If it's a tight contest, the players on the pitch during those final 20 minutes are crucial. They are the deciding factor and although maintaining harmony in the camp was difficult, I needed the subs to know that they had a part to play.

My priority had to be creating a winning plan. I believed that we were good enough to become world champions in France and I was confident after we were drawn in a group with Colombia, Romania and Tunisia. A place in the last 16 was well within our reach and I felt that I had the players to go even further.

The challenge was working out who to name in my 22-man squad for the finals. Some players picked themselves, others had much to prove, and I was beginning to worry about Gazza. His form was a concern, he was having problems off the pitch and he was struggling to stay fit, forcing me to think about using other players in his position.

I didn't welcome the situation. Gazza was great during qualifying, especially when we drew with Italy, and I wanted him in my squad. I tried to motivate him. I tried to get through to him before we faced Chile in a friendly at Wembley in February. Despite being injured he still came to training, and

I was desperate to make him realise that his place was on the line. We sat by ourselves in a little corner, away from everyone else, and I spoke from the heart, reminding him of how he took the world by storm in Italia 90 and pleading with him to take better care of his mind and body.

It was a dilemma. Gazza understood our shape and he was a gem of a player. Yet the injuries were piling up. He always seemed to have a problem with his calf and he had some bother with his knee as well. The knocks kept coming and I knew from my playing days that you end up succumbing to injuries in other areas because of the body overcompensating.

I wanted to help Gazza find his way through the mist. Although you can't be with him all the time, he's a lovely guy. I couldn't help but feel, however, that it was in one ear and out the other. He kept saying, 'Yes, gaffer,' but I don't think he took anything on board. He heard what I was saying, but he wasn't listening properly.

I sensed that a difficult decision was on the cards. We were a better team when Gazza played and we didn't play well when he was missing against Chile. We picked the fixture as part of our preparations for facing Colombia and we were surprised by Chile's quality. They gave us so many problems and I was impressed with Marcelo Salas. He scored twice and his first goal, a stunning volley, was a peach.

We couldn't have any complaints after losing 2–0. The defeat brought us down to earth. We still had room to improve and although the pressure was off after Rome, I found it hard to relax. That nervous wait for the real thing to start is tough for international managers and I found the friendlies awkward because I always worried about injuries disrupting my plans.

Warm-up games can be strange affairs. The result matters to fans and the media, but the performance is more important.

I wanted to experiment with our tactics and give fringe players a chance to impress. There was no point playing our
strongest team all the time. You always have to be ready to
find something new, and even though there was scrutiny if we
went three games without a win, the only way of finding out
if someone was capable of stepping up was by playing them.

If that meant the friendlies were a bit of a mish-mash at
times, so be it. I gave Rio Ferdinand his debut in a friendly
win over Cameroon, and had Scholes and Gazza playing off
Fowler. We had a look at using a back four in a dour 1–1 draw
with Switzerland in March, and the Chile game was notable
for the presence of an exciting young debutant in our attack.

His name was Michael Owen. I had so many strikers at my
disposal, but this boy was special and had been on my radar
for a long time. I'd heard about him before I became England
manager, listening with interest when a coach told me about
a sensation who was always playing above his age group at
Liverpool. Michael was already making waves and his class
was obvious when he burst on to the scene at the end of the
1996–97 season, scoring on his debut after coming off the
bench against Wimbledon.

Michael bowled me over. I watched him live against Crystal
Palace and couldn't believe my eyes. His speed was terrifying
and he knew how to use it. He was so clever. Some players
have pace, but they can't time their runs and always end up
offside. Not Michael. He was ready when he was 17. He knew
how to bend his runs, he knew when to come to the ball, he
knew when to spin away from a defender, and his confidence
was incredible. Although he was an unassuming guy, he had
so much belief in himself. He wasn't arrogant; he was ruthless.
His finishing left no room for debate and I think he felt sorry
for defenders. It was almost as though he looked at them

before the game and thought, 'You're not going to be able to live with me today.'

It was incredible to watch. Michael's temperament was magnificent and he gave us another dimension. He had Wrighty's movement and Les's pace. He was small, sharp and intelligent. His composure was unrivalled and he took to playing up front in the men's game like a duck to water, running riot after breaking into Liverpool's starting 11.

All Michael needed was the right service from midfield. I had no doubt about calling him up for the Chile game and was excited about working with him. Yet I wasn't going to build my attack around Michael straight away. Alan was available again after recovering from his ankle injury and it was worth having a look at his partnership with Teddy when we faced Portugal in April. Alan and Teddy complemented each other well at Euro 96 and they worked in tandem against Portugal, helping to earn us a solid 3–0 win.

Portugal were no mugs. They played a 4–3–3, which challenged our system, and they had Luís Figo out wide. We switched from 3–5–2 to 4–4–2 without the ball, and I was delighted with the way that Scholesy shuffled out to the left to help out defensively.

The danger with three at the back is that you end up inviting pressure by defending with five. We needed to be flexible and I spent a lot of time working on our tactics on the training ground. Part of my thinking was that we didn't need three centre-backs against Portugal's lone forward. I wanted Graeme Le Saux to swing back from wing-back to left-back when we lost possession, Gary Neville moved from right centre-back to right-back and I told David Beckham, who started at right wing-back, that he didn't have to worry about tracking back.

David almost played as a winger, secure in the knowledge that Gary was covering behind, and the team performed magnificently. They understood my demands. I told Graeme to bomb on when we won the ball, promising him that Figo wouldn't like tracking his runs, and our approach stifled Portugal. Ince and Batty dominated midfield. Scholesy sprang back behind the strikers when we attacked and we forced their wingers to drop so deep.

I knew that we were causing them problems when I glanced at their bench. It was a proper game, even though Portugal hadn't qualified for the World Cup, and it boosted our confidence. Alan scored twice, Teddy once, and I was able to bring Michael off the bench in the closing stages. Everything was coming together nicely.

My squad for the tournament was starting to take shape. Michael was nailed on to make the plane. His form for Liverpool made him a certainty and, barring any late injuries, I had a good idea of which players to take. Gazza, however, was a concern. I wasn't happy with his lifestyle after his move from Rangers to Middlesbrough in March. The culture at Middlesbrough wasn't professional enough and although Gazza still had so much to offer when he was fit, those days were becoming increasingly rare.

I grew pensive when he missed three consecutive friendlies. I was willing Gazza to sort himself out and we kept watching him when he was available. We sent scouts to Middlesbrough's games and every so often they'd tell me about Gazza having a blinder, which was encouraging to hear. At other times, though, the scouts reported back to say that Gazza didn't play.

The clock was ticking. Yet I wanted to leave it as long as possible before making a final decision on Gazza, and he was in when I named a preliminary 30-man squad at the start of May.

My intention was to give myself time to run the rule over several hopefuls and see whether Wrighty, Andy Hinchcliffe, Jamie Redknapp and Darren Anderton could shake off their injury problems. Unfortunately there was heartbreak for some players. There was no room for Andy Cole, Stuart Pearce, Chris Sutton and Matt Le Tissier. Chris hadn't done himself many favours by refusing to play in a 'B' international – we've made up since then – and I couldn't quite find a spot for Andy, even though he was in wonderful form for United.

I have since been criticised for saying that Andy needed three or four chances to score a goal. I need to clear that up. There is no doubt that Andy was a fabulous striker and a clinical finisher at club level. Yet he played in a team that created so many chances for their forwards. Playing for England was different. International football is often attritional and sometimes you only get one chance a game. We weren't going to be as dominant as United and I needed players whose finishing left no room for debate.

After all I was planning to reach a World Cup final. I needed killers and I had so many options up front. Alan, Teddy and Michael were guaranteed to be involved, I wanted to give Wrighty a chance to prove his fitness and I felt that Les offered something different with his physicality, giving him the edge over Andy. In the end I picked players who were better suited to international football.

Nevertheless I was open-minded. I wanted to have a look at Dion Dublin following his outstanding performances for Coventry. People had pre-conceived views on Dion, but I had been aware of his ability ever since coming up against him for Swindon when we faced Cambridge. He was dangerous in the air and he could also play in defence. His versatility gave him a chance and there were places up for grabs when we faced Saudi Arabia in a friendly at Wembley.

Unfortunately we didn't do much to excite the crowd, drawing 0–0. Gazza came on after an hour and he didn't impress. He was running out of time when we went to our training camp in sunny La Manga. We had arranged to go to Casablanca to face Morocco and Belgium in a mini-tournament, and the onus was on Gazza to realise that his place was on the line.

The overall picture had become clearer by that stage. The tournament came too soon for Jamie Redknapp, who could have played as a sweeper in my system, and there was further disappointment when Wrighty suffered a hamstring injury during our 1–0 win over Morocco. He knew it was over when he limped off and made way for Michael, who came on to score his first England goal. It was a crushing blow for Wrighty. He would have gone to France if he'd been fit.

Michael's goal lifted the mood, yet all eyes were on Gazza. I was pleased that he made it through the 90 minutes, but I wanted more from him when we faced Belgium two days later. It was crunch time. Gazza had missed a few days of training and his injuries remained a cause for concern, but I was going to pick him if he made it through the Belgium game unscathed. I tried to get through to him before kick-off: 'Gazza, just take three touches maximum on the ball,' I said. 'Just get through the game. Keep it nice and simple. We just want to get your fitness up.'

The message didn't sink in. Early in the second half Gazza tried to take on a Belgium defender, who wiped him out. The writing was on the wall. Gazza's head was bandaged and he had to come off with a dead leg. I was praying that it wouldn't come to this, but the evidence was impossible to ignore. The medical staff told me that Gazza wasn't going to be fit for another three weeks and my mind was made up by the time we returned to La Manga.

It was the saddest decision I ever made and it has been well documented that Gazza didn't take it well when he found out. Yet it was a football decision. Gazza left me with no choice and I couldn't bring him when I had other players available in his position. Scholesy was impossible to drop and I was pleased with Paul Merson's performances for us.

I didn't relish having to leave players out. With Darren free from injury, the other main conundrum was whether to take a back-up for Graeme Le Saux on the left. I knew that we couldn't afford an injury to Graeme. Andy Hinchcliffe had a thigh problem, ruling him out, and I decided to gamble by disappointing Phil Neville, who was unlucky to miss out.

That left me with three more players to cut. Ian Walker, Dion and Nicky Butt were the unfortunate ones. Dion was close to making it but I decided that I had enough cover in defence and attack.

Much has been made about how the players were each given five-minute slots with me when I delivered the news, and people made a fuss about Kenny G playing in the background when individuals entered the room to find out their fate in one-on-one meetings. It was seen as insensitive, but I thought that it was the best way to approach a delicate topic. I was surprised by the reaction. I think it's how any adult would want to be treated. There isn't a great way to tell a player that his World Cup dream is over and I feel that my way was better than sending a text message or slipping a note under the door of someone's hotel room. I wanted to look my players in the eye and speak from the heart. I never wanted to hurt anyone.

* * *

The whispers about my man-management never went away. I was grateful when Steve McManaman issued a denial after a newspaper claimed that he had likened the camp to a cult, but I was surprised to hear that there was a feeling that I wanted to exert control because of my youth.

I was thinking about how to gain an edge. I used Dr Yann Rougier, a medic who had joined Arsène at Arsenal. He spoke to the players about how they digested food and it had a big effect on Tony Adams. They listened to him and it transformed them physically, making them better players.

Diet, sleep and fitness were important to me after my time with Arsène at Monaco. But I didn't, for instance, have any say in an FA official stopping Gary Neville having a sandwich brought to his room one day. Why would I bother myself with that?

Footballers have a habit of reading a lot into their manager's behaviour. I sometimes did it when I was a player, over-analysing small things. But as a manager my main concern was building a cohesive unit. Basic standards on the pitch mattered to me from a young age. I burned inside if I allowed the ball to run under my foot during training. It hurt my pride if I made a silly mistake and I expected a lot from players who were internationals.

The beauty of managing England was that I didn't have to do a lot of coaching on individual attributes. These were the best players in the country. But they still had a responsibility to their talent. If they dropped their standards, I was ready to come down hard on them. It happened when I saw a couple of reserve players not paying attention during a drill on set-pieces before a qualifying game. They were messing around and I picked them out, asking them to run me through our routines.

Maybe my response didn't land well with them. But is that really bad management? Surely it's good management. You have to be strong at times and there's no excuse for not concentrating during training, particularly when a loss of focus could cause us to concede a silly goal from a set-piece. It annoyed me. Being a sub for England isn't easy – I should know – but you always have to be ready.

We were in France to win a World Cup. The idea that I wanted to show off by joining in during training isn't true. I was reluctant when Johnny G pushed me in to make up the numbers in a couple of small-sided games, but it was the only way to make the sessions work if a couple of players were carrying knocks. We weren't a club side, so we couldn't just drag a player over from the reserves. We had to adjust and I was still fit enough to join in. I wasn't looking to impress the lads.

Certain portrayals of me don't correspond to reality. My critics also say that I grew frustrated with players who weren't as talented as me. My response is to point out that I started my managerial career at Swindon Town. I brought in a big centre-half, Shaun Taylor, and marvelled at his heading ability. I admired him.

I didn't have everything in my locker as a player. I wasn't a good header of the ball. Yet I understood players' attributes. When Arsène first spoke to me about going into management, he told me that I could reach players. 'You can teach them because of your ability,' he said. 'And you have patience with players, too.'

Arsène's words hit home. I watched Shaun leap into the air in training and loved his determination to win his headers. I couldn't do that and I would never have dreamt of discarding someone just because they didn't possess bags of skill.

My job was to find ways to capitalise on my team's positive qualities. Tony Adams and Sol Campbell didn't need me to coach them but they did benefit from my advice at times. It helped if I told them that they were giving away fouls in the air because their starting position was too deep. I couldn't win their headers but I could make things easier for them by telling them to push higher at goal-kicks.

My way was never to tell someone that they weren't good enough or couldn't pull off a certain skill. I encouraged my team to play with freedom.

It makes me laugh when I hear that I was jealous of David Beckham's fame. This is a player I wanted to sign on loan when I was at Chelsea. I gave him his England debut. David's technique was incredible and I've never seen anyone cross the ball as well as him. His passing range was impeccable and I think that he could have played more in central midfield for club and country when he was older. He could have sat deep and would have found more passing angles than when he was on the right.

Going into our opening game against Tunisia, however, I could tell that David wasn't focused enough in training. My decision to replace him with Darren caused a fuss but it was the right call. It was nothing personal. David would have played at right wing-back if his mind was clear but he was distracted by events off the pitch before the game.

I was honest with David when I sat down with him. 'I don't think you're focused,' I said. 'I'm going to leave you out of this game. Your mind is somewhere else. I don't know what it is, but you've got to get your mind right.' I looked him in the eye and made sure to give him some encouragement. 'You will play at this World Cup,' I added. 'You're too good to leave out but I need you right at it.'

It jolted David. He wasn't happy but his response was excellent. He must have thought about our chat because he was on it when we trained the next day. I was interested in his attitude after being dropped and it was spot on. He hit a new level and showed me that it wouldn't be a risk to play him in midfield with Incey further down the line.

The matter was over as far as I was concerned. But the press had other ideas. David was a huge name and his omission was a big story. It certainly didn't go down well with Ferguson – and I wasn't exactly flavour of the month at Old Trafford. I had left out Phil Neville and had issues with another United player when I had to discipline Teddy after he was pictured on a night out in the build-up to the tournament.

Dealing with United wasn't easy. There were problems getting players to report for duty at times and I had a row with Ferguson over two of his players before one friendly. His conduct was unprofessional when we spoke on the phone. I wasn't going to use the players in the game but I wanted them to join up with the squad because we were preparing for the World Cup. But he wasn't having it. He was ranting and raving, even when I said I would send them back once the meetings were out of the way.

I can't repeat what he called me. I just put the phone down. He called back to apologise but he wasn't happy. It all became a bit of a battle, and he used his *Sunday Times* column to criticise me when David and Gary Neville were put up at a press conference shortly after our win over Tunisia. Apparently it was insensitive to have them meet the media after they'd been left out of the game. Again, I'm not sure I understand the logic; there was no big strategy on my part. I wasn't trying to humiliate David. It was down to the press officers to select players and I gave them the thumbs up when they suggested

David. I knew that the media wanted to speak to him and I thought it was a good idea to give them what they wanted on a quiet day, especially as David was guaranteed to play sooner rather than later. It was a trivial affair as far as I was concerned. But it was spun into something else. It often was.

In the months before the World Cup I heard that there was a story coming out about me bringing in a faith healer, Eileen Drewery, to work with the squad. I decided to act pre-emptively, revealing it in a press conference before the article was published, but I was well aware that it would be turned into a negative in some quarters. I knew it would be twisted inside out and it wasn't long before there were stories about players being left out of the squad if they refused to see Eileen.

Those tales were utter garbage. Some people were simply closed-minded. There is nothing strange about healing and it wasn't like someone had randomly asked me to try it out of the blue. I had sought Eileen's guidance ever since she helped me overcome a hamstring injury when I was 18. Dad's sore back was cured in one session and I merely saw healing as an extension of our medical offering. Players didn't have to see her and I had nothing to hide. I told Mike Varney, Tottenham's physio, about seeing Eileen when I was a player. It was powerful, and if people had been more willing to look at it with open eyes they'd have realised that Eileen gave players a better chance of shaking off injuries. She did wonders for Darren's career.

It wasn't for everyone. Some players saw her and some probably took the piss. Either way it wasn't going to hurt the team. It was just another option and I had a good understanding of the benefits of healing.

I didn't think about the public reaction. I thought about making the team as fit as possible. I had asked for Eileen's help in my previous jobs and not introducing her to England's players would have been like having a brilliant free-kick up your sleeve and never using it.

Yet those were different times. I once asked a sceptical reporter if he would consider suggesting healing to a relative if they were really ill. He wasn't happy because he couldn't say no. Why wouldn't you do everything to help your family? Healing isn't invasive. It doesn't hurt. Why would you say no?

You need an open mind to understand it. I didn't have any faith in healing at first; I was a kid when I first came across it, and it wasn't until I was approaching the end of my 20s that I began to talk to Eileen in greater depth about healing. For a long time I went to see her for a session and went on my merry way when it was finished. Sometimes the cure arrived straight away, sometimes it took longer, but almost 10 years passed before I asked Eileen how it worked.

It's been a huge part of my life. I wouldn't have come back from my knee injury at Monaco without healing. I found a healer, Dominic, when I was recovering at Monaco and Eileen also helped when she visited me on holiday. I am convinced that my career would have been over without those sessions.

Plenty of people will still say it's a load of rubbish. If you've experienced it properly, though, you'll know that it works, and I didn't think twice about mentioning it to my players. In fact, we'd already been using Eileen for six months before the story came out. She'd even helped me throughout my reign at Chelsea.

I knew that some people wouldn't understand. I knew that some people thought I was odd. Football is a macho environment and some things simply aren't accepted. But I often ask people what happens if they cut their hand. The answer is obvious: the cut heals and disappears if you don't pick at it.

We all have that healing energy inside of us. The cut on your hand heals on its own. You don't have to go to a healer or a doctor for something that small. Your body does the job on its own, but the process speeds up if you're someone who's ready to embrace spiritual methods.

Framed that way, it would have made no sense for me not to introduce the players to Eileen. My job was to do everything in my power to make the team better and I wasn't scared about talking to them about healing. I knew it would help certain players and I wasn't worried about the ones who weren't interested. It wasn't an obligation for them.

I didn't think bringing Eileen in was brave. Call me naive, but I thought it was natural. Other than not asking Eileen to join us in France, I have no regrets about her role. It was part of my life, and if my faith in healing ever helped anyone look into it and improve their life, then the media circus was worth it. I was trying to win the World Cup but I wasn't defined by my job. There's more to life than football.

The fuss over Eileen wasn't as big a deal as the press made out. The mood in the camp was good as we prepared for Tunisia. Spirits were high. Before travelling to France we took the players and their partners to the West End to see the musical *Chicago*. Somehow someone got hold of our route to the theatre and inevitably the roads around London were blocked as we made our way there. People spilled out of pubs to cheer us and it was good for the players to see that support, even if most of them didn't enjoy the show.

It was a reminder of how much England meant to people. The reaction brought back memories of Euro 96 and gave us a boost before making our way to the World Cup. It was manic on the streets and the patriotic fervour gave me a greater appreciation of the responsibility on my shoulders.

The country was about to come to a standstill. For the next six weeks I was going to be as important as the prime minister and I was full of pride as we walked out to face Tunisia on a baking hot afternoon at the atmospheric Stade Vélodrome in Marseille.

The conditions were stifling, which suited Tunisia, and I asked for a professional performance. We couldn't afford to lose our opening game, and although I wasn't particularly worried about Tunisia's threats, I went with the solidity of Incey and Batty in midfield.

The points were all that mattered in that heat. It wasn't a flowing performance but we went ahead through Alan in the first half and sealed the victory when Scholesy lashed one in from 20 yards during the dying stages.

It was a big moment for Scholesy, given that he had effectively taken Gazza's place in the team. Watching from the bench, I was willing him to shoot and kill the game off when he found space on the edge of the area. I backed Scholesy to flourish and he took his chance perfectly, cracking a rising shot past the Tunisia goalkeeper.

I always say that Scholesy is the best player I managed. He had everything. He could play in the hole, as a No8 and as a second striker, and he even played in a deeper role when he was older. He had so many strings to his bow and was a 9 out of 10 wherever he played. His ability was enormous and he knew how to simplify the game. His passing was immaculate, he timed his runs into the box expertly, he scored headers despite his lack of height and he could create goals.

What more could you want from a midfielder? Scholesy was so astute and I loved how he just got on with the job.

Nothing fazed him, although I felt it was important for him to get off the mark against Tunisia. It helped me relax too. Getting off to a strong start was vital and, for all the drama over David having to do that press conference after the game, the vibe was positive when we returned to our training base.

Yet challenges reared their head as we prepared to face Romania. We had a setback when Gareth suffered a freak injury in training, going over on his ankle after kicking a stray ball during a run. I had to change our defence and I woke up with a bad feeling on the day of the game.

I couldn't shake it off. It felt awkward. We'd expended a lot of energy during our first game, battling in the heat, and were slightly off the pace against Romania. It was scrappy, we struggled to find our flow, and although I didn't want to make the players tentative, I knew that a draw wouldn't be the worst result.

There were a number of little worrying signs. It was strange for Incey, who was such a fierce competitor, to go off after 30 minutes. We tried to be assertive with the players before the game and at half-time, but we couldn't get the ball down and play. Our rhythm was off and although we were a solid defensive side, we fell behind after conceding a sloppy goal to Viorel Moldovan at the start of the second half.

Sometimes you get those feelings in games. You try to fight them, but nothing works. Michael scored a late equaliser after coming on for Teddy, but we weren't out of the woods. Romania won when Dan Petrescu, a player I brought to Chelsea, scored a last-minute winner after a mistake from Graeme.

We had put ourselves under needless pressure. Yet it wasn't all doom and gloom. Michael had made a huge impact after coming off the bench and David impressed after replacing Incey. I was delighted with David. It was the perfect response to being dropped and I liked him in the centre, using his wand of a right foot to hit those wonderful passes.

David and Michael had both done enough to start against Colombia. But I wasn't bowing to outside pressure by playing them. Although there was plenty of clamour for Michael to be in the team from the opening game, some opponents suit different styles. I'd always planned to start Michael against Colombia, who played a very high line. We weren't going to need Teddy to drop off against them.

All the same, Michael's cameo against Romania was a sight to behold. As soon as we went on the pitch he looked like he owned the place. He had an aura about him and knew when he was going to change a game. He had ice running through his veins.

Colombia weren't prepared for Michael's pace. He scared them to bits and I knew that we were going to get the win we needed to reach the last 16. I had watched plenty of tapes of Colombia, and despite being talented they weren't organised enough at the back. David and Scholesy could deliver the ball to Michael and Alan, putting us in business, and we went in front when Darren, who could run up and down the right flank all night long, scored with a powerful shot.

We were in control. David played superbly. His passing was splendid in that tournament and he announced himself on the world stage when he whipped home a free-kick just before the hour-hour mark, giving us a 2–0 lead to take back to the dressing room at half-time.

The scoreline could easily have been more emphatic. We had so many chances and I laughed when I saw Sol run the length of the pitch before being tackled on the edge of the area. 'Is this the same guy who didn't want to play in a back three?' I asked Johnny G.

We looked like a good, strong team. We handled a pressurised situation with ease and deservedly went through after finishing second to Romania. Confidence was building and we weren't scared of facing Argentina in the second round. We fancied our chances as we made our way to Saint-Étienne.

It was the last 16 of the World Cup and we were ready to confront Argentina. We were going to come up against tough opponents, but we had shown what we were capable of by winning Le Tournoi and standing up to Italy in the lion's den in Rome.

Our self-belief was now considerable, but the intensity rose and the interest was magnified because it was Argentina. Graeme had to deal with nonsense in the press because his wife was Argentinian, but I wasn't worried about him. I knew that he was sensible enough to ignore it. We had a team full of unflinching characters, our system worked, we had bags of creativity and our attack was capable of destroying any defence. I planned to stay in France until the very end.

I didn't have many issues with my selection. The main question was how to play Alan and Michael together. There was no puzzle when Teddy partnered Alan. Teddy was comfortable dropping deep, playing astute passes and making late runs into the box. But that wasn't Alan's game. I didn't want him to become the deeper player all of a sudden and we spent a lot of time working with Alan and Michael on their positioning during training.

I didn't want them playing square and just standing next to each other. Alan was a traditional No9 and Michael liked to play off the shoulder, but we asked them to be unpredictable with their runs. Luckily they were intelligent enough to understand our demands.

Defenders don't like it when strikers pull away from them to receive a pass. They don't like following a striker who moves into midfield and links the play. You have to keep defenders guessing with good movement and that's what Alan and Michael gave us, dovetailing a lot and creating space for midfielders like Scholesy or Rob Lee to run beyond them.

Michael was a little baby assassin. He believed that he could rip defences apart, but he was also a team player. Some bright spark in the press once put it to me that Michael wasn't a natural goalscorer. I said that he was more than a goalscorer because of his awareness. When Michael went through on goal he didn't think twice about passing if he saw a team-mate in a better position. It's rare for an 18-year-old to be that unselfish.

That was Michael. It was hard to find a weakness in his game. He was utterly lethal and the only area that needed to improve was his left foot. He told me that he didn't do much work on it at Liverpool and I pulled him aside at training one day, telling him that we were going to do a session on his left side.

'I know you can do it with your right,' I said. 'But I think you've got to improve your left because once you get this reputation, people will put you down your left side. People will say, "Don't let him go right side." You've got to get better at that. Just ask one of the coaches for help. Do it whenever you want. Do it with no goalkeeper. Put some cones out in the corners and try to hit the different areas.'

At that World Cup, though, our opponents were still a little naive about Michael. Argentina didn't seem to have much of a plan for him. We backed ourselves, and we had a lovely balance to our side with Incey, David and Scholesy in midfield.

Yet we soon found ourselves a goal down. Argentina caught us out with a clever move and Diego Simeone got to the ball moments before David Seaman. It looked like a penalty from my position and we were behind when Gabriel Batistuta converted from 12 yards.

Incredibly, it didn't affect us. There was a long way to go and I knew that we had goals in us. We just had to keep the faith, and Argentina looked jittery as soon as Michael started running at them. I don't think they understood how quick he was. He had this way of stopping and starting again, and he got us back into the game when Roberto Ayala sent him flying in the area.

Was it a penalty? It was tight but we were all up off the bench, appealing for Kim Milton Nielsen to point to the spot. I'm sure that these days it would be given by VAR, and we were back in it when Alan blasted us level.

What a response. We were playing. We were brave. We were good and we knew it. Argentina were rattled, although even I wasn't ready for what was about to happen next.

It was one of the greatest goals ever scored in a World Cup, a moment that left everyone in the stadium speechless. Michael was 18. You aren't supposed to do that when you're 18. You're supposed to be raw and rash at that age.

Not Michael. He was wise beyond his years. Something that pleased me about his goal was that it stemmed from our work with Alan and Michael on the training ground. Look at it again and you'll see that Michael drops back into midfield to receive the ball from David, who was having a terrific game. David plays a lovely little pass to him and Michael just goes.

There was a moment at the start where it was touch and go about whether he was going to shake off Chamot. Once he was away, though, there was no stopping him. That was the beauty of Michael. Defenders didn't want him running on to balls over the top but they also couldn't do anything when he moved into midfield, turned and zoomed at them. He had everything, and the entire bench went up as soon as Michael set off, all of us certain we were on the verge of witnessing something historic.

I actually thought that he was through as soon as he went past Chamot. I didn't realise that he still had to take on Ayala, whose decision to drop ridiculously deep showed how frightened Argentina were of Michael.

'Where the fuck's he come from?' I thought. But I wasn't worried when I saw Ayala's body position. He was facing Michael square on and he didn't have a prayer. The only way out for Ayala was to chop Michael down, but then he would have been sent off for a last-man foul. It was an impossible situation for Ayala, although I have no idea what he was doing back there. Argentina didn't play with a sweeper system. There was only one explanation: they simply had no idea what to do with our boy wonder.

This much was clear from the way that Ayala didn't even try to show Michael on to his left side; instead Michael swerved to the right so easily and the finish into the top corner was impeccable. I laughed when I saw Scholesy popping up out of nowhere and almost taking the ball off Michael. No chance. Michael was too quick for him as well.

I still get goosebumps thinking about that goal. I can see Michael running towards the corner. He must have felt like he was dreaming. He had announced himself to the world and we were all pinching ourselves on the bench. It was the most incredible feeling.

It was ridiculous. I suspect that Michael thought that he had a chance of scoring as soon as he got the ball off David. It was like watching Ronaldo or Maradona at their absolute best, and the amazing thing about Michael was that he didn't let it go to his head. He wasn't giddy after putting us 2–1 up. He was focused.

So were his team-mates. Although it was a chaotic start, we looked organised. We were excited but we kept our shape and didn't get carried away. We had a handle on Ariel Ortega, their No10, and were unlucky not to go 3–1 up when Scholesy missed a golden chance.

Then we conceded a free-kick on the edge of our box. We set up well and had Graeme standing to the left of our five-man wall. We always put someone there in case someone made a run down the outside. We wanted to block every path to our goal.

Yet the gap was slightly too big this time. Graeme was a bit too wide and we sensed danger on the bench. We were screaming at Graeme to move closer to the wall but the message never reached him. Graeme edged the other way and it was too late to respond when Juan Sebastián Verón slipped the ball through to Javier Zanetti, who peeled into space before equalising.

Credit to Argentina. That routine wasn't in any of our scouting reports and it was a very clever ploy. Sport is about peaking at the right moment and Argentina pulled that move off brilliantly. Zanetti's finish was class.

Yet I didn't panic when the half-time whistle blew. I was happy with our performance and I didn't say too much to the players beyond telling them how well they were playing. The players knew it. I didn't need to address anything tactically. We just had to get the equaliser out of our system and we were optimistic when we went out for the second half.

* * *

I wasn't worried about David before the game. He could be hot-headed at times but his attitude had been spot on after being dropped against Tunisia. His free-kick against Colombia was world class and there was every chance of him doing it again against Argentina. That was until the moment when Simeone barrelled into him from behind and then wound him up by ruffling his hair while he was sprawled on the ground. I don't know if Simeone said something to David or somehow got inside his head. I don't know why David reacted, but Simeone did know how to get under an opponent's skin. David was naive to fall for it, but I wasn't too concerned when I saw him flick out at Simeone. I thought it was silly from David, but it was a yellow card. I was shocked when, after booking Simeone, Nielsen brought out the red. It was pure injustice. I felt like running on to the pitch to ask the ref what he was playing at. I felt powerless. All I could do was tell Terry Byrne, our masseur, to take David to the dressing room and look after him.

The incident never made me think that I was right to question David's focus at the start of the tournament. It was something that came out of nothing, and Nielsen made the wrong call. David was certainly petulant, but it wasn't violent play and he didn't deserve to be cast as the villain by the media. The reaction back home was disgraceful, and it showed how strong David was that he answered his critics by winning the Treble with United a year later. Like me, David viewed football as a labour of love. He had enough in his bank account to hang up his boots long before he retired, but he kept going for as long as possible. His desire deserves respect.

Standing on the touchline in Saint-Étienne, however, I didn't have time to think about what I was going to say to David. I had 30 seconds to make a decision. Johnny G was looking at me, waiting for me to make a call, and I felt like asking him to give me five minutes.

I didn't have that luxury. Multiple scenarios ran through my mind in a matter of seconds. The easiest decision would have been to take off Michael and stiffen the midfield, but that would have invited Argentina to pile forward. It was all still to play for, and it soon dawned on me that the best move would be to keep both Alan and Michael on the pitch, giving Argentina something to think about at the back.

It was a 4–4–1 with a difference. The game resumed but we got the message to the players, moving Darren next to Incey, Scholesy to the left and Michael to the right flank, with Alan on his own up front.

I probably would have taken Michael off and tried to defend if we'd been winning. But we needed his pace and he quickly settled into his new role. Michael's inexperience wasn't a factor. He tracked their left-back diligently and gave us no reason to make a replacement.

After a while we told Alan to swap positions with Michael every five minutes. The plan worked to perfection and Argentina created nothing. We smothered their attack and I never thought about hanging on for penalties. I reckoned we could win with the two strikers dovetailing and thought we'd gone ahead when Sol headed in a corner. But the emotional highs and lows of the game were extraordinary. One minute we were celebrating Sol's header, the next we were watching Argentina steam upfield on the counter. The goal was harshly ruled out for a foul on the keeper by Alan, and half our team were celebrating in the corner when Argentina broke. I was sure they were going to score. I felt numb and confused when I saw them attacking. Somehow we escaped. In the heat of the moment I didn't even realise that the flag was up for offside when Darren whipped the ball off Hernan Crespo's toes.

We stood firm. We lost Graeme to injury and Gareth had to come on at left-back, but Argentina never hurt us. The only danger was fatigue. I didn't want us to press when it went to extra time, even though Argentina's defenders were average on the ball, and I needed to make changes. Scholesy looked shattered with 10 minutes left of normal time. He was young and the intensity of the tournament caught up with him. His socks were down by his ankles and I had no option but to bring on Paul Merson, who was a penalty taker.

I did think about introducing Teddy, who also would have taken a penalty. Yet we still had to hold out. It would have been a huge risk to bring on a third striker when I decided to substitute an exhausted Darren. We needed the insurance of David Batty in midfield, even though it meant we didn't have many penalty takers on the pitch for the shootout.

But it should have never got to that point. As if Sol's disallowed goal wasn't bad enough, Argentina got away with one again when Chamot handled in their area in extra time. It was blatant. Yet none of our players appealed. Only Alan saw it, and he didn't make a big fuss. I think it gave Nielsen an out; I saw him motion to go for his whistle and then he seemed to change his mind. I'm certain that he was influenced by the Golden Goal rule – it would have been game over if Alan had put the penalty away, with us not Argentina facing Holland in the last eight.

Instead we were through to a shootout. I had Alan, Michael and Merse, but we were short of specialists. Darren, David and Scholesy all could have taken one, but they weren't on the pitch. We needed volunteers, and Incey and Batty were brave enough to step up. They didn't deserve the agony of missing the vital penalties.

The lads left everything out on the pitch. We were so close to pulling off an astonishing victory and it could have been a different story had we shown more ruthlessness when Seaman briefly put us in control of the shootout by saving Crespo's penalty, only for Incey to spurn the chance to hammer home our advantage.

Instead the tie remained on a knife-edge, and when Ayala made it 4–3 to Argentina the pressure was on Batty to keep our hopes alive. But it didn't feel like we had lost when his kick was saved. Argentina didn't beat us. We just didn't go through. I didn't have a single negative thing to say to the players in the dressing room. They were magnificent and their performance merited a win. They deserved better from the officials.

The pain was immense. I've never been able to watch that match back. It was an emotional rollercoaster and I struggled to cope during the aftermath. I felt sick and I broke down when I saw my wonderful PA, Michelle Farrer, and Joanne Budd, who worked in the FA's press team, in floods of tears while I was waiting to go into my press conference. I was still holding back the tears when I spoke to the media. It was that kind of night.

Outside the stadium we saw the Argentina players going berserk on their bus. They were waving their shirts above their heads celebrating and the bus was almost rocking. I'll never forget that behaviour and it left a bad taste in the mouth. Our players had to watch that as they boarded our bus, only adding to our sense of injustice.

It was disrespectful from Argentina, who should have waited until they had driven away before starting their celebrations. Instead they chose to rub our noses in it. 'No class,' I thought. 'You're not showing any class at all.'

I was seething. At least Anne, my middle daughter Zara and my son Jamie were with me and helped me keep things in perspective. Jamie was only six and his innocence disarmed me. I looked down at him and he almost made me well up again. 'Never mind, Dad,' he said. 'It's only a game.'

Kids, eh? What could I say? Zara was laughing and I felt a wave of emotion wash over me as I ruffled Jamie's hair. 'I love you, son,' I said.

12

AN OPEN MIND

'Get me to the hotel,' I said. 'I need a beer.'

I couldn't hang around that stadium. I wanted to block the events of Saint-Étienne out of my mind. The image of the Argentina players celebrating on the bus, followed by my boy's words of wisdom, had floored me emotionally. The dream was over, destroyed by misfortune and injustice, and our time in France had come to a tearful, premature end.

I maintain that my team were strong enough to go all the way. Our belief would have soared if we'd beaten Argentina with 10 men. We would have built up great momentum before facing Holland in the last eight, even though David would have been suspended, and beating Brazil in the last four wouldn't have been beyond us.

Yet it was all ifs, buts and maybes. There was nothing to be gained from torturing ourselves by dwelling on our defeat, and at least we finally had a chance to let our hair down. We didn't have to worry about training anymore, and the lads enjoyed themselves back at the hotel. They went about it the right way. There was no wallowing. Or sleeping. They stuck together, and I was amused to see some of them out on the golf course when I looked outside my window at 6am.

It was time to move on. I went on holiday to recharge my batteries, but I was hungrier than ever. The talent was there, and I was excited about the youngsters who had broken through under my watch.

I wasn't on the back foot. I was only thinking about qualifying for Euro 2000 and building a team capable of winning a major tournament. Judging by our performances, I had no reason to fear for my job.

Off the field, however, the mood had shifted. The press were talking about my future and painting a picture of an unhappy camp. There was talk about the way that I told players that they hadn't made the World Cup squad and I was criticised for not putting my arm round David's shoulder after his red card against Argentina, which was unfair given that Johnny G was on hand to speak to him when we returned to the dressing room. Managers have to keep their distance sometimes. I had to make sure that I was in the right emotional state before speaking to David. I didn't want to say the wrong thing and I spoke to him when we were on the plane home the next day.

But sometimes it's hard to stop a narrative taking hold. The story goes that I made my bed by releasing my World Cup diary a month after the tournament was over. I supposedly committed the cardinal sin of betraying dressing room secrets, apparently damaging my relationship with the players.

The backlash surprised me, especially when I faced questions from certain influential figures at the FA, as the reality was much more mundane. Presumably no one had told them that I wrote the book in conjunction with David Davies, the FA's press officer. The FA knew all about it from the start and I made it clear when the publishers initially approached me that I wasn't prepared to write with someone from outside the organisation.

The FA didn't have a problem with the project. They knew that my contract allowed me to do external jobs as long as they were involved. I had a sponsorship deal with Mitre, for example, one of the FA's sponsors, and the book was no different.

The reaction was over the top. The book was hardly warts and all. I was careful not to include any major revelations and I wouldn't have written it if I felt that it was going to cause problems down the line.

Yet it was portrayed negatively. There were rumours of an unhappy camp, but no player ever came to me to complain. There were no alarm bells. I never had a meeting that left me feeling that I needed to regain the trust of the players. Some of them might have been unhappy about not playing more, but that's football. It happens all the time, and nothing made me think that I had to worry about anything more than making sure our qualification campaign went well.

It didn't help my cause when we performed poorly in our opening game. Much like the Romania match in the World Cup, I had a bad feeling when we faced Sweden in Stockholm. Their fans were up for it, their style unsettled us and we struggled to take control of the game.

Sweden always seem to give England problems. I thought we might escape with a draw, but we conceded two careless goals after taking an early lead through Alan, and there was no way back after Incey was sent off for two bookings in the second half.

We simply weren't quite at the races, and we put ourselves under further pressure after a goalless home draw with Bulgaria. But it was way too early to panic. We recovered after losing at home to Italy during qualifying for the World Cup, and we had plenty of home games to come. There was time to recover, and I felt better after watching Rio impress for us in a 3–0 in Luxembourg.

I had big plans for Rio, who was such a classy defender. I envisaged using him as a sweeper because of his ability on the ball, and he had an enterprising role against Luxembourg, giving him freedom to push on from right centre-back and support our attacks by becoming an extra full-back. It was clear that he was destined for the top and he had another fine game when we beat the Czech Republic 2–0 in a friendly at Wembley in November.

I was pleased with a polished win over awkward opponents. The Czechs had lost to Germany in the final of Euro 96 on their previous trip to Wembley, and beating them without the injured trio of Scholesy, Michael and Alan told me that we were on the right track. If only everyone else had agreed.

I sensed the agenda changing before our home friendly against France in February 1999. The coverage remained negative and spooked the FA, whose press officers told me that it would be a good idea to regain some favour with the media by arranging a series of interviews with different journalists before facing the world champions.

I was nonplussed. My view was that the only way to win people over was by winning games and I was confident that we were going to get back on track sooner rather than later. The rumblings of discontent were to be expected after a couple of disappointing results, but I trusted my team to turn it around.

Yet if people want to make things awkward for a manager, they will latch on to anything. The background noise about irrelevant off-field issues coloured perceptions of me and I suspect it informed the FA's thinking. They wanted me to do the interviews and I reluctantly went along with them.

I never made it past the first one.

Looking back, I wonder if there was a bigger problem brewing behind the scenes, waiting to engulf me at a moment's notice. I had certainly sensed a shift in attitude from the FA's committee before I was due to have my first one-on-one chat with a sports writer from *The Times*. The atmosphere had become frayed. The press had managed to oust the FA's chairman Keith Wiseman and the chief executive Graham Kelly, and, with the benefit of hindsight, it's hard not to assume that I was next on their hitlist.

If that was the case then I needed support from my bosses. Yet it was a time of upheaval. Once Keith and Graham, two allies, had left the building, there wasn't as much communication as before. We were working from offices outside Wembley because the FA were in the middle of leaving their headquarters in Lancaster Gate and, in contrast to managing at a club, I didn't have much contact with board members from one day to the next.

All the same I wasn't overly concerned when I sat in my office one morning and picked up the phone for my 20-minute interview with a sports journalist from *The Times*. It was, however, a surprise that no press officer was on the call. Someone should have been with me, but David Davies wasn't around and he hadn't asked anyone from his team to make sure the interview didn't lead down any unnecessary paths.

Even then I wasn't worried when I started the interview. We spoke about the world champions coming to town, my thoughts on Rio's development and how we were going to prepare for Zinedine Zidane. The focus was on football and we were coming towards the end when the journalist caught me off guard by saying that he was fascinated by my belief in reincarnation, adding that he was interested in the topic.

Perhaps a press officer would have stepped in at that stage and ended the interview. I was on my own, however, and I didn't see any harm in talking about it if he was interested. Nothing had happened when I spoke about reincarnation with the BBC's Brian Alexander on the radio before the World Cup, explaining I believed that the body was an overcoat for the soul, and I assumed that the journalist wanted to dig deeper after hearing that interview.

But I was surprised when he started bringing up examples about mental and physical disability. Reincarnation is about growing spiritually and handling the opportunities we face in our lives, both negative and positive.

I don't think he understood the topic. He returned to the subject of disability twice, after which I started to have misgivings over the direction that the conversation was heading. The subject was too broad to tackle in a 20-minute interview. Reincarnation takes a lifetime to understand. More than half the world believes in it, and I decided to end the interview when he kept bringing up those examples.

I wasn't worried when the interview was over. I thought it was a strange way to end things but I didn't think about calling David to alert him to a potential problem. I put the phone down and continued as normal, thinking nothing more of it until I took a phone call on a Friday saying that a story was about to come out in *The Times* about me claiming that disabled people were being punished because of sins from a past life.

I was astonished and appalled. The last thing I wanted was for anyone with a disability to think that this was my view. It couldn't have been further from the truth. My belief is that the soul chooses to come back to learn about life. You choose your opportunity to come back. It's a spiritual decision to return and experience positive and negative challenges. The soul is here to learn from its past mistakes; it's never a punishment.

I never spoke about punishment. I never used that word, nor did I talk about karma working from another life or disabled people having to reap what they sowed. I never said it. I believe that the soul has a choice when it returns to this world. There are no inevitabilities with reincarnation; free will at a spiritual level is involved. I accept that reincarnation isn't an easy topic and that it can be misunderstood by people who don't believe in it. I didn't understand it until I was in my 30s, which is when I began to search for meaning on a deeper level.

I don't hide my beliefs, but reincarnation wasn't supposed to be on the agenda during my interview. I would have gone into further detail if I'd spent more time with the journalist, but I was there to talk about playing France and could have spoken to him properly about reincarnation on another day. I hadn't been at all comfortable with his focus on disability. I gave him other examples, and I don't know how that got construed as me talking about punishment.

Yet there it was on the front page of the newspaper. Dennis Roach, my agent, got in touch, and we called David to talk about the story. At that stage I still viewed it as a bit of a nuisance. I didn't want people to believe that I held such abhorrent views, but I remained confident that it would blow over and I got on with my job on the weekend, heading to Highfield Road to watch Coventry beat Liverpool.

It was when Tony Blair criticised me on television that my mood changed. 'We might have a problem here, Glenn,' Dennis said. 'You're going to need the backing of the FA.'

It wasn't forthcoming. The prime minister's unhelpful and inappropriate input inevitably made my life harder. He should have known better than to comment when he didn't know the full story. But I could tell which way the wind was blowing and I was counting on the FA to back me.

I think that they would have held firm if the chairman and chief executive had still been in their posts. It wasn't so long ago that the conversation was about giving me a 10-year contract after our triumph at Le Tournoi. Now I was under siege, Public Enemy No1, and I was short of allies who were prepared to protect me.

It was evident that the FA had already made up their mind when I met the committee for crisis talks at Lancaster Gate. A sense of resignation fell over me when I walked into the room. I told them that I didn't believe in punishment for past sins – but it had no impact. I could tell that they were looking for any reason to sack me. I told my side of the story but I had already been found guilty in the court of public opinion.

I knew that I was in trouble while I was in that room with those men from the FA. Although a couple of committee members told me in private that they were on my side, the majority didn't want me to continue. It was frustrating, and I told Dennis that they were weak. There was all this peripheral talk about healing and some of the figures on that committee were pouncing on the interview in order to make my position untenable.

It was hard to take. I would have understood it had I been sacked for footballing reasons. Yet we had won our two previous games. We had proven our worth at the World Cup and I knew that we were going to improve.

Yet I was hung out to dry by the FA. I walked away from that meeting telling Dennis that I didn't want to work for people who had shown themselves to be so feeble. Not many managers are sacked after winning their last two games and I felt an immense sadness when it was over. I was worried about the effect on my children, who struggled to deal with the back-lash. It had a massive impact on them, and I was devastated that disabled people would think that I held dreadful views about them.

They are not my beliefs – they never have been and never will be. Reincarnation is something that people have to study for themselves. It's not up to me to define it. What I do know, though, is that plenty of people believe in it. It's a philosophy that's existed for thousands of years and it was only the Western world that found the subject difficult. I encountered closed minds in 1999 and I lost a job I cherished.

People saw me as a kook. Yet an open mind is one of the greatest gifts anyone can have. It's not so long ago that virtually everyone thought the world was flat and accused anyone who disagreed of being mad. There's nothing wrong with exploring philosophies from different cultures and I think that we have now become more open to new experiences.

We always have opportunities to grow and develop. I don't bear a grudge towards the journalist who wrote the piece. I don't know him, and at first it was hard to see him if we happened to be travelling to the same game for work. Yet sitting near him at an airport gave me an opportunity to think more deeply about our conversation and offered me a chance to forgive him in my mind.

I believe that is what life is about. That particular journalist came into my life to teach me about forgiveness. It took a few years for me to think more positively about the situation, but in the end he helped me grow spiritually and I would be the first person to come to his aid if I saw that he was in trouble. You have to move on. You can't allow yourself to become consumed by negativity. It's unhealthy.

When I was sacked, though, I wasn't thinking that way. I left that meeting with the FA and returned to the embrace of my family. I knew that I could count on them. I spoke to my parents and wanted them to know that I was going to survive. 'Move on, son,' Dad said. 'It's their loss.'

Dad was right, but it wasn't easy. I still feel that I had unfinished business with England when I left. I had experienced players at my disposal and I was planning to build around Rio, Scholesy, David and Michael. We would have had a great side.

I see frustration when I talk to players from that squad now. Rio even said that my departure held the team back by a decade. I've had little chats with Rio, Scholesy and Michael down the years and their disappointment about the way English football went always comes across.

Of course, some players would have been less upset to see me go. Some of them would have been hoping to play more under the new manager and I would be lying if I said that I haven't noticed their comments about my man-management down the years. On reflection, I think that I should have put aside more time to speak to players individually. It was easier to have those chats at club level and I feel that I made a mistake by not making more of an effort to build those human connections when I was managing England. It would have strengthened my position, and although I think that our performances showed that there wasn't a problem with the squad's morale, it is something I would do differently now.

Looking back, I also feel that I wasn't canny enough with the press. I didn't play the game well enough. After my sacking I remembered that one of my main reservations when I took the job was how my life would change off the field. I knew that the media were going to be a problem when I took over. They always were for England managers in those days, and the best way to sum up my relationship with certain outlets is that I found out later that my phone had been hacked.

On its own, though, that wasn't a reason to turn the FA down when I was approached in 1996. It was a magnificent job and I held my head high when I left. I judged myself on results and mine were good.

Yet I didn't realise that the game didn't start and end on the referee's whistle. It's going on all the time. Some managers are always thinking about how to use the media to their advantage; they look forward to press conferences and use them to push an agenda.

That wasn't me. Although I did them because they were part of my duties, I wasn't there to offer the journalists easy stories. I was happy to talk about tactics, but I soon discovered that from Monday to Wednesday they were happy to talk about anything apart from the game. They had to fill their papers before the weekend and most of them didn't want to hear me banging on about our formation.

I was naive. I should have embraced my press duties more as England manager and given the pack juicier tales. Yet I sometimes regarded the briefings as a nuisance. I tried to run through where we were as a team, and it was a relief when I was able to keep the press happy by telling them about an injury.

Nobody can argue that during my time as manager we weren't developing as a side. We produced big performances against top teams and our system gave us flexibility on and off the ball. But England reverted to type after I left. I watched the France game because Johnny G stayed on to help Howard Wilkinson, who had been placed in caretaker charge, and we were already back to 4–4–2. It wasn't a surprise when France picked us off, winning 2–0.

There's nothing wrong with 4–4–2. Defensively, it's probably the best way to play. Yet it isn't suited to a possession game at international level and it didn't allow us to make the most of our talent. I found myself watching managers, including those who came from foreign shores, struggle to find a way to get the best out of Joe Cole, Wayne Rooney, Frank Lampard, Steven Gerrard and Scholesy. I was exasperated when I saw Scholesy or Steven stuck out on the left wing. I laughed when people said that Frank and Steven couldn't play together. The individuals weren't the issue. The problem was a system that forced England to play in straight lines, making them far too predictable. Arsenal defended with two banks of four under Arsène, but nobody could tell their shape when they had the ball. Their movement in a nominal 4–4–2 was exceptional. England, on the other hand, were painfully rigid.

Do you think that Frank and Steven would have been questioned if they'd played for Germany or Spain? They were fantastic footballers. Two goalscoring midfielders in the same side? Hallelujah! Every manager wants to have that luxury, but England couldn't make it work. Sven-Göran Eriksson and Fabio Capello were as flummoxed as any homegrown manager. But they just needed to find a sitting midfielder. It could have been Michael Carrick. It could have been Owen Hargreaves. It even could have been Scholesy, who was able to control a game for fun. Yet England tried to cram everyone into a 4–4–2. It was hard not to think about what might have been.

I had to move on, though. I went off to lick my wounds after my sacking, but I wasn't going to hide away. If you worry about what people say you'll never make it out of your front door. I was never going to walk away from football. I just needed the hunger to return and the right opportunity to arrive.

I wanted to wait before jumping back in. A few offers came and went, but nothing grabbed me at first. I needed time to heal. In a way the break was a blessing in disguise. There was something to be said for stepping away for a few months and allowing myself to take a breather. Football had dominated my life since I was a boy and, although I loved it, it's a relentless industry, particularly as I jumped straight into management as my playing days were coming to an end.

Yet life's like a magnet. You draw good things towards you when you reject negative thoughts. Doors start to open and it's up to you to decide whether to see what's on the other side. I was soon ready for a new adventure. I missed the smell of the grass and I was intrigued when Southampton approached me in January 2000.

I clicked with Rupert Lowe, Southampton's chairman, when we met at his farm in Gloucestershire. Rupert knew sport and he was passionate about his club. It felt right, even though Southampton were just above the relegation zone in the Premier League when I replaced Dave Jones.

Southampton reminded me of Swindon. They were a family club and their old ground, The Dell, was a tough place to play. It was a tight, atmospheric little stadium and it already had a special place in my heart. I felt wistful when I looked up at the directors' box when I was having my picture taken on the pitch during my official unveiling and remembered playing for

Tottenham when we won promotion by drawing with the Saints in 1978.

The signs were positive and I was confident that we were going to stay up. I came in with a reputation after managing England, but I liked the look of my squad. We didn't need a major overhaul. I made a few tweaks but I wasn't dogmatic about playing a back three. My centre-backs, Claus Lundekvam and Dean Richards, were happy playing in a back four and I liked Jason Dodd at right-back.

Although we sometimes shifted into a back three, we often ended up playing more of a 4–3–3. I brought the little Latvian wizard Marians Pahars out to the left flank so he could face up to defenders and asked Kevin Davies to play wide as well. The players were good, in a squad that lacked any egos. The players gave their all and responded to our tactical drills. We asked our midfielders to push into the box and I was a big admirer of James Beattie up front.

We were involved in some exciting games and we stayed up with relative ease, giving ourselves an opportunity to build by finishing 15th. It was an exciting time for the club. They were preparing to move to St Mary's and I enjoyed having a bit of input into the design of the dressing rooms.

Everyone was pulling in the same direction and I had a good relationship with Rupert. We'd speak on the phone when I drove home after training and he always wanted to know about the team. He sought information about potential signings and he was an astute businessman.

I enjoyed Rupert's company. I was closer to him than the other chairmen I worked for during my career and I found his attitude refreshing. He was rational after defeats, preferring to look at the bigger picture, and he was ambitious. Rupert loved Southampton and he wanted to take them higher.

It was an enjoyable time. The facilities were acceptable and the spirit was strong. I took Johnny G with me and I quickly bonded with the other coaches, Stuart Gray and Dennis Rofe. Everyone was pulling in the same direction and our camaraderie made us stronger. I felt good going into pre-season. I knew that I had made the right choice.

The only problem at Southampton was the lack of funds for new signings. We had to be canny in the transfer market. We brought in Mark Draper and Uwe Rösler for peanuts, and focused on drilling the team during training, improving their tactical understanding as we prepared for the new season.

The one disappointment when it came to picking the team was Matt Le Tissier's injury woes. Matt was a fabulous talent but he had a persistent calf problem. He wasn't getting any younger and his body was starting to let him down. I tried my best to work on his fitness, sending him to Arsène's old pal Dr Rougier for nutritional advice and waiting for the situation to improve. But there were no guarantees. You can't trick your age, and I remembered running round Ascot racecourse when I was 37, wondering why I was still putting my body through that grind.

Ultimately you have to put in the hard yards if you want to extend your career. Matt was different to me, and it was frustrating that he wasn't available on a more regular basis. He would have made us much better.

But it was an easy squad to manage. They liked a night out, but there were no superstars and they showed that they could play as the 2000–01 season progressed. We weren't in a relegation battle and everyone could see that we were on an upward trajectory. England was in the past and I felt happy again.

13

HEAD VS HEART

The thought of leaving Southampton could not have been further from my mind when I went on holiday to South Africa near the end of the 2000–01 season. I was settled at The Dell and felt optimistic about the future. Free from relegation concerns, we were on course for a top-half finish and I was starting to wonder if we were capable of pushing even higher in the long run.

Our belief kept growing. I brought in John Syer, my old sports psychologist from Tottenham, and he worked wonders with our defence, playing a massive role in them forming an incredible bond. He had a way of making people open up and express themselves. His techniques could be deceptively simple, at times nothing more complicated than passing a pen round a big circle and saying something to the group when it was in your hands.

Some people found this uncomfortable at first. Wayne Bridge, our gifted young left-back, turned red when it was his turn. Bridgey was painfully shy as a youngster and he only managed to say a few words before handing the pen to someone else.

Still, at least he said something. The hard part was over and Bridgey was clearly more confident when we went through the exercise again a week later. I saw him starting to come out of his shell, and John told me to watch out for a change in Bridgey's attitude in training after doing a private session with the defence.

Positive reinforcement goes a long way. According to John, Bridgey swelled with pride when Claus Lundekvam, Jason Dodd and Dean Richards told him that he was good enough to play for England. There is nothing quite like praise from your team-mates, and John's trick was to make players be honest with each other.

It doesn't come naturally to footballers. They spend a lot of time with each other, but it's hard to cut through the banter. They can go years without having a genuine conversation, and it takes someone like John to put them in situations that allow true connections to build.

I experienced it when I played for Tottenham and I watched it work for Bridgey, who went on to have a wonderful career, playing for England and winning titles with Chelsea. He was a fantastic talent and he played a big part in Southampton becoming one of the toughest teams in the league to break down.

We had a stingy back four protecting the dependable Paul Jones. Bridgey flew up and down the left flank, Dean Richards and Claus Lundekvam were rocks in the middle, Jason Dodd was experienced at right-back and Francis Benali was a reliable reserve. They trusted each other implicitly and became such a strong unit that we went into games knowing that we weren't going to concede.

It was lovely to watch from the touchline. We went on a brilliant run after the turn of the year, repeatedly shutting teams out. We looked unbeatable if we scored the first goal, and we signed off for the March international break in style, recording our seventh consecutive clean sheet in the league with a 1–0 home win over Everton.

The mood around the club was serene. We were eighth in the league, five points behind third-placed Ipswich, and Rupert told me to go and have a good break during the internationals, promising to leave me alone until I came back from a week at my agent's house in South Africa.

Neither of us knew that our relationship was about to take a turn for the worse. I wasn't thinking about work when the phone rang while I was spending the day in a secluded little vineyard. The scenery was beautiful and I was in the middle of a picnic when I was jolted out of my blissful state, although the signal was so bad that I couldn't hear anything more than someone saying 'David Buchler' on the other end of the line.

I was mystified when I put the phone down. I racked my brains, trying to place the name, and eventually remembered that there was a David Buchler on the board at Tottenham. Gradually it dawned on me. I tried to focus on the holiday but it was impossible not to wonder why someone from Tottenham was trying to call me in the middle of an international break.

I was deep in thought on the drive back to where we were staying in Stellenbosch. I couldn't help but wonder, given that Tottenham were looking for a new manager after firing George Graham, and my suspicions were confirmed when I spoke to David again after reaching somewhere with a better signal.

I hadn't seen it coming, even when George was fired. I was settled at Southampton and I wasn't waiting for an approach from Tottenham. It came completely out of the blue, and it was strange to think that the offers always seemed to come when I was at my most content. The similarities with my departures from Chelsea and Swindon immediately came to mind, and instead of relaxing I found myself deep in discussion with my agent, trying to work out what to say to Tottenham.

After a day of contemplation, however, I realised that I couldn't say no to Tottenham after having turned them down in 1993. This was my club calling, and it was time to go back. I listened to my gut, and all I could do was hope that everyone at Southampton would understand why I wanted to return to White Hart Lane.

Not that it was an easy decision. I found working at Southampton invigorating and I was excited about where we were heading before Tottenham called. Leaving was a wrench, and that call from David ruined my holiday. I was on the phone most of the time and Rupert wasn't pleased when he found out that I wanted to take the Spurs job. He was intent on persuading me to stay. He could see what we were building at Southampton and he wasn't thrilled about the prospect of losing me.

Yet Southampton were fighting a losing battle. Rupert soon realised that I wasn't going to stay and there was a fierce backlash from the fans when I said that I was going. I was a pariah in their eyes, and I wasn't in Rupert's good books either after leaving.

At least my friendship with Rupert wasn't beyond repair. We didn't have a huge falling-out, and although we didn't speak for a few years, Rupert knew that I'd done a good job for him. His feelings towards me mellowed over time and he even tried to bring me back to Southampton in 2004. I was ready to work with him again and knew that it would only take a few wins to win the fans over, but the deal collapsed after other board members made it clear that they didn't want me back.

I wish that people at Southampton could have accepted why I chose Tottenham. It wasn't an ordinary job offer. It was a chance to go home. The head didn't matter. I was following my heart. Perhaps that was where I went wrong.

The problem with making decisions based on sentiment is the danger of blinding yourself to reality. Although Tottenham were my boyhood club, my time there as manager was the unhappiest of my career.

The negotiations were tricky. I should have put my foot down when David Buchler called me in South Africa and told me that David Pleat would be staying at Tottenham as director of football. I played for David and I wasn't impressed when he told the media that Tottenham would be better without me after I joined Monaco in 1987. It was an unnecessary comment after everything I'd done for the club, and I should have explained to David Buchler why I felt uncomfortable about reviving that relationship. It wasn't constructive to have a manager and a director of football who didn't see eye to eye. Rather than worrying about how it would be received if I'd been seen to be making too many demands before taking the job, I ought to have been firmer with the board.

At the same time the director of football model wasn't going to stop me returning to White Hart Lane. Although Tottenham hadn't produced much of note for a few years, I was thrilled about following in the footsteps of the great Bill Nicholson and managing the club I had adored since I was a boy.

I needed all the positivity I could possibly muster. I thought about stepping into Bill Nick's shoes and the nostalgia seeped over me when I looked up at the cockerel I used to polish when I was an apprentice at White Hart Lane. I was a Tottenham fan, a part of the crowd, and picking up maximum points on a Saturday afternoon meant even more now that I was manager.

Yet all this baggage only added to the pressure. I was beyond desperate to succeed, and something I've learnt over time is that when your mind craves something that badly, it can become harder to grasp.

I didn't feel that there was any discernible style of play when I arrived. The squad contained a lot of holes and I only had five days to prepare for my first game – the small affair of an FA Cup semi-final against Arsenal at Old Trafford.

It was some way to start. I was up against Arsène, who had a brilliant team, and we had loads of injuries. We were straight in at the deep end and we couldn't afford to play an expansive game against the likes of Thierry Henry and Robert Pires. We lined up with five across the back and gave ourselves something to hang on to when Gary Doherty put us ahead early in the game.

Yet Arsenal were the better team on the day. I was worried when Sol Campbell, our defensive rock, injured himself while conceding a free-kick on our left midway through the first half. We had worked on defending zonally from wide free-kicks and the plan fell apart without Sol covering the near-post area. He was receiving treatment when the ball came into our box and, with the lads unable to hear my cries to shuffle across to close the gap, Patrick Vieira was free to dart into the vacant space to glance in the equaliser.

Sol would have headed it away had he been on the pitch. Ultimately, though, we couldn't have any complaints. Arsenal deservedly won 2–1, killing my hopes of a dream start, and I spent the final weeks of the season working out where we needed to improve.

I needed players who could fit into my system after finishing 12th. First, though, we had to find a way of convincing Sol to sign a new contract. His deal was up and plenty of top clubs wanted to sign him on a free. I worked on winning him over, inviting him to my place for dinner and holding talks with his agent, and I was relieved when he told me that he was going to stay.

So I wasn't quite as ecstatic when I found out that Sol was joining Arsenal on a free transfer. He was within his rights to move but it was a shame that he'd kept us in the dark about his true intentions. The fans were livid, and although I wasn't sure how the board had managed to let the situation drag on that far, the way that Sol handled his departure left a sour taste in the mouth.

It was hard to take the loss of such a great player. I wasn't too bothered about him going to Arsenal; the damage to my defence mattered more to me than the rivalry with our north London neighbours. Although we responded by somehow managing to persuade Southampton to sell Dean Richards, I was gutted not to have Sol in my team. It would have been wonderful to see him in a back three with Deano and Ledley King.

We didn't quite have the quality to play a back three without Sol. Christian Ziege and Stephen Carr were perfect wing-backs for our system, but we couldn't find the right balance in the middle and often reverted to playing a back four.

Nevertheless we had the makings of a decent side. Ledley was a fabulous player and I'm pleased that he has become a coach at Tottenham, but when he was younger he needed to work on being more vocal. I eventually brought John Syer to Tottenham and he tried to help Ledley become more expressive. We wanted Ledley to be more demanding on the pitch and bark out orders. I knew from experience that you earn respect from your peers when you lead during games. I was a shy kid but I was a different animal when I stepped over that white line. Football meant the world to me and that made me more willing to change my personality on the pitch.

I wanted to see the same attitude from Ledley. He was smart enough to spot patterns during games, but he wasn't a great communicator. He needed the confidence to be forceful with a team-mate who hadn't tracked a runner. It would have made him an even better player. He was two-footed and could play anywhere in a back three. He was versatile, read the game well and was deceptively fast. He didn't look quick but he had a huge stride and he covered the ground impressively.

Ledley's emergence softened the blow of Sol's exit. Yet my first transfer window didn't exactly set pulses racing. I was at a big club but funds were limited. It's one of the biggest frustrations I experienced as a manager. I never worked at a club with a massive budget and so I always found myself having to make compromises. I had to count the pennies at Chelsea, I dipped into my own pocket to buy Shaun Taylor at Swindon and I wasn't flush with cash at Tottenham.

This forced me to improvise in the transfer market. Although their best days were behind them, I signed Gus Poyet and Teddy Sheringham on free transfers. Ziege came in from Liverpool for £4m and Goran Bunjevčević was a cheap buy from Red Star Belgrade. I wasn't exactly shopping at Harrods.

Yet there was cause for optimism when I bought Deano for £8m from Southampton. I knew him inside out and the future looked bright when he put us 1–0 up on his debut against United in September. The fans at White Hart Lane could hardly believe it. We tore into United, the defending champions, and were 3–0 up by half-time.

Our football was unbelievable, but I knew that United weren't going to roll over and I told the lads to be careful during the first 10 minutes of the second half. Then I watched Andy Cole pull one back a minute after the restart.

I could feel the belief in the stands draining away as United turned the screw. They were so difficult to stop once they gained momentum and it wasn't long before they were level. They embarrassed us in the end, winning 5–3, and it was one of those games where you find yourself groping helplessly for clarity on the touchline. My head was telling me one thing, my gut was telling me another, and before I knew it United had put the ball in our net five times. It was horrible to watch us go from an inventive, free-flowing team to one reduced to holding on. It hurt that I couldn't find an answer.

On the other hand those first 45 minutes were as good as anything I had seen from Tottenham for a long time. There were positives to take from the game in spite of how it unfolded and we went on a promising run after that loss to United. Gus scored goals from midfield, Teddy had a dangerous partnership with Les Ferdinand and we had a chance of winning silverware when we set up a League Cup semi-final with Chelsea after beating Bolton 6–0.

It was massive. Tottenham used to beat Chelsea with our eyes closed when I was playing, but they had moved past us during the Premier League era. I had started the foreign revolution at Stamford Bridge when I signed Ruud, and they continued to progress after my departure, signing big players and playing in the Champions League.

We were the underdogs and it looked like we weren't going to make it to the Millennium Stadium for the final after losing the first leg 2–1 at Stamford Bridge. Chelsea had a great record at White Hart Lane – their fans called it Three Points Lane

– and it was clear that we'd have to be at our very best to beat them.

Yet the form book went out of the window. We were sensational on the night, obliterating Chelsea from start to finish. We won 5–1 and although I knew that we were a long way off becoming a great team, I felt that lifting a trophy would act as a springboard for future success.

My hope was that winning would strengthen my position and give me the clout to demand more money from the board. Our ageing squad was crying out for a revamp and I needed support from the club. I wasn't asking for the world. I simply wanted us to show more ambition.

I wouldn't have faced so much pushback from the board if we'd beaten Graeme Souness's Blackburn in the final. The little obstacles that stopped my vision from becoming a reality would have fallen away if we'd made the most of our superiority over Souey's team. Yet it simply wasn't to be. We played well on the day and created enough chances, only to find Brad Friedel in inspired form in goal for Blackburn. Friedel made so many saves, and we lost 2–1 after a poacher's goal from Andy Cole in the second half.

I wish it had turned out differently. I should have been experiencing the most joyful time of my managerial career. Instead, it was the most demoralising. Losing to Blackburn meant that we missed an opportunity to improve the club's self-belief and I found it hard to deal with my emotions after the game.

I was absolutely gutted when we met up with the families in a venue near the stadium. I needed to get away from everyone, and my parents joined me when I went upstairs to find some privacy in an empty bar.

Mum and Dad were always there for me. We sat there talking for an hour, away from the crowd, and they made me feel better. You can always count on your family in the low moments. I sat next to Dad on the plane back to London, chatting away and enjoying his company, and I decided to go back to my parents' house in Harlow after we landed in Stansted.

It was a blessing. I didn't sleep much that night and I was still raw when I woke up early the next morning. Yet it was a new day. I needed to head to our training ground in Chigwell and I was about to open the front door when I turned around and saw Dad standing there.

Dad wasn't the type of person who expressed his emotions easily. Something must have got into him. Perhaps this was his soul telling him that his eldest boy was going to be fine because it caught me completely off guard when he gave me a great big kiss on the cheek.

It meant so much. I immediately kissed him on the cheek and hugged him, before saying something that probably hadn't come out of my mouth since I was a little boy.

'I love you, Dad.'

It was the last thing I ever said to him.

I never saw Dad again. I heard the news the next day. I was having a meeting with the players on one of the training pitches, trying to lift their spirits, when I turned and saw my secretary Irene walking towards us. She said something to Johnny G, who had left the circle, and he sprinted towards me as soon as the conversation was over.

'You've got to go,' John whispered. 'Your dad's been taken to hospital.'

My whole body went numb. I felt dizzy. But I ran. We told Chris Hughton, one of my coaches, to take the session, and

John, who's very close to my family, joined me as I made my way to Harlow hospital.

I was in shock. Dad had suffered an aneurysm and although he was on a life-support machine, there was nothing the doctors could do to save him.

I couldn't believe it. There had been no signs that Dad was unwell. He'd looked a bit grey on the plane, but at the time I just thought that he was stressed about the final. I didn't think anything serious was about to happen. Dad was only 67. He still had so much time.

But why did he kiss me that morning? I believe that our spirit knows when our time has come. I think it was Dad's way of saying goodbye, and it's amazing that the last thing I said to him was telling him that I loved him.

Men don't normally hug and we often struggle to share our feelings with each other. Yet it was sincere when I embraced Dad. I felt blessed to have that moment and I know that he is up there now, still watching over me.

Dad was always by my side. He played football with me for hours when I was a boy, and he was Tottenham through and through. He loved taking me to games and he never pushed me too hard when I was starting out as a player. Dad never told me what I could have done better. It wasn't his style. He was a steady influence, kind and supportive, and his unde-monstrative personality helped me keep my feet on the ground.

Mum was similar. I am grateful to my parents for how they brought me up. Dad wasn't a simple man, but he liked the simple life. He didn't seek confrontation and he was never in your face, although that doesn't mean that he wasn't strong. He showed his tough side when he met Ken Bates for the first time in the directors' box at Stamford Bridge when I was at Chelsea. Ken liked to attack people when he was introduced to them, just to see if they were weak, and the first thing he did when he met Dad was make an acerbic comment about his jacket.

It might have floored someone else. Not Dad, though. 'Well, look at your shirt,' he replied. 'At least my shirt's been ironed properly. Look at your collar – creases everywhere.'

Mum told me that Ken loved it. He liked people who stood up to him and he always had a bit of banter with Dad, who never thought twice about having a laugh at the expense of Chelsea's chairman.

That exchange was typical of Dad. People warmed to him when they met him. There was never a hidden agenda with my parents. They gave me a calm upbringing and it was funny to think that I went from growing up in a council house in Harlow to living in Monte Carlo.

I enjoyed having my parents visit me when I was at Monaco. I wasn't a betting man but I wanted to go to the casino when I was with Dad. I made him wear a white tuxedo and he looked a million dollars when he walked up to a table and slapped 500 francs down straight away.

There was only one problem: he had no idea what he was doing. I was walking around with Mum, minding my own business, and Dad looked a bit flustered when we found him.

'How much did I use, son?' he said. 'How much was that?'

'That was £50, Dad. Why? What's happened?'

'I put it on red over there,' Dad said. 'Before I knew it, it was taken and the fella only gave me one chip back. I put it on red and it came up black. And that was it.'

Poor Dad. He had no idea that the table was a 500 franc minimum. He thought the guy was going to give him some change back and he didn't have a clue that it would be taken away. It was a real Del Boy moment. I couldn't stop laughing.

We dined out on that story for years and his sisters loved winding him up about it over Sunday lunch.

I'm grateful that we stuck together as a family after Dad passed away. I was worried about Mum, but Uncle Dave lived nearby and my cousins Mark and Michelle weren't far away either. I could count on them to look after Mum when I went back to work.

I didn't take much time off. I was back in the dugout when we hosted Sunderland a week after losing to Blackburn and I was touched by the club arranging a minute's silence before the game, which we won 2–1 thanks to goals from Les and Gus.

It reminded me that Tottenham were my second family. Dad was a popular figure at White Hart Lane and I wrote a letter to the supporters' club to thank them for paying him such a lovely tribute. I also thanked the Sunderland fans, who behaved impeccably. It meant a lot to know that people were looking out for me.

Yet it still took a while for the despair to leave me. The healing process isn't simple. A couple of years later I was at a spa hotel having a reflexology session when my emotions suddenly came pouring out. I didn't realise that I hadn't finished grieving for Dad – that I still had to shake something out of the bottle.

It caught me completely off guard and it was awkward for the reflexologist when I burst into tears. I apologised, went back to my room and lay on my bed for two hours, sobbing my heart out.

It was a moment of release. I hadn't realised that I'd been carrying that pain around for such a long time.

* * *

My growing frustration with life at Tottenham didn't help my mood after Dad passed away. I wanted to build a younger squad after finishing the 2001–02 season in ninth place. It was time for the club to show ambition.

Yet I kept running down dead ends when it came to signings. It often seemed that I wasn't on the same page as the board. I found it strange that I never had a single conversation with the owner Joe Lewis, and I wasn't the last Tottenham manager to discover that transfer talks tended to drag on when the chairman Daniel Levy was involved.

I got on with Daniel, who had been given responsibility for running the football operation by Lewis, but there was always something to negotiate over with him. It wasn't easy to accept and I felt cut off at times. There was no link to the very top of the club, where the owner's silence was deafening, and I struggled to build a rapport with David Pleat. There was a wall between us and we drifted further apart instead of trying to find some common ground.

Ultimately everything felt too political. It wasn't that I had unwanted signings foisted on me from above. The problem was more that we dithered when we needed to be decisive, which stopped us progressing. We had some promising young defenders, but other parts of the squad looked tired and frayed. We needed more energy in midfield, given that Darren Anderton and Tim Sherwood were getting on, but the lack of funds forced me into compromises like signing Jamie Redknapp on a free transfer from Liverpool.

It wasn't the behaviour of a club looking to challenge the elite. Most of our best players were approaching retirement. I loved Jamie but his contract had to be incentivised because of his knee problems, and I also knew that we couldn't expect our main strikers, Teddy and Les, to last for ever.

We needed more firepower. Sergei Rebrov, signed for £11m by the previous regime, had failed to adapt to the Premier League despite making a name for himself with his performances for Dynamo Kiev in the Champions League. It was time for a different approach, and I was buzzing when it looked like we had a chance of pulling off an extraordinary coup by signing Fernando Morientes from Real Madrid and Samuel Eto'o from Mallorca.

Morientes, one of the best strikers in the world, was out of favour at Real after the arrival of Ronaldo that summer, and Eto'o, only 22, was a thrilling young talent. It only would have cost around £12m to sign both of them and I had already made my mind up about Eto'o after watching him play at the Bernabeu. He absolutely terrorised Real. Mallorca kicked off and Eto'o was on it straight away, dropping a shoulder to beat one defender before winning a free-kick on the edge of the area after another piece of skill. It was clear that he had something special. There was a murmur in the crowd, who knew what they were watching, and I felt like telling his agent that I had already seen enough.

Premier League defenders wouldn't have had a clue how to handle Eto'o and I liked him when we met in a hotel after the game. I'd heard a few negative whispers about his character, but I found him to be enthusiastic and hungry. We spoke for an hour and it was clear to me that he just wanted to play football. The stories about Eto'o being headstrong didn't matter to me. He was a young guy from Cameroon adjusting to life in Spain. He just needed time to settle and I didn't have any concerns about him succeeding in England.

The same applied to Morientes, who had just won his third Champions League. When push came to shove, though, we weren't decisive enough. Daniel couldn't agree a fee with Real for Morientes after flying to Spain for negotiations, and the deal for Eto'o also fizzled out. I suspect it was because the club had listened to the rumours about him being difficult.

We missed the boat. We would have been a serious force with those two up front, but we weren't prepared to take the plunge. I should have had more backing. It puzzles me why we weren't bolder, particularly as it wasn't long before Tottenham became more aggressive, building an impressive new training ground and spending more on big players.

Yet I couldn't mope after missing out on Eto'o and Morientes. I remembered a piece of advice from Ken Bates, who used to say, 'It's no good crying over spilt milk – go and find another cow,' and I was more optimistic when we signed Robbie Keane from Leeds. Robbie was a wonderful player and the fans adored him. He loved playing football and, unusually for someone of his quality, he stayed at Tottenham for a long time.

Signing Robbie was an encouraging step. Yet I still didn't feel that everything was working in perfect harmony. I thought that the stars were aligned when I took over at Tottenham, but the opposite was true. The budgetary constraints weighed me down and the 2002–03 season fizzled out after a promising start.

I felt that the writing was on the wall during the final weeks of the campaign. I was fighting against the tide and I heard rumblings of discontent from the crowd. Nobody abused me outside the ground, but I knew that the fans were dissatisfied. The atmosphere wasn't great, making the players edgy, and chances to relieve the pressure by picking up a positive result or two kept passing us by, the unrest growing when we ended the season with heavy defeats against Blackburn and Middlesbrough.

Yet I didn't want to give up. The job meant so much to me and I tried to stay positive during the summer. Freddie Kanouté, a quick and skilful forward, was a bargain from West Ham at £3.5m; Bobby Zamora, who had scored for fun in the lower leagues, was worth the risk at £1.5m; and Hélder Postiga, signed for £6.25m, was regarded as one of the most promising forwards in Portugal.

I was content with these additions to my attack, even though it wasn't possible to pay as much attention to other areas of the team. We had support for Robbie after allowing Teddy and Les to leave. Kanouté became a top player after moving to Sevilla and Zamora had a solid Premier League career. Postiga, meanwhile, was a terrific young talent. I believed in his quality and it was a shame that he didn't enjoy more success in England. It had nothing to do with a lack of ability. Sometimes a signing just doesn't work out.

The problem, though, was that I needed a strong start to the 2003–04 season. I was aware that I was on borrowed time and feared the worst after we only picked up four points from our first six games.

It was inevitable. I knew what to expect when Daniel called me. It was the first time I had been sacked for a poor run of results, but I understood the club's reasons. Although I should have been more assertive on signings, I couldn't use the lack of money as an excuse. I had experienced just the same thing in my previous jobs and it was up to me to deal with it at Tottenham.

My failure to come up with the right answers stung and I was absolutely gutted when the end arrived. I deeply regretted not being able to bring success to my beloved Tottenham and I spent a long time walking around my garden, running things through my head and looking at where I had gone wrong.

It hurt. I knew it was going to take some time to recover emotionally.

14

A NEW CHALLENGE

I felt guilty about falling short at Tottenham. I went away to lick my wounds and it was a while before I was in the right frame of mind to return. A lot of offers simply didn't grab me, and I experienced another setback when Rupert's attempt to bring me back to Southampton in February 2004 was met with opposition from board members who were worried about upsetting the fans.

I had to be patient. I registered my interest in managing France after Euro 2004, only for Raymond Domenech to get the job, and I spent some time doing punditry work until my agent got in touch just before Christmas to ask whether I fancied taking over at Wolves on a caretaker basis.

It was an intriguing proposition. Wolves had just been relegated after a year in the Premier League, but they were a big club with a lot of history and I fancied the challenge. I wasn't worried about how much time I'd have to spend travelling to work and I was full of motivation when I arrived, backing myself to lift the mood around the place.

We had to start smiling again. Some of the players were on too much money, which had an impact on the club's spending power, and there was a hangover after relegation. Yet there was no need to panic. The Championship is a wildly unpredictable league and although we were quite far off the pace, we still had a squad capable of putting a run together and challenging for a play-off place. Stuart Gray, an old colleague from Southampton, was already on the backroom staff, and I was pleased to be reunited with Incey, who was still going strong in midfield.

The team's potential was obvious. Joleon Lescott was a fine defender and we had dangerous strikers. Kenny Miller could score goals out of nothing and Carl Cort was a good target man, despite his lack of ruthlessness.

If only we had developed more of a cutting edge during my first season. It was infuriating to miss out on the play-offs after only losing once in 24 league games. Draws were our Achilles heel. We played good football and the crowd expected us to go up, but we didn't handle the pressure well enough and contrived to finish ninth despite ending the season with an 18-game unbeaten run.

The punishment was often self-inflicted as I didn't see a team lacking in ability. Poor finishing was the main issue and we often didn't get the rub of the green. The travails of Tomasz Frankowski, a Polish striker I signed in my second season, summed us up. He'd been banging them in when he was playing in Spain for Elche but he kept finding new ways to miss for us. We once more failed to gain promotion in my second season, finishing just below the play-off spots.

By then I was starting to feel my hunger ebbing away. I didn't have much money to spend and the travel was wearing me down. I was honest with myself. I didn't feel fully invested in the job anymore and we were about to head to Spain for a pre-season tour when I decided to tell Jez Moxey, the chief executive, that I was leaving.

At least it gave Wolves time to find a replacement. They tried to make me change my mind but I didn't want to leave them in the lurch two games into the new season. I had to be honest with Jez. I wasn't 100 per cent committed. I didn't think that the budget was big enough for a promotion challenge, which made me think that Wolves hadn't mapped out a journey to the Premier League, and I told him that I wouldn't be doing the club a favour if I forced myself to continue.

I had never felt like that before. It's not in my character to walk away from a challenge but I couldn't see myself taking the team any further. I thought about it long and hard, telling myself to see how I felt travelling up and down for a week of pre-season, but I soon realised I had to quit.

The travel took a toll. Management isn't a healthy job. The emotions a coach goes through during a game put a strain on your body – look at what happened to my heart in Rome – and there are times when it can feel as if you're putting out fires all day.

Although it isn't a lonely job, there's only so much your backroom staff can do to lift the burden of responsibility. You spend a lot of time in your head, thinking about the next game, the next training session, the next signings. There are contracts to deal with and an entire squad of players looking to you for guidance.

I still leant on John Syer's old advice about compartmentalising problems, but there were more things to stick in every drawer as a manager. It was sometimes hard to know where to find the positives, and I soon discovered that I needed to focus on small wins. I loved the peace and quiet of a 40-minute drive after a game when I was truly alone with my thoughts.

Although I knew I had to switch back into family mode as soon I was out of the car and through the front door, it was difficult to forget about work. You think you're spending time with your kids – or you think you're at a party – but you don't realise that other people are wondering if you're fully present. There's always something going on in the background, something forcing you to divert your attention from the things that really matter in life.

Managers have to be prepared to make sacrifices and I saw no point staying at Wolves once I felt the passion for the job fading away. It wouldn't have been fair on them if I'd lied to myself.

I still enjoyed much of my time at Wolves. I was never lonely when I had my little brother, Carl, as part of my backroom staff, and I cherished having the opportunity to work with Carl. We thought about football in the same way and he made an impression on everyone at Wolves. He got on with people easily, winning them over with his sense of humour, and his knowledge of the game made him an invaluable asset.

It meant a great deal to me to have Carl with me. I'd had so much success in football, but this was different. This was special. It was me and my brother working side by side, and it was great to spend so much time with him. I was very close to Carl, who was nine years younger than me. I looked out for him when we were growing up and it was inevitable that we bonded over football, spending countless hours kicking a ball around the garden.

I loved helping Carl improve his skills. He was a talented player, strong, two-footed and technically gifted, and I was desperate to see him flourish when he started playing in the recreational league in Harlow. It was odd. I had just broken into the first team at Tottenham, but I was never more nervous than when I watched Carl's games. I sensed that he was under pressure because of my name. It wasn't fair on him, and I badly wanted him to succeed on his own terms, especially when he followed in my footsteps and started to train at Tottenham.

Carl did well, and it was a wonderful moment for our family when Tottenham took him on as an apprentice. Mum and Dad were so pleased, and I knew that Carl had a chance of making it. He was a good player and he looked like me. We had similar characteristics and I always tried to watch him in training when I had a spare moment.

Carl's one weakness, though, was that he struggled to get round the pitch because of his size. He shot up when he was a teenager and it was a horrible day when Tottenham decided to let him go at 18. I was in tears and I wondered if I could have done more. I was gutted for Carl, as leaving Tottenham hit him hard. He dropped into the lower leagues, joining Barnet before spells at Bishop's Stortford and Leyton Orient, and he had to adjust to a tougher style of football.

I felt for Carl when I watched him at Orient. He was a technical player but the ball was in the air all the time. It wasn't the right fit, and it was a relief when he returned to Barnet, who played on the floor a bit more.

That was a better time in his life. I even ended up facing him during my first season as Chelsea manager. I was watching the draw for the third round of the FA Cup and for some reason made a pact with myself, vowing that we were going to make the final if we landed Barnet.

Sure enough, Barnet were the name out of the hat. The only frustration was that I missed the match with a calf strain. Carl had a good game and Barnet were unlucky not to beat us. We escaped with a 0–0 draw, won the replay 4–0 back at Stamford Bridge and lost to United in the final.

I think about Carl all the time. I was beyond devastated when he passed at the age of 40 in 2008. I was on holiday in Barbados and I went numb when I was told that Carl had died. I cried out in pain, unable to believe that my brother was gone, and I broke down in tears. He had complained about having bad headaches a few weeks earlier but the doctors couldn't identify the problem. It was well hidden. They call it a ticking bomb. It was like an aneurysm and it could have happened when he was 18.

That didn't make it any easier to accept. The whole family was in shock, although my belief in the afterlife made it easier to overcome losing Carl. I still have a connection with him. I check in with him, tell him his two beautiful daughters are well and acknowledge his presence.

It has nothing to do with religion. I believe that our spirit lives on after we die, and there are times when I feel Carl nearby. The Cars song 'Drive' was played at his funeral, and it's been played on the radio more than once when I've been thinking about him while driving.

I just wish he hadn't left us so soon. I don't know if I've truly grieved for Carl. There's a part of me that still feels bad about my success making it harder for him. He was a good footballer, but I sometimes wonder if I inadvertently stopped him achieving more in the game.

Carl's story goes to show how fine the margins are in football. Releasing players when they are 18 isn't an exact science. Although players like Wayne Rooney arrive fully formed, some are still developing. Academies have to make tough decisions, but it's tricky to predict if someone will go on to succeed at that age and it can be hard for young people to bounce back from the disappointment of being told that they aren't good enough.

That hit me at the start of my spell at Swindon. It wasn't long before we had to make decisions on who to release. It wasn't fair. I hadn't seen the youngsters yet and I had to go on what the youth coaches said. I was making snap decisions and I hated leaving kids heartbroken. It was a horrible job, far tougher than leaving a player out of a World Cup squad, and I vowed to take a slightly different approach when decision time arrived a year later.

I wanted the youngsters to have hope and I set out to reassure one kid, Wayne O'Sullivan, after telling him that his contract wasn't going to be renewed. Wayne had ability, so instead of dumping him on the scrapheap I told him I was going to play him in the reserves for the rest of the season, giving him the opportunity to impress scouts from other clubs. This had a liberating effect on Wayne. He became a different player when his anxiety about whether he would get a professional deal disappeared. He relaxed and started playing so well that I had no choice but to change my mind about not giving him a contract, kickstarting his career.

It was the same story at every club I managed. I kept having to release kids when they were 18, and I was convinced that there had to be a different way of doing things. Some players just needed another chance to prove themselves. I thought back to how I was at 18 – a skinny, bony kid still learning his trade – and I realised that I could help by creating an academy for youngsters who needed a path back into the professional game.

Leaving Wolves gave me the chance to make my vision come true. I went on holiday to Spain, just to switch off, but the idea came back to me when I bumped into a friend, Chris Moore, who lived in Sotogrande. I was talking about how much talent was out there, and how I wanted to unleash it all one day, and Chris said that he would see if he could drum up some investment in the academy from his friends in London.

There was nothing mapped out. I wasn't thinking about the academy after saying farewell to Wolves. It simply felt like the timing was right when I spoke to Chris, and after a while I went back to England determined to make it happen.

First, though, I had to go back to Wolves to meet Jez Moxey. He suspected that I'd been tapped up by another club and wanted me to sign a document stating that I couldn't take any other management job for a further year. I refused. I was honest with Jez, promising him that I was starting an academy, and I told him that I would make sure Wolves would receive compensation if a managerial job came up within 12 months.

That was an unlikely prospect. I was fully invested in the academy when it opened in 2008. It was a hell of a project to get off the ground. I relied on Chris to make the financial argument to potential investors, while I took care of presenting the footballing argument. I explained that there was so much talent lost to the game, and we soon had some backing. We decided to set ourselves up in Montecastillo in southern Spain, reasoning that the warm weather would allow us to train all year round, and quickly began the process of finding players.

Yet it was difficult at first. We held trials at Chelsea's training ground and managed to drum up some interest from television, but most players were more interested in finding a new club straight away. We were a new venture and we had to tweak our approach by going to the Professional Footballers' Association trials, where it was easier to scout those rough diamonds.

We were on the move. I brought Johnny G on board and asked George Foster, my chief scout at Wolves's academy, to help. We went to trials to note down players we liked and told them about how the academy worked.

Being in Spain enabled us to train in a calmer way. The warm climate meant that we could lay on two sessions a day, even in winter, and we had a lot of time to work on improving our players' technique. They had come from lower league clubs and we were able to offer a level of coaching they had never previously experienced.

There should be more of these academies. We were picking up players from small sides, but they had ability. In fact, part of the challenge was rewiring them mentally. We had to make them think more positively, as it's hard when you've repeatedly been told you're not good enough. We needed them to know that we believed in them.

We weren't lying. We found Ikechi Anya, who was stacking shelves in Tesco after being released by Wycombe. He played in the Premier League for Watford and went on to represent Scotland. Sam Clucas, released by Lincoln, played in the Premier League for Hull and Swansea before joining Stoke.

Jordan Hugill already looked like a man when he walked into our academy at the age of 17. He had never been coached properly but I knew that we could work with his physique. Jordan was so powerful and he has gone on to have a very good career as a target man in the Championship.

It was enjoyable watching these boys develop. They weren't necessarily the most talented players, but they were strong mentally. They were desperate to learn and in the second year we started playing friendlies against Spanish clubs. We took on Real and Atlético Madrid's B teams at their training grounds, and Ikechi played so well against Sevilla B that they asked if they could give him a two-week trial.

That was music to our ears. It was the whole point of the project. The idea was that we could make it self-sustaining by receiving transfer fees for our players, and we were overjoyed when Sevilla gave Ikechi a two-year deal in their B team. It showed that the academy was working.

We had the vision. We kept our players grounded, asking them to muck in and carry out the menial tasks I had to perform in my apprentice days, and we put a good coaching system in place. The coaches used to head out on six-week rotations and the standard was high. The youngsters were being coached by former internationals. Johnny G came out, and we had people like Graham Rix, Nigel Spackman and Dave Beasant involved. It was hard work organising everything, but it was worth it. The project had so much potential.

I wanted to take it further in our second year and an opportunity arrived when we bought Jerez Industrial, a small local club who were in danger of going out of business. We only had to pay around £50,000 to keep them going. They were in the Segunda División B, the Spanish fourth tier, and had no players, so I realised that we could help each other out if we filled the club with our talent.

The arrangement allowed us to play competitive games. We took on good amateur teams in the league and there were some fierce contests at times. It was England versus Spain and we weren't very popular with our opponents, but that didn't stop us. We had scouts coming to watch our boys, and we were top of the league in January.

Yet problems cropped up when I returned to England to speak to the FA about the project. They classed us as agents and refused to let the academy keep a small percentage of the transfer fee if a player joined an English club. They had it all wrong. I wasn't anyone's agent. The players had their own representatives. We were just providing them with a platform on which to perform. Their expenses were covered, they stayed in a wonderful hotel with great facilities and they didn't have to worry about anything other than improving as footballers.

It wasn't hard to see that we were helping the game. Yet the right people refused to back us. The PFA didn't do enough to help us and the FA wouldn't budge, saying that the rules didn't allow us to make money on transfers.

Their argument was that it was akin to third-party ownership, but that wasn't our model. Take Sam Clucas, who went back into the Football League after his spell at Jerez ended in 2011. Swansea ended up signing Sam for £16.5m from Hull in 2017 and I pointed out that we could put money back into the academy if we were allowed a cut of the fee, giving us the opportunity to keep growing every year.

But this cut no ice with the FA. I was exasperated. I pointed out that I would be forced to send our players to countries with looser third-party rules, but it made no difference. It was a sad state of affairs. The FA's position left us in a bind. We were providing great coaching but we could no longer bring the players back to England, which is where most of them saw themselves playing in the long run.

So many kids need more time to prove themselves. The FA, the PFA and the Premier League should come together to create six of these academies around the country. They have the finances, but do they have the will? I'm not sure they do, yet we demonstrated that it can be done. We provided good coaching and found players who wanted to grab that second chance with both hands.

But the rug had been swept away from under our feet. It happened just as the academy was getting stronger and it didn't help when Jerez asked us for money to pay off further debts. They were in huge financial trouble, yet we weren't in a position to bail them out anymore. We had no option but to bring our players back to England, after which the writing was on the wall. We kept training for a while, but the finances no longer made sense. Although we tried to create links with Oxford and Swindon, telling them that they would receive the bulk of our players, it didn't come off and we had to dissolve the company in 2014.

It was incredibly frustrating. Nobody was flexible enough to see what we were offering. It could have worked brilliantly.

I had envisaged our academy graduates returning a few years later to speak to the new intake. They could have come back to work the youngsters and speak about their experiences. I wanted to stay connected with our former players. We could have continued to mentor them, offering them advice and helping them make the right career choices. I still speak to some of the boys, but it would have been great to have a more professional relationship.

We would have improved. Nobody knew anything about us at the start – nothing like what we were doing had ever been done before and some players were suspicious when we explained it to them. They weren't sure if it was going to succeed and we had to work hard to sell ourselves. Convincing them was a challenge, particularly if they had already played at a high level. We had no evidence to fall back on and we ended up with a lot of players from the lower leagues. Yet if we had kept going, parents and agents might have seen the academy thriving and told players released by bigger clubs to give us a chance. Standards would have been raised.

Yet the system stood in my way. I felt sad for the coaches and annoyed that nobody in power believed in our concept when it came to the crunch. I wanted to continue but it became too much of a grind. We couldn't find players their moves and I ended up constantly putting out fires. It was no longer enjoyable and the time had come to move on.

15

EXTRA TIME

I don't have any regrets about walking away from management to invest all that time and energy into starting the academy. I am proud that we were able to give so many kids a life-changing experience and I wasn't in a rush to return to football when the project was over. I had been away from the industry for seven years and was happy to let my agents take care of any job offers that came my way.

I never felt a need to chase after a new club after leaving Wolves. I was happy focusing on other projects, although I never shut the door on management. You never say never in football and I had opportunities to manage again. I turned down an offer to lead Nigeria at the 2010 World Cup – the conditions weren't right – and I was in with a chance of replacing Zola at West Ham in March 2010. West Ham sounded me out because they were in relegation trouble and I thought that I was going to be offered an interview after they lost at home to Stoke on a Saturday afternoon. Yet there was a split at board level and Karren Brady said that the owners David Gold and David Sullivan wanted to give Zola more time when she called me the following day. We didn't speak again.

I wasn't too upset about missing out on going to West Ham. The only time I was really excited about the possibility of a comeback was when Tottenham spoke to me about taking over from André Villas-Boas in December 2013.

The academy was winding down and I was ready to talk when Daniel Levy called me late one evening. He was under pressure after sacking Villas-Boas. Tottenham were yet to find a new manager and Daniel was coming round to the idea of waiting until the summer before settling on a permanent replacement.

He had a plan. He wanted to know what I thought about Louis van Gaal, who was set to quit as the Netherlands manager after the 2014 World Cup, and he asked whether I would be prepared to come in on an interim basis until the end of the season.

On the surface it seemed like a wonderful opportunity. But I had to be honest with Daniel. I didn't think that Van Gaal was right for Tottenham and I wasn't particularly interested in a caretaker role. 'What happens if we do well and qualify for the Champions League?' I said. 'You'll have pressure from the crowd to keep me. If I come in for this sort of job then I want it to be long-term.'

Perhaps Daniel expected that kind of response from me. We carried on talking and eventually he asked whether I'd be happy working alongside Les Ferdinand. It seemed that we were on the right track. We spoke about backroom staff and I went to bed thinking that I had a chance of managing Tottenham again.

Yet everything went quiet after that conversation. Daniel never called again and I was left hanging. I was in the pub with my son watching Arsenal play Chelsea on a Monday night when it was announced that Tottenham had appointed

Tim Sherwood as their interim manager until the end of the season.

It left a bad taste in my mouth. Someone should have told me I wasn't getting the job, although I couldn't take it up with Daniel until he came over to me at a game a few years later to complain about a newspaper column in which I'd said that the club was at a crossroads.

Here was my chance. 'I understand what you're saying about the column, but it was quite a constructive piece,' I said. 'And by the way, why did you never phone me back about the job?'

Daniel said he had no idea what had happened – that it was news to him. I told him the full story and he insisted that it was up to Franco Baldini, Tottenham's director of football at the time, to tell me that they were going with Sherwood.

Daniel was under the impression that Baldini had called me. But perhaps missing out on the Tottenham job was a blessing in disguise. When I looked back I realised that it would have been very difficult to combine managing a Premier League team with looking after Mum, who was close to passing away from lung cancer. I lived 90 minutes away from her and I wouldn't have been able to spend much time with her if I'd gone back to Tottenham. Mum was on her own after Dad's death and she needed family by her side. She had wonderful support from relatives who lived nearby, but I wanted to be there as much as possible.

Mum battled cancer for five years and it was horrible when she had to go into a hospice. Her passing was one of the toughest things I've ever experienced. Mum was a beautiful person. She loved acting in her younger days and had a great sense of humour. We could always rely on her to rise to the occasion when we played charades at Christmas and she was an expert at pulling Dad's leg.

Mum knew how to make people happy and I was devastated when she passed away. I wouldn't wish that kind of pain on my worst enemy. Losing my parents and my brother in the space of 12 years was incredibly hard to take, and I was grateful to one of the nurses in Mum's hospice for reminding me that it was OK to grieve.

'Glenn, you've been looking out for your mum and you're being brave for everyone in the family, but you've got to look after yourself,' she said. 'You're an orphan now.'

Bereavement has taught me never to take anything for granted. Life is unpredictable and some things are out of our control. Sometimes luck is the only explanation – the difference between us reaching the end of the road or living to see another day.

And I was close to not even making it past the age of two. It was all so mundane but I shuddered when Mum told me about the time a trip to watch Dad play football for Hayes FC on a bitterly cold winter's day nearly ended in unspeakable tragedy.

I only survived because Mum had the weather in mind when she got me dressed before we went to the ground. It was the only reason why she picked out a pair of thick trousers with turn-ups at the bottom. She was worried about her baby catching a cold and she readily accepted when one of her friends, whose aunt lived in a flat overlooking the pitch, said that it would be better for me if they went inside to watch the game.

We were safe from the elements after heading up to the eighth floor, only for Mum to get the fright of her life. She wasn't thinking when she turned around after opening the window. One moment I was in Mum's arms, the next I had fallen through the window after slipping out of her grasp.

Luckily Mum reacted quickly, sticking out her hand and grabbing the turn-ups on my trousers. I would have been a goner if she had put me in a different pair that morning. It was pure chance. Mum hadn't given the turn-ups a second thought until they saved her son's life.

Some people don't get a second chance. Nobody caught Dad and Carl when they fell, but I survived. I was lucky that Mum had sharp reflexes and I was fortunate that I was in BT Sport's studio in Stratford when I had another near-death experience nearly 60 years later.

I wasn't supposed to be working on 27 October 2018. It was my 61st birthday and I was meant to have tea and cake with my daughters and my grandchildren Rosie and Teddy in the morning. Everything was arranged and I don't know why I said I would try to change my plans after my agent Terry Ellis called during the week to ask if I wanted to do some punditry for *BT Sport Score* that Saturday.

Normally I would have turned the offer down. For some reason, though, I told Terry that I would see if my girls could switch our plans to Friday. I assumed it was a long shot but it turned out that they were free, and I had a lovely time when they came to spend the day with me and my partner Lisa. I was content after playing with my grandkids and opening my presents, and I was ready for work when my driver Johnno came over to pick me up on Saturday morning.

I didn't feel ill. I'd been tired for a few months, but there was no sign of anything serious. I wasn't breathing heavily and there was no cause for alarm when we arrived at Stratford. I was fine when I jumped out of the car and told Johnno that I'd see him again at 5.30pm. I wasn't sweating when I walked in and said hello to the presenter Jules Breach, who was with some of the other guests – Harry Redknapp, Steve Sidwell, Paul Ince and Robbie Savage.

Everything was normal. Mark Pougatch was there because he was presenting the show after ours, and I went into the green room to discuss the schedule. But I can barely recall anything from the show,. nor can I remember taking Robbie on in a Teqball match. The credits were rolling and we were still playing when I collapsed, tumbling backwards and smashing my head on the ground.

I was gone for several minutes, lost to this world, and I wouldn't have come back if I'd told Terry that I wanted to spend that Saturday with Lisa, my girls and my grandchildren. It would have been horrific if it had happened in front of my family. They wouldn't have known what to do when I fell and it was just as well that I was at work when everything went black.

I was out of it – powerless and unable to cry out for help. But it wasn't my time, even though I suppose that it would have been fitting if I'd died while I was mucking about with a football. I was in a room full of people, and our sound engineer Simon Daniels knew exactly what to do.

Simon was incredible. He was a volunteer policeman at the time and he didn't hesitate when he saw me on the ground. You only have three minutes to receive CPR after having a cardiac arrest and Simon took over straight away, jumping to my aid and telling the others to get the defibrillator while he kept me going until the ambulance arrived.

Simon's a pretty mild-mannered guy, but his decisiveness was mind-blowing. You have to be forceful when you perform CPR and Simon didn't hold back, breaking seven of my ribs while he was pounding my chest. Even the paramedics were impressed, telling him to keep going until they were ready to load me into the ambulance.

But I wasn't out of the woods yet. First they whisked me off to the Royal London Hospital in Whitechapel to check if I'd suffered a brain injury when I hit my head on the floor; then I was on my way to St Bartholomew's Hospital to receive treatment on my heart. I briefly regained consciousness when I was back in the ambulance, and it meant so much to see my son Jamie looking down at me when I opened my eyes.

I couldn't do anything apart from squeeze Jamie's hand. It's one of the few things I remember before arriving at St Bart's. Everything else was a blur. All I recalled was saying goodbye to Johnno in the morning, joking about my age when Paul Ince and Robbie surprised me with a birthday cake, and, most bizarrely of all, seeing a lizard on the set.

At first I assumed that the medication was giving me hallucinations. But I was relieved when people told me that the lizard had actually made a guest appearance on the show because Harry was about to go into the jungle on *I'm a Celebrity ... Get Me Out of Here!*

I had to rely on others to fill me in on the details surrounding my collapse. I knew nothing about Simon's heroism and I couldn't hear anything when Steve and Incey, my former midfield general, rushed to my side and urged me to keep fighting.

I wasn't fully aware of my surroundings until I woke up in a room at St Bart's. I had stents in my chest and was stunned when the doctor told me that I'd had a cardiac arrest. I couldn't understand it. I didn't know that a cardiac arrest was different to a heart attack. I was in a state of utter shock and they waited before telling me that I still needed to have a quadruple bypass. I had come so close to death and, overcome with emotion, I couldn't help but feel like my life wouldn't have meant anything if I had gone that day.

* * *

I struggled to shake off those thoughts as I lay in my hospital bed. I was gone, but I'd been given a second chance. I realised that the journey means more than the final destination. It's how we achieve things that matters. I believe that the spirit passes on when we die but this was a reality check – a reminder that we can't take our house and our car with us when the end arrives. All you can take with you is the love you've shown to people. Your success means nothing if you treated others badly while you were on your way to the top.

Your bank balance won't help you in the next life. All you have in the end is how you lived your life, and I had a lot of time to think about that during my four and a half weeks in hospital. I felt overwhelmed when my surgeon, Steve Edmondson, told me that I had to wait 10 days before having my quadruple bypass because my lungs and kidneys weren't functioning properly.

It was so much to absorb. My broken ribs were incredibly painful and I was in a daze when Steve explained that three of my main arteries were blocked. 'How you haven't had a massive stroke in all this time is beyond me,' he said. 'You were living off the final 1 or 2 per cent of your last main artery.'

I had to go under the knife. Mr Edmondson removed a big haematoma during my operation, they cut my arms and legs open to use my veins for the bypass and I realised that I had been living in a state of blissful ignorance. I didn't pay much attention to my feelings of fatigue in the months leading up to the cardiac arrest. I had lived with atrial fibrillation for a long time and there were times when the medication made my breathing heavy, but I thought that I was fit. I went to the gym and I swam a lot. I assumed that I was doing all the right things.

I couldn't have been more wrong: my body was waiting to give up on me. I was so lucky to have survived and I was emotional when my family told me about Simon's role in my escape. I had never met him before and it was odd to think that I owed my life to a complete stranger.

It all had a profound effect on me, changing the way that I view life. For a long time I'd believed that the body was just an overcoat for the soul. I experienced healing when I was 17 and I started to think about spirituality more deeply when I was 28. I found out about Eastern philosophies while I was at Monaco and looked inside myself more. It has nothing to do with religion. We all have a spark inside us, an energy, a connection to the creator, and I have always been looking for answers about the meaning of life.

But they were just theories. This was the first time I'd experienced it on a practical level. Almost dying made me realise that nothing matters more than how we conduct ourselves. I'm in extra time now, and I've never been more determined to do the right thing.

I try to savour every moment and focus on what matters. I always make sure to look upstairs and express my gratitude whenever I'm with my grandchildren, Rosie, Teddy, Jack and Bertie, who was born earlier this year.

It doesn't mean that I think I'm still here to fulfil some great purpose. I didn't see a light when I was unconscious in the BT studio; I didn't have an epiphany. It simply motivated me to make the most of my time left on this earth.

It was humbling to watch the staff at St Bart's go about their business. I was surrounded by beautiful people and saw the NHS at its best. You don't realise how brilliant it is until you experience it properly. The organisation has been astonishing during the Covid-19 pandemic, somehow coping under the most intense pressure imaginable, and that's because of the people who make it so special.

I wasn't thrilled when I needed to have a second operation to have a defibrillator installed while I was there, but it wasn't a problem when I said that I didn't want it to stop me playing golf. A different surgeon to Steve did the procedure and he didn't mind putting the defibrillator in my back, ensuring that my swing wasn't compromised. It summed up the efficiency, professionalism and kindness at St Bart's, and it was an honour when I went back to launch a fundraising campaign for the hospital's charity.

Yet my fight wasn't over after I was discharged from hospital. I was shattered and despondent after walking again for the first time. 'I'm never going to be able to deal with this,' I thought. 'How am I going to get back to any sort of life if I can't walk 200 yards?'

I needed Lisa, her daughters and my children to remind me that I had to take it day by day and focus on small victories. I went 300 yards, then 400, and eventually I was able to walk four miles. But it was tough. I was emotionally and physically drained, and I marvelled at how Lisa looked after me after I left the hospital, nursing me through my recovery and making sure that my medication was in order.

It was a worthwhile battle. Every walk was special. I felt grateful every time I walked on my own and listened to books or music. I had to let time be the healer. I'm determined, but I realised that I couldn't push it. I allowed my body to heal naturally and although my scars will always be there, I eventually began to improve.

After a few weeks I was well enough to invite Simon over for tea. It was fantastic to be able to thank him properly. We chatted away for four hours and I didn't mind hurting my ribs when I gave Simon a huge hug at the front door. The pain was nothing compared with my gratitude to the man who saved my life.

I call Simon my earth angel. I speak to him a lot now and it was wonderful to give him an award at an event for the British Heart Foundation. It's important to make people feel valued, and I enjoyed taking Simon and Steve, my surgeon, to Tottenham for a game against West Ham in April 2019.

Daniel Levy was extremely generous, pulling out all the stops. Simon loves football and I didn't realise that Steve had played with my old Tottenham team-mate John Lacy back in the day. Steve was delighted when I brought John up to meet him.

It was an unforgettable day. In the evening I went to see my son play his first live gig in London. Jamie's band is called Mona Vale and I couldn't stop myself becoming tearful when I watched him on stage. It hit me: I never would have seen my boy perform if I hadn't survived.

The emotional punches kept coming. It was tough when I finally went back on *BT Sport Score*. I said that I didn't want them to make a fuss, but they didn't listen. The cameramen and engineers formed a guard of honour and applauded me on to the set, and I had to work hard not to break down on live television.

Sitting in that studio brought it all back. But it was a beautiful gesture and I loved doing punditry again, even if my family weren't particularly pleased to see me jumping around the studio with Gary Lineker and Rio Ferdinand when Tottenham fought back from 3–0 down on aggregate to win their Champions League semi-final against Ajax in May 2019.

I blame Rio. He isn't even a Tottenham fan and he was the one who pushed me in the chest when Lucas Moura scored the winner. But it was an unbelievable game. You can't blame me for losing control. It's what football does to you. I couldn't believe that I'd witnessed my childhood team reaching the Champions League final.

It was like I was a little boy again, kicking the ball around Mum's living room. I was back to being a fan, and I was bombarded with text messages from friends and family when the clip of my celebrations with Gary and Rio made it onto social media. I didn't have much of a comeback when my kids reminded me that I'd just had a quadruple bypass.

But it was such a special night for the club. We stayed overnight in Amsterdam and we were in a bar full of Tottenham fans after the game. Everyone kept buying us drinks and at one stage I had 16 beers in front of me. Des Kelly, BT's lead interviewer, took a photo of us and I decided to wind my kids up by sending it to them. 'Look, I've got to drink all of these by 1.30am!' I said.

I wanted to enjoy myself. It was disappointing when we lost the final to Liverpool in Madrid, but at least I was there to see it. I didn't want to be restricted. I was ready to live life to the full, so I decided to go for it when I was asked to be a contestant on *The Masked Singer* in 2020.

What did I have to lose? I'd never had much of an interest in appearing on reality television, but I'd always told my agent Terry to let me know if anything musical came along. I've always been passionate about music. Uncle Dave was a big influence. He introduced me to the Beatles when I was five – 'A Hard Day's Night' was my favourite song – and it wasn't long before I was singing all the time. I was an Eagles nut when I was a teenager, I went to watch Queen and Elton John, and I often visualised myself on stage, playing in front of a huge crowd as I sang along to David Bowie.

I'm always listening to something. I inspired myself before games by losing myself in my Sony Walkman, I never hear the engine of my car because I always turn the radio up and I love going to watch smooth jazz. I hired a wonderful saxophonist, Dave Koz, for my 60th birthday, and he wowed everyone at a jazz club in Holborn.

My one regret is that I never had time to learn an instrument. But I've always been able to pick up a tune, even though I've never had singing lessons. I can harmonise and I think Jamie has inherited my love of music. He's very talented. He can sing and play the drums, the guitar and the piano.

I'm not quite as versatile as Jamie but I can sing, and I made a bit of a name for myself in the music world when I recorded 'Diamond Lights' with my Tottenham and England teammate Chris Waddle in 1987.

Our old pal Pat Mitchell was responsible. He used to come to Tottenham's training ground and we did a few things with him. Pat gave Chris and me sponsored cars, and we were happy to help out when he asked if we would come to a big function in Coventry one evening.

We went with our wives after a game and had a good time. We had a few beers and before we knew it everyone wanted us to go up to the stage and sing with the band. We were only having a laugh, but Pat was buzzing when we sat back down. He didn't realise that I'd been miming and he surprised us when he came to the training ground with a big idea a week later.

'Guys, you sound fantastic,' Pat said. 'You've got to make a record.'

'What are you on about?' I said. 'We don't want to make a record!'

But Pat wouldn't stop pestering us. He told us that he'd found a songwriter, Bob Puzey, and he eventually ground us down, convincing us to have a meeting at the guy's house. The walls were closing in on us. Bob played us his song, a slow number called 'Diamond Lights', and we were beginning to feel guilty about refusing to take part, particularly when Pat started tugging on our heartstrings by pointing out that the guy had six kids to support.

It became increasingly difficult to walk away. Pat badgered us for another two weeks, chipping away at our resistance until we finally agreed to do the song. Now we were in trouble. We headed off to a studio in south London after training and we were still there in the early hours, trying to get the song right even though we had training in the morning. It was surreal. At one stage I went to the toilet and found myself standing next to Boy George.

We were in way over our heads thanks to Pat. By that stage, though, we were completely invested in the song. The production team had won us over by livening it up, making it pacier, and we were impressed when we heard it again at Bob's house a few weeks later. It sounded amazing and we couldn't believe it when we found out that it was going to be released.

There was no way out now. The wheels were in motion and the demands were ridiculous. Tottenham had just made it to the FA Cup final, heightening the attention on us, but we had to find time to publicise the song. We even appeared in a video, trying very hard to look like actors while a woman danced around us.

Six weeks after recording the song we had another call from Pat, informing us that we were required to appear on a live recording of *Top of the Pops*.

We were allowed to mime the song, but there wasn't going

to be a second chance if one of us fell off the stage. We couldn't afford to make any mistakes and I made an important request when Pat told us that a driver would come to the training ground to take us to the BBC's studios in Shepherd's Bush on the day of the show.

'Pat, the only thing is that he must have a cassette of the song in the car,' I said. 'We can't remember the words.'

It was damage limitation time. We jumped in the car when training finished at 1pm and spent the journey singing along to the cassette. It was our only chance to practise the song and it was a bit worrying that the driver was better than us.

We were terrified when we made it to the dressing room. 'Bloody Pat Mitchell,' I said, looking at Chris. 'We're going to make ourselves look so stupid.'

We didn't know what we were doing.

Taking a penalty in an FA Cup final was a doddle compared with going on *Top of the Pops*, so there was only one solution: alcohol. Our wives were taking the mickey out of us back in the dressing room and we felt better after getting stuck in to a few beers. The nerves started to disappear and I felt more confident when it was time go on, even though we had to follow Five Star and I looked like something out of *Miami Vice* in my white jacket. I tried to help Chris calm down as well, telling him to relax and enjoy himself.

Somehow we made it through unscathed. We went out with our wives after the show and had a great night. The pressure was off and no harm had been done. We had good fun doing it and even recorded another song, 'Goodbye', only to have to pull it when I went to Monaco.

It was disappointing for Bob. He wanted us to do an entire album, but we decided to quit while we were ahead. I donated my fee for 'Diamond Lights' to Helen & Douglas House, a children's hospice in Oxford, and the only time I ever regretted doing the song was when my kids threatened to put it on whenever they wanted something from me. They knew I'd give in.

I found myself in a similar situation when I was dressed as the grandfather clock during rehearsals for *The Masked Singer*. There were times when I wondered why I had agreed to stuff myself into that costume, but I always went back to my cardiac arrest. I didn't have to take myself seriously and although I wasn't sure about the show's concept at first, I was hooked when I took a closer look at it.

I had to sign a non-disclosure agreement after being invited on, while Lisa, her daughter Sophia, Terry and my driver Johnno couldn't say anything either. My identity had to remain top secret. It was a proper cloak and dagger operation, right down to having to put on a hoodie, a balaclava and gloves when Johnno was driving me to the show.

I couldn't remove my disguise until I was in the dressing room, and it had to come back on whenever I went outside to do some voiceovers and practise my songs. But it was such an enjoyable experience. I wasn't there to win and it wasn't about collecting three points; I just wanted to have a good time and I didn't hesitate about picking the grandfather clock costume. I knew that Rosie, Teddy and Jack would love it when I was finally revealed.

The only problem, though, was working out how to sing when I was crammed into that great big box. That was where I missed a trick – I should have adjusted to my new surroundings by practising with a cardboard box on my head when I was at home. I didn't realise that it would be so hard to breathe when I was in costume. It was incredibly hot and I also had to deal with the nerves that came with performing live on stage for the first time.

Those were the moments when I questioned why I was putting myself through all that hassle. But I quickly got over my self-doubt. 'No,' I thought. 'Enjoy it and love it. You're in extra time and this is what it's for – to do the things that you want to do.'

It wasn't long before I was having the time of my life. I met some wonderful people and I was delighted to make it through the first few rounds. I had some real humdingers up my sleeve if I'd gone further.

I also made an impression on the singing coaches along the way. One of them, Mark Delisser, gave me a lot of confidence and taught me how to breathe when I was in my box. He also made me think more seriously about singing and told Terry that I should make an album. I've released two singles since then – 'Cuz We're England', a song for Euro 2020, and 'The Life You Give', as well as raising money for the NHS with another song, 'Unsung Heroes'.

At least none of the judges guessed my name before I left the show. There were a few clues about the 1986 World Cup and some hints about the times I had to go in goal for Tottenham, but I was chuckling under my mask when I heard shouts of Ian Wright, David Seaman and John Barnes.

Admittedly I did receive some messages from my family and friends when the show was on television. A few of them were asking if I was the grandfather clock, and I had to pretend that I was watching the football and had no idea what they were talking about.

I couldn't tell the truth, not even to my kids. Interestingly, though, Rosie, Teddy and Jack guessed that it was me before the big reveal. They watched a few episodes and they could tell who it was from my voice. 'That's Poppa G!' they said.

It must be because I'm always singing around Rosie and Teddy. They're only five and Teddy always says, 'Put Poppa's music on' when he's in my car. I turn on the jazz and we have a good sing-song.

I've learnt to cherish those moments even more since my cardiac arrest. Nothing matters more to me than family and nothing fills me with joy more than hearing about Teddy forcing Zara to put *The Masked Singer* on all the time or seeing Rosie wearing England colours on her way into school, singing my song, 'Cuz We're England'.

Every day is precious now. Every day gives me a chance to smile. I played football with Teddy recently and he had me in hysterics after booting the ball past me.

'Poppa,' he said, turning round to face me, 'I thought you used to play for Spurs.'

PICTURE CREDITS

Page 7, bottom: Ross Kinnaird/Allsport/Getty Images

Page 8, top: Jon Buckle/EMPICS Sport/PA Images/Alamy Stock Photo

Page 8, bottom: ITV/Vincent Dolman/Shutterstock

INDEX

GH indicates Glenn Hoddle.

INDEX